UNLOCKING THE BIBLE STORY

UNLOCKING THE BIBLE STORY
VOLUME 1

Colin S. Smith

Moody Publishers
Chicago

All Scripture quotations, unless otherwise indicated, are
taken from the *Holy Bible, New International Version*®. NIV®.
Copyright © 1973, 1978, 1984 by International Bible Society.
Used by permission of Zondervan Publishing House. All
rights reserved.

Scripture quotations marked NASB are taken from the *New
American Standard Bible*®, © Copyright The Lockman
Foundation 1960, 1962, 1963, 1968, 1971, 1972, 1973, 1975,
1977, 1995. Used by permission.

Scripture quotations marked NKJV are taken from the *New
King James Version*. Copyright © 1982 by Thomas Nelson, Inc.
Used by permission. All rights reserved.

ISBN: 0-8024-6543-9

3 5 7 9 10 8 6 4 2

Printed in the United States of America

For Mum and Dad,

who taught me the Bible,
led me to Christ,
and continue to be examples
of a God-centered life

CONTENTS

ACKNOWLEDGMENTS

A friend of mine was once asked how long it took him to prepare a sermon. "Forty years," he said, quoting his age at the time. As I look back on more than forty years, my heart is filled with a sense of gratitude to God for the many people who, from childhood onward, have taught me the Bible and been a means of God's blessing in my life.

I am deeply thankful for the example of my own pastors Campbell Henderson, who is now with the Lord, and Derek Prime. I am also indebted to Tony Lane of London Bible College who supervised my studies in historical theology, which gave me a theological grid that continues to be an invaluable tool in studying the Scriptures. I am also grateful to Stuart and Jill Briscoe and Warren Wiersbe, who were part of God's providence that led to our family's coming to the United States and who have been models to me of the proper use of imagination in preaching. The influence of all these friends and teachers are interwoven into my life and therefore into this book.

I am especially grateful to my friend Jonathan Stephen for his insights on the theophanies in the early chapters of Genesis, and warmly commend his book *Theophany: Close Encounters with the Son of God* (Epsom, England: Day One Publications, 1998). His fresh approach has shed new light for me on God's visible presence in the Garden of Eden. I am also indebted to another friend, Charles Price, for his work on the purpose of the Law of God, which has helped me to see how the Law is a reflection of God's glory.

I am also grateful to my friend Dr Raju Abraham of the Emmanuel Hospital Association in India who drew an Old Testament time line for me on a napkin over lunch, and gave me his permission to use it! Raju is an insightful Bible teacher, and I am thankful to God for the stimulus of our many discussions. The time lines throughout the book are based on the work of Walter Kaiser, president of Gordon-Conwell Theological Seminary. Dr. Kaiser's dates appear in his outstanding work, *A History of Israel* (Broadman & Holman).

Those who are familiar with the writing of Dr. Martyn-Lloyd Jones may find his influence throughout this series of books. I have tried to soak my mind in his writings. In this book, I am especially grateful for his image of Christ advancing against the sword guarding the entrance to Paradise, which I found in an unpublished sermon on Genesis 3.

There must be many other insights, phrases and stories, accumulated in my mind over the years, whose source I have forgotten. I am deeply conscious of my debt to many pastors, friends, and colleagues whose ministry I have appreciated over the years, and have attempted to identify sources of ideas that I received from others. If there are those whose influence I have forgotten, then I hope that they will forgive my oversight.

One of the joys of working on this book has been my deep sense of the hand of God on this project. Quite unbeknownst to me, a member of the congregation at Arlington Heights sent a sermon tape to Bill Thrasher, the general manager and associate publisher at Moody Press. Since discovering the series, Bill has been relentless in his drive and enthusiasm to make this material available in print. I owe him a profound and lasting debt of gratitude.

It has been a joy to work with the publishing team at Moody, several of whom have become good friends since the snowy day on which we first met to talk, dream, and pray about this project. It has been a special delight to work with Greg Thornton, Dave DeWit, and John Hinkley. My editor, Jim Vincent, has worked tirelessly in editing and shaping the manuscript and has made significant improvements to it. I am also deeply indebted to my secretary, Susie Von Busch, who continues to support me with skill, speed, and a joyful spirit.

I would also like to express my gratitude to the two churches I have been privileged to serve. The Enfield Evangelical Free Church of London took a risk with a twenty-two year old college graduate who had no pastoral experience and called him to be their pastor. Karen and I served the Lord there with great joy for sixteen years until 1996, when I became senior pastor of the Arlington Heights Evangelical Free Church. "The boundary lines have fallen for me in pleasant places" (Psalm 16:6), and it is a special privilege to serve a congregation with a deep hunger for the Word of God. Their faithful prayers and kind encouragement continue to be a rich means of God's blessing in my life.

On a more personal note, I want to express a special word of thanks to my family. Karen and I have been married for twenty-one years. We began in the pastorate together three weeks after we were married, and have never known anything else. I owe more to Karen than I can ever express in words, and with every year that passes I feel a deeper appreciation of the gift God has given to me in her. Our two sons, Andrew and David, have taken ownership in this work, and have gladly extended their patience and made sacrifices for it. Without their love, support, and encouragement, I would never have been able to complete this task.

A special word of thanks to my younger son David, who at the age of thirteen has developed a sharp eye for detail and played an important role in preparing this book for print. As I worked on editing each chapter, David made corrections, and looked up every Bible reference. We worked long hours on this project together, broken only by short stops for meals and a longer break for a game of tennis. Our three weeks together are a special memory for us both, and I am full of admiration for the commitment and enthusiasm with which David gave himself to this task.

Through parents, family, teachers, colleagues, friends and churches, God has poured out more gifts and opened more doors of opportunity in my life than I had ever expected. I can say with deep gratitude to "from the fullness of [God's] grace we have all received one blessing after another" (John 1:16). It is my prayer that some of the blessing I have received over the years may be shared with others and that God may use this book to unlock the Bible story so that you may know Him, through His Son Jesus Christ.

INTRODUCTION

"I've been in church for years. I don't feel that I have a good grasp of the Bible. But I wish that I did."

I've lost count of the number of times I've heard a comment like that. Many people know stories from the Bible but do not know the story of the Bible. That's like having a handful of pearls with no string to link them together. *Unlocking the Bible Story* will give you the string, and show you how the pearls of God's truth fit together.

It begins with two people in a beautiful garden and ends with a vast crowd in a magnificent city. All the way through, it points us to Jesus Christ. *Unlocking the Bible Story* will show you the big picture and help you to discover the breathtaking sweep of the whole Bible story.

These volumes began as a series of sermons preached over a period of two years at Arlington Heights Evangelical Free Church in Illinois. I had been planning to teach the story of the Old Testament, and when the chairman of our elder council suggested the idea of encouraging the congregation to read the Bible in a year, the two ideas came together and ignited a spark.

We presented the challenge to the congregation and offered the gift of *The One Year Bible* to everyone who would make a commitment to read it. We promised that every Sunday the preaching would come from the Bible book we were reading, and would show how each part fits into the whole. We ordered four hundred Bibles. But the response was overwhelming. Fourteen hundred people made the commitment!

Now, two years later, I am deeply moved by many testimonies of how this journey through the Bible has touched and changed people's lives.

"Though I have been a believer most of my life, I have never continuously read through the Bible from beginning to end. I have studied different passages and books, which was great, but they did not give me comprehensive message of the Bible....I especially appreciate understanding the Old Testament and find it enriches my understanding of who Christ is." —Hyacinth, a human-resources manager

"The most significant benefit of these two years of unlocking the Bible has been seeing how God's plan is so intricately woven through the Bible. Many of the stories in the Bible used to seem disconnected and now are wonderfully brought together. What an encouragement."—Jeff, an engineer

"The messages of *Unlocking the Bible Story* [have] given me a new way to talk to seekers about the Bible as a whole and how it impacts them."—Liz, a nurse and mother

What has happened for these folks can happen for you!

There are two ways to use *Unlocking the Bible Story*. You may choose to read the Bible in a year, and use these volumes (this is volume one of four) as a road map for your journey. At the end of this book you will find a Bible reading plan based on *The One Year Bible* published by Tyndale House. You may want to use this approach.

Alternatively, you can use *Unlocking the Bible Story* as an aerial photograph, to gain a big-picture perspective on the Bible so that when you are "down on the ground" in your own study, you will have a better sense of where you are. Either way, welcome to the journey.

Each of the eighty chapters in this four-volume series begins with a key question to unlock, and ends with a summary of the answer from the Bible. At the beginning of each chapter there are signposts that point out discoveries you will make, truths you will learn, and insights that will help you to worship. Finally, in each chapter of the Old Testament volumes, you will find a "Spotlight on Christ" which will help you to see how the whole Bible points us forward to Jesus Christ.

Unlocking the Bible Story does not cover every chapter or even every book of the Bible, but it will take you through the whole of the Bible story, and show you how it fits together. It will also introduce you to the major themes of the Bible.

The Bible uses some specialized words, like prophet, priest, atonement, and revelation. If we want to fully appreciate what God is saying to us in the Bible, we need to understand the words that He uses. Many areas of life have their own distinctive vocabulary. When I came to America five years ago, I had a very limited understanding of baseball. The basic idea was clear to me, but I quickly discovered that other people were seeing and enjoying things that I missed. The commentators talked about a "curve ball" and a "slider." Of course, I didn't need to know what these words meant to enjoy the game, but I soon realized that if I wanted to appreciate what was going on, I needed to learn some new words.

Unlocking the Bible Story will help you to understand the Bible's vocabulary. Each chapter introduces a key word in the Bible story, and as you grasp the Bible's major themes, you will begin to enjoy insights that otherwise you would have missed.

Unlocking the Bible Story will show you how the whole Bible points to Jesus Christ. He is the focal point of the whole story. If you take a diamond and move it in the light, each facet will reflect a different shade of color. The diamond sparkles as the light reflects on the stone at different angles. *Unlocking the Bible Story* will help you to worship as you see new facets of the glory of our Lord Jesus Christ.

PROLOGUE: RAISING THE CURTAIN

Suppose you and a friend have tickets to a major play called *The Bible Story*. But because of traffic (and bad planning) you arrive late at the theater. In fact, you are so late that you have missed the whole of act one in the great drama of the Bible story, and so you know nothing about the Old Testament. You're frustrated, but figure, Well we might as well stay, and besides the New Testament is the best part.

You walk into the lobby to discover it's the middle of intermission. You've arrived just in time to hear the buzz of conversation about act one. You lean in to listen, when the lights flicker low then go up again. Time to get a seat. You find it just in time for the beginning of act two.

The curtain rises, and the scene at the beginning is in a stable. A manger and a newborn child are at center stage, with animals nearby. As the scene unfolds, you learn this is not an ordinary child. Unlike any other character in human history, He has no father. He is born of a virgin, and an angel announces that He is the Son of God. He is "God with us" (Matthew 1:23), and His Name is Jesus, because "he will save his people from their sins" (Matthew 1:21).

In front of you, you spot a couple who were talking in the foyer during the intermission. The wife, nudges her husband.

"This is it!" she says. "He will be the one who was promised. You wait and see; it will all center around Him. He'll be the answer to the problem."

But you have just arrived, and you don't know what the problem is. And when you hear that He is the Son of God, you don't know who God is. When you hear that He will save His people, you don't know who they are, or why they need saving or what they need saving from! Having missed act one, you struggle to grasp what this story is about. You don't know the problems and you don't know the promise, so all you see is a baby lying in a manger, surrounded by a few animals.

That is precisely the situation of many people today. They hear about the story of Jesus, but they do not understand it, because they don't know the big story of the Bible. Many people today have concluded that God is some kind of impersonal force located within us, and that getting in touch with God is therefore essentially a matter of getting in touch with yourself. And if God is an impersonal force located within us, then presumably sin is about hurting ourselves, and if sin is hurting ourselves then the solution to it is simply that we need to forgive ourselves. People who think like this conclude that if we can learn to be in touch with ourselves and forgive ourselves, then we will enjoy spiritual health.

If you come into act two with ideas like that, the story of Jesus will never make any sense. What need would you have of Christ? And why would it matter who He was? What could He do for us that we could not do for ourselves?

If you don't know who God is, and you don't know what the problem is, and you don't know what the promise is, the coming of Christ will seem nothing more to you than a sentimental story, a wonderland of children, angels, babies, and animals in cattle stalls and snow and Father Christmas. It will all be a blur.

This is why we need to unlock the Bible story. Act two won't make sense to us until we have grasped the main themes of act one. The living God has revealed Himself. He is the God of Abraham, Isaac, and Jacob. He has made the world and everything in it, and He causes you to live and move and breathe right now. He is holy. He is love. He reaches out to you and wants you to know Him.

THE BIBLE STORY:
ABRAHAM TO JESUS CHRIST

ABRAHAM

2000 B.C.   ISAAC
             JACOB

             FOUR HUNDRED YEARS OF SLAVERY
             IN EGYPT

1500

             EXODUS FROM EGYPT (MOSES)
             ENTRANCE INTO CANAAN (JOSHUA)

             THREE HUNDRED YEARS OF CHAOS
             (THE JUDGES)

             SAUL
             DAVID
1000   SOLOMON

             FOUR HUNDRED YEARS OF DIVISION
             (NORTHERN AND
             SOUTHERN KINGDOMS)

             BABYLONIAN CAPTIVITY

500

             REBUILDING OF JERUSALEM
             (EZRA, NEHEMIAH)

             FOUR HUNDRED YEARS OF SILENCE

0   BIRTH OF JESUS CHRIST

Life

GENESIS 1:1–2:25

Who is God

and why does

it matter?

Who am I and

why am I here?

1 Life

GENESIS 1:1–2:25

DISCOVER

how God is directly involved in every home, job, and marriage.

LEARN

why your life has unique value and how you cannot know yourself until you know God.

WORSHIP

as you consider the good gifts God has poured into your life.

IMAGINE yourself at a theater for the first performance of a new play. The curtain goes up, but the stage is empty. Then the author walks on and introduces himself to the audience. He tells you who he is, why he wrote the play, and what it is about. The author does not present an argument for his own existence. When he walks onto the stage, he simply introduces himself and begins to speak about himself and his work.

THE AUTHOR TAKES THE STAGE

The Bible begins with God walking onto the stage and introducing Himself.

> In the beginning God…(GENESIS 1:1)

This is His story, and so right at the beginning God introduces Himself to us. As we follow the Bible story, we will discover more about who He is and what He has done, but the first thing God wants us to know is that He is here. He also wants us to know what He has done.

> In the beginning God created the heavens and the earth. (1:1)

The Author wants us to know that what we are about to see is entirely His work. This is of great importance because the Creator has the rights of the owner. We live in a world of trademarks, registered service marks, and patents. If I say, "Have it your way," you will immediately think about Burger King. If I say, "Just do it," you immediately think about Nike. The slogan is owned by its creators.

A creator always has the rights of ownership, and God owns all that He has made. If your life were an accident arising from millennia of human history, then you would be a free agent, accountable to nobody but yourself. But if you were created, then your Creator has the full rights of ownership over your life. One or the other of these things must be true, but both of them cannot be true. Either

1. you are an accident of history and therefore completely at liberty to do whatever you please with your life—to indulge it or trash it or end it—and if that is the case your life is ultimately meaningless; or,

2. you are a created being, and if that is the case, your Creator has absolute rights of ownership over your life.

God introduces Himself as our Creator and therefore our owner. You are not your own. Your life is a trust given to you from God. You are not worthless or aimless; God chose to bring you into being. He did it on purpose, and you will discover that purpose as you get to know the One who created you.

UNDERSTANDING OURSELVES

If we do not know our Creator, we will not understand ourselves. When people start believing that they are meaningless accidents, human life becomes cheap. And if human life is cheap, it becomes disposable when it is inconvenient. First the unborn, then the handicapped, then the elderly or others who are a drain on the economy become nuisances and even expendable. Then come those who are the "wrong color," the "wrong race," or the "wrong religion."

The most monstrous evils of our time have been built on the assumption that human life is an accident. The future direction of our society will in large part be determined by whether we choose to believe that we are accidents of history or the special creation of almighty God.

When we open the Bible, we are confronted by God. He is the Creator, and He has the absolute rights of ownership over all things.

After God tells us who He is, He explains two things that He wants us to know about ourselves: (1) We are made in His image, and (2) we are absolutely dependent on Him.

THE IMAGE OF GOD

Then God said, "Let us make man in our image." (1:26)

Did you notice the plural pronoun there? God says, "Let *us* make man." This is a fascinating hint about the nature of God to be revealed more fully later.

After five days of creation, the crowning moment has come. It is almost as if God has a conversation with Himself. "Let's do it! Let Us make man in Our image, in Our likeness." An image is a reflection, and so God is telling us that He made us in such a way that we would be able to reflect something of His own nature and glory.

"Man" is used as a generic term here; it includes male and female. We are specifically told "God created man in his own image,…male and female he created them" (v. 27).

This image of God is what distinguishes people from the animals. The animals were made by God, but none of them was made like God. That is why no man or woman should ever be treated as an animal or behave as an animal. The difference between man and the animal kingdom is of enormous significance.

Early on in the Bible story, we will discover the devil taking on the form of an animal. At the center of the Bible story, we will find God taking on the form of a man. The Son of God is the image of God, and so when He took flesh, it was in the form of a man, because man was made in the image of God.

Men and women who believe that they are simply developed animals have missed the most fundamental thing that God says about them. We are made in the image of God!

THE KISS OF LIFE

Man is made in the image of God, but he must always remember that he is not God. In fact, man is rather fragile. God made the first man from the dust of the ground, so we should not be surprised if there are similarities to the animals at a biological level. But there is more to man than chemical or biological life.

> The LORD God formed the man from the dust of the ground
> and breathed into his nostrils the breath of life, and the man
> became a living being. (2:7)

God formed a corpse, and a skeletal frame lay lifeless on the ground. Then God breathed His own breath into this biodegradable corpse. He gave man the kiss of life, and the lifeless corpse became a living, self-conscious being.

God is always doing what He did that day. "He [God]…gives all men life and breath and everything else" (Acts 17:25). God sustains you one breath at a time. So if you want to sin against God intentionally, try to do it without breathing! It would be a sad thing to draw breath from God and use the energy of that breath to grieve His heart.

Here is the second key to knowing and understanding yourself: You are absolutely dependent upon God. If you can grasp those two truths—you are made in His image and dependent on Him—you will discover a great dignity and at the same time a profound humility.

God gave Adam four special gifts that made his life wonderfully rich. They were God's presence, a place, a purpose, and a partner.

TAKING A WALK WITH GOD

God is Spirit. That means that God is invisible to the human eye. Yet right at the beginning of the Bible we read about "the *sound* of the LORD God as he was walking in the garden in the cool of the day" (3:8; italics added).

God revealed Himself in a beautiful garden called Eden. We call each revelation a *theophany*, and that means an appearance of God in visible form. The Old Testament has many examples of this, and they are very important. In the earliest theophanies, God did for Adam and Eve in a visible way what He does for all His people in an invisible way.

God is eternal and invisible, and He wants to establish a relationship with the man and the woman so that they may know Him and enjoy Him. Later in the Bible story, we will see that God became a man, so it should not seem strange that in the Old Testament He should appear in a visible form. These theophanies show us the intense desire in the heart of God to establish fellowship with man.

It is almost as if the Son of God could not wait to come. He burst out of heaven, entering human time and space, and came to earth so that He could walk with the first man and woman in the garden.

Notice that "they *heard* the sound of the LORD God as He was walking in the garden." They heard the cracking of twigs and the rustling of leaves. They walked with the Son of God in Eden as surely as Peter, James, and John would walk with the Son of God in Galilee.

Adam and Eve walked with God. They asked questions and enjoyed conversation. Can you begin to imagine what this would be like? God was interested in what Adam had done in the day. He was listening to whatever was on Eve's mind. God spoke with them. The man and the woman were walking in fellowship with God.

We will see in the next chapter that this fellowship between God and man was broken, and that it has remained broken throughout the generations of human history.

Christ came into the world to restore that broken relationship and to make it possible for man to walk with God again.

That is the whole story of the Bible. Jesus Christ gives us access to the Father. We cannot see God, but when we come to Him with faith and in the name of Jesus Christ, His presence is as real as it was when He appeared in visible form to Adam. Think about that next time you pray.

A Place Called Home

Now the Lord God had planted a garden in the east, in Eden;
and there he put the man he had formed. (2:8)

It is difficult to be precise about the location of Eden, but it is important to grasp that it is a real place. We are told that it was in the east. The book of Genesis was part of the revelation God gave to Moses at Mount Sinai, so we are talking about a location east of Sinai. We are also told about four rivers (2:10–14), the Pishon and the Gihon (which are not known to us), the Tigris and the Euphrates, which run through modern Iraq. We cannot be certain about the garden's location, but it is clear that the Lord planted one somewhere in this area. (See the map "A Garden in the East.")

The significant thing is that the Lord put the man there. God appeared to Adam in a theophany and placed him in this garden. It is possible that God created Adam outside the garden and then brought him to Eden, saying, "This is the place I have prepared for you!" God created a particular place where Adam would know and enjoy the blessing of God.

I find it helpful to remember that God does the same thing for us. He has determined the exact places for all of us to live (see Acts 17:26). Try to imagine God walking with you into your home and saying, "This is where I want you to be." Or, imagine Christ walking with you into the church and saying, "This is the place I have prepared for you to grow." None of us is where we are by accident. When we know, as Adam did, that God has placed us where we are, we will find strength in the most difficult times.

There's Work to Be Done

Now the Lord God had formed out of the ground all the beasts
of the field and all the birds of the air. He brought them to the
man to see what he would name them; and whatever the man
called each living creature, that was its name. (2:19)

A GARDEN IN THE EAST

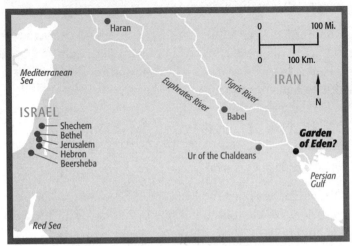

In Genesis 1, God gave names to the day and night. Now Adam was invited to participate in God's work of naming things. Science is all about giving things names. The scientist observes, reflects on what he sees, and then describes it. That was the first work that God gave Adam to do.

Right from the beginning Adam was occupied with work. "The LORD God took the man and put him in the Garden of Eden to work it and take care of it." (Genesis 2:15).

Work is a good gift from God. It existed before sin entered the world, and it will continue after sin has been cleared out. The entrance of sin into the world has affected our work and introduced frustration into it, but the first thing to say about work is that it is a good gift from God.

Notice that God brought the animals to Adam. God took a personal interest in Adam's daily work. That's worth thinking about at your desk, on the shop floor, in the school, or by the kitchen sink. God cares about your daily work and wants to be a part of it.

A MARRIAGE MADE IN HEAVEN

> The LORD God said, "It is not good for the man to be alone. I will make a helper suitable for him."…The LORD God made a woman from the rib He had taken out of the man, and he brought her to the man. (2:18, 22; emphasis added)

Once again the Lord appeared to Adam, and He said, "Adam, I have someone I want you to meet." I have no doubt that Adam's jaw dropped wide open. He certainly seemed pretty pleased! He said, "This is now bone of my bones and flesh of my flesh" (2:23).

Notice, the LORD Himself brought the two together. The first wedding service was conducted by almighty God. Try to picture it in your mind: The Lord God takes her hand and puts it into his hand, and says, "Here is the partner I have made for you!"

We will see in the next chapter that this marriage had more than its fair share of troubles. When Eve was tempted, Adam became a passive observer who did nothing to help his wife when she needed him to stand with her. Then we find both of them trying to avoid their responsibilities and pass on the blame for their troubles. But whatever their problems in the future, neither of them could ever have doubted that the reason they were together was that they had been *joined by God.*

There will be times in every marriage when a husband and wife need to come back to this. Marriage is the joining of one man and one woman by God. As the Scripture says, "For this reason a man will leave his father and mother and be united to his wife, and they will become one flesh" (2:24).

Marriage is a wonderful gift from God. When two people marry, God does in an invisible way what He did for Adam and Eve in a visible way. If you are married, try to picture God taking your hand and the hand of your spouse, and joining them together. As He does that, God says, "Be partners together, love each other, and forgive each other. Go through life together." If you are married, this is what God has done, and when you know God has joined you and your spouse together, it will help you to weather the most difficult times.

If you are looking for a marriage partner, remember that God brought the woman to Adam. The pressure of trying to find the right person can be intense. God brought Eve to Adam. You can trust God to bring the right person to you, or bring you to the right person. I am not suggesting that you should be passive, but I am suggesting that there is no need to panic. You can trust the Lord God with every area of your life.

Can you see the overwhelming goodness of God, who lavishes good gifts on the man and the woman? The Creator gives the first man a place, a purpose, and a partner, and together they share the joy of His visible presence. It was literally heaven on earth.

SPOTLIGHT ON CHRIST

In the next chapter we will see that sin brings strain into the marriage, frustration into the workplace, and leads to the first couple being evicted from their home and losing the joy of the presence of God. But even then, God will not remain at a distance from man.

Christ came into the world. The Son of God who walked with Adam in the garden took the form of a man and was born in human likeness. And when He came, the presence of God was made visible among us. He came to heal and restore what was spoiled and broken by sin. He said, "I have come that they may have life, and have it to the full" (John 10:10).

UNLOCKED

God wants you to know that He is the Creator and therefore has the right of ownership over all things, including you. God also wants you to know that He has made you in His image and that for this reason you have unique dignity and worth.

At the very beginning of human history, God made it possible for our first parents to know Him and enjoy Him. He will do whatever it takes to make this possible. God appeared to them and walked with them.

God poured out His blessing into their lives. He brought the man and his wife together. He led them to their home and gave them their work. He provided all that they needed and shared in their life. What God did for them, He continues to do for all His people. The only difference is that we don't see Him do it. We walk by faith and not by sight.

PAUSE FOR PRAYER

Thank You for the gift of prayer in which I may know Your presence as truly as Adam did in the garden. Thank You that through Your Word You speak to me as clearly as You spoke with Eve.

Thank You for the blessings You have poured into my life. I recognize Your hand in my home, my work, and my relationships. I also see how sin can spoil each of these good gifts, and steal the joy of what you have given. Pour out your blessing in a fresh way on my home, in my work, in my relationships, and in my personal walk with You. Help me to bring all these things under Your Lordship and Your control. Amen.

2

Curse

GENESIS 3:1–24

If God made

everything good,

why is the world

as it is today?

2 Curse

GENESIS 3:1–24

 DISCOVER the two greatest problems that confront every person born into this world.

 LEARN your enemy's top strategies and how you can defend against them.

 WORSHIP as you see how Jesus Christ stands up to your enemy and opens the way back into the presence of God.

IMAGINE life in Eden, the place God gave the first man and woman. Adam's work is fulfilling and fascinating. He enjoys the companionship of his wife and the company of God. When he is hungry, he reaches up and picks his food from the trees. His whole life is one of blessing and joy. That's the picture at the end of Genesis 2.

By the end of Genesis 3, everything has changed, and Adam finds himself struggling to make a life in a very different world. The man and the woman are now outside the place where God blessed them. They are excluded from this paradise called Eden, with no way back. They are away from the Tree of Life and find themselves in a wilderness where all kinds of wild animals threaten, and where they must work to get their food. They experience pain and fear and guilt, and when the evening comes, they no longer see God. Something has gone terribly wrong. Genesis 3 tells us the story.

When we feel ill and visit the doctor, we are usually looking for two things. The first is an accurate diagnosis, and the second is an appropriate prescription. Any doctor who gives prescriptions without diagnosis is to be avoided. This principle holds good in every area of life. If we don't understand the source of sickness, then we will not be able to recognize the cure. Diagnosis is where we must begin.

RECRUITING FOR THE REBELLION

The first carrier of the sickness that infected Adam and Eve is known by various names, most commonly as Satan, the devil, or the father of lies. He is the enemy of God and of mankind.

Satan wants to communicate with the woman, and so he must find some visible form in which to come. Remember that spirits are invisible to us. Satan had no entrance to the man or the woman at this point, so he approaches them through a part of the animal creation. He comes as an alluring serpent.

The Bible never gives us a full explanation of the origin of evil. It does not tell us how a being in the presence of God could find rebellion against God attractive. But it does indicate that the devil was at first an angel of light.

Angels are spirits who are in the presence of God in heaven. When "God created the heavens and the earth" (Genesis 1:1), angels were part of that invisible creation in heaven.

As one of those angels, the devil became inflated with pride in his own position and tried to usurp the position of God (see Isaiah 14:12–14). Why he should have done this is not revealed to us.

Satan's rebellion was unsuccessful and led to his being excluded from the presence of God and cast down to the earth. So right from the beginning of human history, there was an enemy bent on destroying the work of God.

This enemy came to the woman in an attempt to recruit the human race into his rebellion. His first aim was to introduce the man and the woman to the experience of evil.

READING YOUR OPPONENT'S PLAYS

A good basketball team will spend hours working on their plays. They will also study the opposition's plays so that they can work out an effective defense against them. Satan used all his best plays in his first game in the garden. Once we learn these plays we will be able to detect them and defend against them.

The First Play: Confusion

> "Did God really say, 'You must not eat from any tree in the garden'?" (v. 1)

Satan's first play is to pose a question. God had given one simple instruction to the man and the woman, and Satan's first action is to question it. If Satan could undermine the clarity of the Word of God and generate enough confusion about it, then it would be much easier for the man and the woman to disregard the Lord's command.

It is very interesting that when Satan launched his assault against Christ in the wilderness, this was again the enemy's first play. "If you are the Son of God, tell these stones to become bread" (Matthew 4:3; italics added). The enemy was attempting to bring confusion into the mind of Christ! He wanted to create uncertainty about Christ's identity, and of course he failed completely.

Whenever Satan tempts you to sin, his first strategy will be to create confusion. He will try to lower your defenses by suggesting to your mind that maybe what you want to do is not really forbidden by God, or at least that the Bible is not clear about the matter.

The Second Play: Presumption

> "You will not surely die." (v. 4)

God had made it clear that sin would result in death (2:17), but Satan suggests to the woman that the consequences of sin have been greatly exaggerated. In effect, the tempter says, "Eve, come on. You can't seriously believe that just a simple act of disobedience is going to lead to something as drastic as death!"

It's not hard to see where this strategy is heading. He wants the woman to presume on the grace of God. "After all, God loves you," he is saying, "so how could He allow anything bad to happen to you?"

Notice that Satan also used this second play against our Lord Jesus Christ. In the second temptation, Satan took Christ to the highest point of the temple, and he said: "If you are the Son of God…throw yourself down" (Matthew 4:6). He tried to suggest to Christ that if He were indeed the Son of God, He could act in any way He chose, including throwing Himself off tall buildings, and nothing bad would happen to Him.

"If You are God's Son," Satan was suggesting, "You are in a position where You can do anything You like! So here is a suggestion. Why don't You do something other people wouldn't dream of doing. Throw Yourself from the pinnacle of the temple. You know You don't need to worry about doing it, because You are the Son of God."

This is the temptation of presumption, and it is the enemy's second great strategy. When Satan tempts you to sin, he will lower your defenses with this suggestion. "The consequences won't be *that* bad. You can do this, and nothing bad will happen to you."

The Third Play: Ambition

> "God knows that when you eat of it your eyes will be opened,
> and you will be like God, knowing good and evil." (v. 5)

The man and the woman had been made in the image of God, but Satan suggests that they could now go one better. After all, why would they want to have God telling them what to do? Would it not be better if they could decide what is good and what is evil for themselves?

Satan knows how much we like that suggestion. Man is made in the image of God, but he is not content with that. Time after time, man wants to be God. Satan's third strategy is to appeal to man's ambition.

As you might have predicted, Satan also tried this third play against the Lord Jesus Christ. He showed Christ the kingdoms of the earth and said, "All this I will give you…if you will bow down and worship me" (Matthew 4:9). Satan was saying, "Think of what you can become, and don't let obedience to God get in the way."

This is one of the enemy's most subtle strategies. His primary and futile objective is to overthrow the authority of God. He loves to suggest that we should take the place of God, not because he thinks well of us but because of his deep hatred for God. He appeals to our pride when he suggests that we do not need God to tell us what is good and what is evil. His message is still the same. "You decide what is right for you!"

The fact that Satan used the same strategies in the Garden of Eden and in his assault on Christ should give us fair warning that these are the plays that he will most likely try to use against us.

The apostle Paul declared that "we are not unaware of his schemes" (2 Corinthians 2:11). Since we already know his primary offensive tactics, it will not be difficult to organize our defense. We must take the Word of God seriously. We must listen to what He says, refusing to twist the meaning of His Word to make it more convenient. We must recognize that sin always brings its consequences and that when God speaks about judgment, He is not making idle threats. We must let God be God. What God has declared good is good, and what God has declared evil is evil.

THE KNOWLEDGE OF EVIL

Earlier (Genesis 2:16–17) God had given Adam a law for life in Eden: "The LORD God commanded the man, 'You are free to eat from any tree in the garden; but you must not eat from the tree of the knowledge of good and evil.' " God's first law was, like all His commandments, a wonderful expression of His love. God had made everything good, and so "good" was the only thing that Adam knew. But it was not the only thing in the universe. Evil was already at work. It had already found expression in Satan's rebellion.

When God told Adam that he must not eat from the Tree of the Knowledge of Good and Evil, it was as if He had said, "Adam, you need to understand that there is a terrible reality in the universe, and I want to protect you from it. It's called evil. You do not know anything about it, but it already exists. I do not want you ever to experience it. So whatever you do, don't eat from this tree!"

But later Adam and Eve felt that they would like to have this knowledge of evil. Perhaps they felt they were lacking something. Perhaps curiosity drew them to this forbidden knowledge. Satan worked with the grain of curiosity, and it was not long before both Adam and Eve were convinced that this was what they wanted. The knowledge of evil!

So the first couple did what God told them not to do. They got the knowledge of evil. And we have all lived with it ever since.

Of course there was a terrible hook behind this bait. Adam found that once he had this knowledge of evil he could not get rid of it. The knowledge of evil changed him. Evil gained a grip in his life—in Eve's too—and it would be the same with all their children. Today it has a grip on us as well. You've been in its grip, and I have too. It's our primary problem.

EXCLUDED FROM PARADISE

The LORD God banished him from the Garden of Eden to work the ground from which he had been taken. (v. 23)

So God drove the first couple out and placed cherubim—angels who represent His judgment and His holiness—at the entrance to the garden, along with a flaming sword flashing back and forth. Together they bar the way to the Tree of Life.

So man is now outside the place of God's blessing. He no longer enjoys fellowship with God, and his life becomes a terrible struggle in a hostile place, where he is exposed to all kinds of danger from the wild animals, and there are thorns and thistles that had never been seen before (see v. 18).

The perfect marriage, which was a gift of God, became strained. Adam blamed Eve for the problems they were facing, and Eve must have noted that Adam had done nothing to help her during her struggle with the enemy.

Over time, the two of them would begin to notice lines and wrinkles on their skin. They would experience pain, and they would realize that this "death" that God had spoken about was a terrible reality that they could not avoid.

When the evening came, they must have wondered if God would come to them, but He never does. They are alienated from God and alone in the world. Paradise is lost and there is no way back.

NO WAY BACK

After God drove the man and woman out, He placed the cherubim and a flaming sword to guard the way to the Tree of Life (v. 24). We are told that the flaming sword was flashing back and forth, so getting around it would have been impossible. (The flaming sword speaks of the judgment of God.)

This sight must have been terrifying for Adam. He was excluded from the place where he once knew fellowship with God, and there was no way back.

So here is the Bible's diagnosis: We are spiritually sick. We have a knowledge of evil, and we were excluded from the presence of God. We can't get free from this knowledge of evil, and we can't get back into God's paradise.

The man and the woman were no longer in paradise, a place where there was only good. Having chosen the knowledge of evil, they were now outside in a hostile environment where they had to work for a living and where they experienced pain, frustration, fear, and finally death. Since then, there has been no joy that is not in some way touched with the shadow of pain.

HOPE THAT BEGAN WITH A CURSE

That is the diagnosis, so what is the prescription? Hope began on the very day that man sinned and was expelled from the garden—and it began with a curse!

> God said to the serpent,… "Cursed are you" (v. 14)

A curse is an "utterance of deity…consigning a person or thing to destruction," according to the *Concise Oxford Dictionary*, sixth edition. So when God curses the serpent, He was announcing that evil would not stand. Satan would not have the last word. Adam and Eve must have been overjoyed at hearing this news.

We can thank God for His curse on evil. Without the curse, we would be stuck with the knowledge of evil forever. But this curse opens the door of hope for us.

If God did not consign evil to destruction, who else could? Throughout human history we have tried and failed. Our newspapers are still reporting another massacre, another atrocity, another dictator. We can't get free from it. But God says "cursed are you," and from that moment on, our enemy was consigned to ultimate destruction.

Then God pronounced a second curse. He turned to the man and began to speak. "Cursed…"

Adam must have held his breath. God had cursed the serpent, and now He was looking straight at Adam as He spoke that dreadful word "cursed." Adam must have thought that He was going to be utterly destroyed, but he was in for a surprise. Instead of saying to Adam, "Cursed are you," as the LORD did to the serpent, God said, "Cursed is the ground because of you" (v. 17).

A CURSE DEFLECTED

Here we discover one of the most important things that we need to know about God. God announces that He will destroy evil. At the same time, He deflects the curse away from Adam so that it falls on the ground and does not fall on the man directly.

God is just, and the curse must go somewhere, but God finds a way to direct the curse away from the man and the woman. At the right time, God would send His Son, and then direct the curse on our sin towards Him. That is what the Cross is all about. "Christ redeemed us from the curse of the law by becoming a curse for us, for it is written: 'Cursed is everyone who is hung on a tree' " (Galatians 3:13).

The man and the woman would live with the effects of the curse on the ground. They would experience frustration, toil, pain, drought, disease and death. Now they lived in a world that was under the curse and one day would be destroyed. But the curse did not fall on them directly. When they experienced the pain and disappointment of life in this fallen world, they were reminded of the curse on the ground. But as often as they thought about that, they must have been thankful that the curse was not on them. On the very day that they had sinned, they had discovered the grace and mercy of God.

At the end of Genesis 3, there was a curse on the devil (v. 14) and a curse on the ground (v. 17). God will not allow the devil to remain as he is or this world to remain as it is. Like a computer disk with a virus, God will wipe it clean. He will reformat it and make a new heaven and a new earth that is free from this virus of sin, which has attached itself to God's creation. God has subjected "the creation… to frustration," but He has also planned a day when "the creation itself will be liberated from its bondage to decay and brought into the glorious freedom of the children of God" (Romans 8:21).

THE ONGOING BATTLE

So the LORD God said to the serpent,… "I will put enmity between you and the woman, and between your offspring and hers; he will crush your head, and you will strike his heel." (v. 14–15)

"Enmity" sums up the relentless battle against evil that has gone on through the generations of human history. Man is always trying to get rid of evil, but is constantly frustrated as he finds it breaking out in another tragedy, another horror, another dictator, another massacre. Man simply cannot get free from this "knowledge of evil."

But God promises that there will be an offspring of the woman. Someone will come into the human line. This person is not described as an offspring of the man but an offspring of the woman. When He comes, He will engage in a great struggle against the evil one.

THE DECISIVE VICTORY

A deliverer will come. He will inflict a fatal blow to the head of the enemy. He will crush the head of the enemy, and in the process, the enemy will bite the heel that crushed him. That is a wonderful picture. Imagine standing on the head of a venomous snake. In the same moment, he bites you and inflicts a wound, but then that wounded foot bears down on him and brings his destruction.

In the fullness of time, Jesus Christ did come into the world. He did not face the enemy in the tranquil beauty of a perfect garden where all the food is provided, but in a barren wilderness, where after forty days of fasting He was weak, hungry, and exhausted. Satan tried all his strategies in a vain attempt to introduce Jesus to the knowledge of evil. But when all his efforts failed, the devil was left with no option but to withdraw in defeat and hope to fight another day.

Three years later, Christ went to the cross, where He suffered and died. Through His death He inflicted a deadly wound to the enemy and opened the way for men and women to be delivered from the power of the evil one (see Colossians 2:15).

*Oh wisest love that flesh and blood
which did in Adam fail,
should fight again against the foe,
should fight and should prevail.*

—JOHN HENRY NEWMAN
"PRAISE TO THE HOLIEST IN THE HEIGHT"

SPOTLIGHT ON CHRIST

If man is ever to get back into the garden, he needs not only to get free from the power of evil, but also to get past the flaming sword and the cherubim, who represent the judgment of a holy God.

Try to imagine yourself standing with Adam and Eve and many others outside the paradise of God, looking back at the cherubim and the terrifying sword of judgment. As you look, someone comes out of the presence of God. He comes to where we are and stands with us. Then He advances towards the flaming sword. We cringe as we look. The flaming sword is flashing back and forth, and we can see what will happen to Him when He gets there. But He keeps walking forward, steadily, relentlessly.

The sword strikes Him and kills Him. It breaks His body, but in breaking His body, the sword itself is broken. The sword that killed Him lies shattered on the ground. By His death, the way back to the presence and blessing of God is opened.

When Christ died, the heavy curtain that hung in the Jerusalem temple was torn in two (Matthew 27:51). The curtain symbolized exclusion from the presence of God. Images of cherubim were stitched into the material of the curtain. So when it was torn, the cherubim were separated.

Could God have given any more powerful illustration of what Christ accomplished in His death? The cherubim were separated. The judgment fell on Him and the penalty was paid for all His people. A new and living way into the place of the blessing of God was opened.

UNLOCKED

We can only begin to make sense of our world when we understand that man has chosen the knowledge of evil and is excluded from paradise. We keep hoping that we will be able to shake free from the power of evil, but it is in us and we cannot get free. We also feel that we can make this world into something like paradise, but we can't.

But God has not abandoned us. He sent His Son into this fallen world and into our ongoing battle with evil. Christ stood His ground against the enemy and triumphed where Adam failed. He faced all the same temptations but with an entirely different outcome.

Then He went to the cross, and through His death broke the power of the enemy. Thus He opened a way past the judgment of God and back into His presence and blessing.

PAUSE FOR PRAYER

Almighty Father,

I bow before You and recognize that my deepest need is to be delivered from evil and to find a way past Your judgment. I admit that these things are beyond my power.

Thank You that You have not left me in this condition, but You have sent Your Son Jesus Christ. Thank You that evil could not attach itself to Him. Thank You that He has triumphed over my enemy. Thank You that the sword of judgment that would have been held over me was broken on Him and that He has opened the way for me to come back to You through His death on the cross. Confessing my need, and believing in what He has done, I come. Amen.

3

Salvation

GENESIS 6:5–22

What do I need

to be saved from,

and how can I

be saved?

_3_Salvation

GENESIS 6:5–22

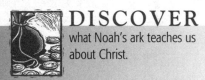

DISCOVER
what Noah's ark teaches us
about Christ.

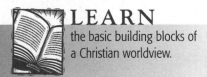

LEARN
the basic building blocks of
a Christian worldview.

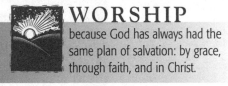

WORSHIP
because God has always had the
same plan of salvation: by grace,
through faith, and in Christ.

NEARLY everything you need to know for life can be summarized in two areas: You need to know who God is, and you need to know who you are. If you get these two things right, you will have a firm foundation for life. If you get them wrong, you will be in serious trouble.

In the opening chapters of the Bible we discover who God is and who we are. God is the Creator and therefore the owner of things. He made us and has absolute rights over us. He filled the world with good gifts for us to enjoy, and from the beginning, God has been reaching out to men and women so that we may know Him.

God made each person in His image. But early on there was a terrible catastrophe that would change the course of human history and our experience of life in this world. Man was drawn to the knowledge of evil. Adam chose to have that knowledge, and the rest of us have had to live with it ever since. The knowledge of evil is in us. That is why Paul said that when he wanted to do good, evil was at hand.

As a result of this knowledge of evil, man has been excluded from the paradise of God. He cannot approach God without facing judgment. The cherubim and a flaming sword bar the way to the Tree of Life.

TIME FOR A DELIVERER
But God gave hope in two ways. First, He promised a deliverer. Someone would be "born of a woman" who would engage in a mighty warfare with the enemy and crush his head with a fatal blow. Second, God diverted the curse away from

man. The curse fell on the ground. Adam's sin brought terrible consequences. But he was not wiped out. There remained room for him to seek the face of God. There was even the hope that some way may be found to save him from this awful curse altogether.

All this pointed toward the coming of Jesus Christ the deliverer. Born of the virgin Mary (He was without human father), He would not come from us, but He would come to us. In His subsequent death on a cross, Jesus would inflict a mortal wound on the enemy. Satan had no hold over Him. When the sword of God's judgment struck Him—in our stead—it broke, clearing a new and living way into the presence of God. Jesus has opened that way to all who will come to God through Him.

BUILDING A BIBLICAL WORLDVIEW

As we learn these foundational truths of the Christian faith, we are building a biblical worldview. A worldview is a set of core beliefs that will determine how we think on any given issue. The reason that people choose very different lifestyles is that they operate on different core convictions about who God is and who they are.

Those who hold a biblical worldview believe that God created them, that He has absolute rights over them, and that every good gift in their lives comes from His hand. If you embrace those realities, your deepest joy will be to know Him and your highest calling will be to obey Him. But, if you believe that your life is an accident and the Bible is a product of human thought, experience, and imagination, then you will conclude that every good gift has come by chance. As a result, your deepest joy will be to discover yourself, and your highest calling will be to be true to yourself.

These are two entirely different worldviews, and both of them cannot be right. Either you

- place yourself at the center, believing that you are an accident of history who must write your own rules, being accountable to nobody but yourself, and that your greatest need is to be at peace with yourself; or you

- place God at the center, believing that He is your Creator, that He writes the rules, that you are ultimately accountable to Him, and that your greatest need is to find peace with Him.

These convictions are like a rudder on a boat. They will determine the direction you take in your life. Convictions formed deep in your heart today will determine where you will be tomorrow.

Men and women who do not know what they believe about God and about themselves are like people sitting in a boat with no hand on the rudder! Their boat will go wherever the prevailing winds and currents are going. If your boat is heading for the rocks, the first thing to do is to stretch out your hand and grasp the rudder.

SAME START, DIFFERENT DIRECTIONS

These two worldviews, one centered on God and the other centered on ourselves, have been with us since the earliest times. Right from the very beginning the human family has been divided in its response to God. Adam and Eve had two children, and the world's first brothers set the rudders of their boats in totally different directions. Abel sought God; Cain struggled against God. This mystery was there from the very beginning.

Cain developed a fierce anger and hatred toward Abel (see Genesis 4:3–5). The world has always hated those who seek to walk in obedience to God. In the end, Cain killed his brother, and God gave Adam and Eve another son whose name was Seth. From that time on, Cain lived a desperately sad life. He was isolated from God and his family.

Cain's actions brought several consequences but God still showed mercy toward him(see 4:10–16). Cain built a city, and his offspring were credited with making significant contributions to music, art, and culture. God protected Cain despite his hostility. The LORD shows kindness even to His enemies. But the focus of the Bible story is on the line of Seth.

When Seth was born, "men began to call on the name of the LORD" (Genesis 4:26). Perhaps up to that time, Adam and Eve had believed that they would make it in the world, but now, after the death of their son Abel, they saw that they desperately needed the help of God, and so they began to seek Him and call on His name.

And so we come to Genesis 5, which is filled with unpronounceable names. When you come to one of these chapters in the Bible, you might be tempted to skim over fast because you don't know who these people are and can't imagine why they matter!

THE RELATIONSHIP THAT MATTERS MOST

But those names are important. The reason? They're the beginning of the line of descent into which the LORD Jesus Christ would be born. In Luke 3, we are given the genealogy from Christ back to Adam, and the names listed in verses 36–38 are exactly the same as those listed in Genesis 5. The story we are following is the story of the line into which Jesus Christ would be born.

We know almost nothing about the characters mentioned in Genesis 5. The one thing that makes their lives significant today is that they were all related to Jesus Christ. That is why their names are recorded.

Similarly, the one thing that will give you significance for all eternity is your relationship with the LORD Jesus Christ. If this world goes on for another thousand years, all of us will be completely forgotten. Nobody will have heard of you or know anything about what you did. But those who have a relationship with Christ are brought into God's purpose for time and eternity.

AMAZING GRACE

God continued to reach out to man even after Adam and Eve were excluded from the garden. God did not abandon people or lose interest in them. All the way through the Bible we find God reaching out to save people by grace, through faith, and in Christ. The pattern is established right at the beginning in the story of Noah:

> Noah found favor in the eyes of the LORD. (6:8)

He found favor, or grace, with God. That is the first occurrence in the Bible of the word that means grace. God looked with kindness and compassion on Noah, and God's grace was expressed in two ways. First, God told Noah that judgment is coming.

> God said to Noah, "I am going to put an end to all people, for
> the earth is filled with violence because of them." (v. 13)

How did God say this to Noah? It is quite possible that Noah actually heard an audible voice. We have seen that when God appeared to Adam, He spoke and walked with him. God also spoke in an audible voice when Christ was baptized and at the transfiguration. In the Old Testament, God spoke to the prophets in dreams and visions. The book of Hebrews tells us that "God spoke to our forefathers through the prophets at many times and in various ways" (1:1). By whatever means, God spoke to Noah and made it clear to him that judgment was coming.

Noah did not keep the message to himself. We are told in 2 Peter 2:5 that Noah was "a preacher of righteousness." He was the first preacher in the Bible. God spoke to him and God spoke through him so that a whole community would hear the Word of God.

The Bible records a number of occasions when God brought judgment on particular communities. They include the flood, the destruction of Sodom and Gomorrah, and the fall of Jerusalem in 586 B.C. These examples of God's judgment in history point forward to the final calamity when God will judge the whole world in righteousness. The first way in which God shows us His grace is that He warns us of the judgment that is coming.

Second, God showed His grace by telling Noah clearly and specifically what he should do in order to be kept safe through it:

> "Make yourself an ark of cypress wood." (6:14)

Knowing about a coming judgment would not be of much help to us unless there were some way in which we could be saved from it. The message of judgment is not the angry outburst of a fierce God; it is the gracious call of a loving God who says, "I must destroy evil, and I will destroy it. But I do not want to destroy you, so here is the way you can escape."

DELIVERANCE THROUGH FAITH

> By faith Noah, when warned about things not yet seen, in holy fear built an ark to save his family. By his faith he condemned the world and became heir of the righteousness that comes by faith (Hebrews 11:7; emphasis added)

When the Bible says that Noah was "a righteous man" (6:9), it does not mean that he was a man of perfect character. He needed the grace of God as much as anybody else. The thing that marked him out as "righteous" was that he believed the Word of God and acted on it. God spoke to him and he believed God, and so he became heir of the righteousness that is by faith.

It could not have been easy for Noah to believe God in his day. God told him to prepare for something that had never happened before. There had never been a flood that had destroyed all forms of life. Why should anyone think that such a thing would happen in his or her lifetime?

God tells us that we must prepare for something that has never happened before. Jesus Christ will come to judge the living and the dead. The world still receives this message with ridicule (see 2 Peter 3:3). That is how it was in the time of Noah. People did not take the warnings of God's judgment seriously then, and many do not take these warnings seriously today.

I have no doubt that if they had aerosol paint cans in the time of Noah, there would be kids who would go to work with graphic slogans like "Noah is nuts." If there had been journalists in that day, they would have written articles with headlines like "The Ship That Will Never Go to Sea." The article would have begun this way:

"Fundamentalist preacher Noah, son of Lamech, has aroused curiosity with a new method of promoting his religious beliefs. Claiming that God has spoken to him, he is constructing a seagoing vessel hundreds of miles from the nearest coastline.

"The work has attracted large groups of sightseers. Those who gather at the construction site are treated to a vintage sermon on the need for repentance and the coming judgment.

"When asked about the response to his preaching, Noah was unable to identify a single person outside his own family who believed his warning."

No doubt at times Noah must have wondered himself. Faith has its questions. If there were no questions, we would not need faith. There are times in the Christian life, when you ask yourself, "Why am I doing this?"

Doubt usually comes to a head when things go wrong, or when God's promise seems delayed. Every time it rained, Noah must have thought that the moment had come. But, as folks would no doubt point out to Noah, it never came to anything. Sometimes he must have wondered if it ever would. Still he believed the Word of God, and because he believed, he obeyed.

FAITH IN ACTION

True faith always shows itself in action. The evidence of Noah's faith was that he built the ark. He believed what God told him and he acted on it. Remember, "Faith without works is dead" (James 2:26 NKJV). Luther described faith as a tree, and he pointed out that faith is not a dead tree, but a living tree bursting with fruit.

Our LORD Jesus Christ commented on this story:

> "As it was in the days of Noah, so it will be at the coming of the Son of Man. For in the days before the flood, people were eating and drinking, marrying and giving in marriage, up to the day Noah entered the ark; and they knew nothing about what would happen until the flood came and took them all away. That is how it will be at the coming of the Son of Man."
> (MATTHEW 24:37–39)

There is nothing wrong with eating, drinking, marrying, and giving in marriage. Noah was married and so were his three sons. They all ate every day. But Noah's great priority was to be ready for the day God had told him about, and the only way to be ready was to believe what God had said and to do what He had commanded.

Scripture tells us that one day God will send a disaster greater than the flood (see 2 Peter 3:10). On that day, Jesus warned, many people will be in the same position as those who heard Noah and did not believe (see Matthew 24:35–39).

WAITING WITH FAITH

God told Noah to get into the ark a full seven days before the rain began (7:4–7). Loading the ark when there was not a drop of rain falling from the sky was an act of faith. There was no obvious reason for getting in there except for the Word of God. Noah must have felt rather foolish.

Then the rain came. It was not just rain coming down, but also springs of water coming up from the earth (7:11). The ship built in the desert rose, and Noah and his family were lifted up and taken into a new world.

SPOTLIGHT ON CHRIST

The flood is past history. It is a judgment that will never be repeated (see 9:8–16). But God warns us about another more terrible judgment to come. Just as God provided the ark for Noah, God has provided a way for us to be saved from the final judgment through Jesus Christ.

CHRIST, THE ARK

All who were inside the ark were safe. All who were outside the ark were destroyed. God has provided an ark for us. *Christ is the ark!*

God spoke to the people through Noah's preaching, telling them that there was an ark in which they could be saved, if they would come into it. The same God is speaking through His Word today. He points us to Christ and tells us that we can be saved if we come to Him.

The apostle Paul describes Christians as being "in Christ." Just as Noah was in the ark, so you can be *in Christ*. When the day of judgment comes, those who are "in Christ" will be lifted by Christ and taken into a new world.

This ark is open to all who will come. Jesus said, "Whoever comes to me I will never drive away" (John 6:37). The people of Noah's time had an open door of opportunity.

God sent a preacher to warn the people. An ark was built in their own community. Some people would have walked past it every day.

GET OUT OF THE RAIN!

One day, some years ago, I was sitting in my study in London writing a sermon for the coming Sunday. The rain was pouring down outside—a real London soaker!

An elderly couple were walking up the street. The rain had obviously caught them by surprise because neither of them had a raincoat or an umbrella. They stood under a tree that was at the edge of our property. It was winter, and the tree was absolutely bare, so it gave them no shelter whatsoever.

I grabbed a coat and went out to them. "You'll get soaked out here," I said. "Why don't you come into the house?" They looked at me, and in true polite English style said, "No, thank you very much; we are quite all right out here."

"But you are getting soaked!" I said. "You can come in and be dry."

To this day I do not know what they were afraid of, but nothing I said could persuade them, and in the meantime I was getting soaked myself. So I left the door to the house open and told them that if they wanted to come in, they were more than welcome. They never moved an inch.

That sudden rainstorm is a good picture of the judgment of God. If we stand alone, the rains will fall on us directly, and we will be overwhelmed by them. But if we are in the house, the downpour will fall on the roof, and because we are inside, it will not touch us.

Jesus Christ is the refuge God has provided for us—the ark that shelters against the storm of God's judgement. When He died on the cross, the judgment of God for our sins fell on Him. And God invites us to come to Him as our shelter. One day the judgment of God will fall, but when it does, it will not fall on us because it has already fallen on Him. "There is now no condemnation for those who are *in Christ Jesus*" (Romans 8:1, italics added).

Are you "in Christ"? Have you come to Him and put your trust in Him as Savior and LORD? Why would you stand outside, when the door is open for you to come in? If you will come *into Christ,* then you will be safe from the judgment of God.

UNLOCKED

Grace, faith, and salvation "in Christ" are not new ideas that emerge in the New Testament. The Bible is one story. God is gracious. He always has been and always will be. He speaks and invites us to believe His Word.

The ark helps us to understand what it means to be "in Christ." Just as Noah and his family were brought safely through the judgment of God because they were in the ark, so we will be brought safely through the final judgment if we are "in Christ."

If you have chosen to believe that God is a product of human imagination and experience, then you will feel that all the talk of judgment is outdated and inappropriate. You will feel that the whole point of life is to find personal fulfillment. But if you believe that at the end of your life you will stand before almighty God and give an account to Him, then you will know that the highest priority in this life is to be ready for that day.

PAUSE FOR PRAYER

Here's a model prayer for those who want to enter the spiritual ark God provides. This prayer is an opportunity to come to Jesus Christ, the Son of God and your Deliverer from God's judgment. (If you pray this prayer, I invite you to write the publisher at the address on the last page of the book for information on beginning the Christian life.)

Almighty God,

I believe You are the Creator and that You have absolute rights over my life. I recognize that I have a knowledge of evil and that I am excluded from paradise. I believe Your Word about judgment to come and recognize that apart from You I have no other hope.

Thank You that in Your grace You sent the LORD Jesus Christ. I believe that if I am in Him I will be saved from the judgment to come. I believe in Him today. I put my whole trust in Him. I come and call upon Him to be my Savior. By Your Spirit, place me in Him, and make me secure, through Jesus Christ.

Thank You, God, for Your grace in delivering me from sin's judgment and giving me this gift of eternal life. In Jesus' name I pray. Amen.

4

Judgment

GENESIS 11:1–12:3

Why did God

cause the peoples

of the world to

speak in different

languages?

4 Judgment
GENESIS 11:1–12:3

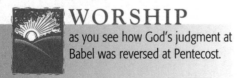

DISCOVER
how prayer began.

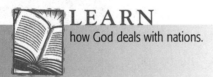

LEARN
how God deals with nations.

WORSHIP
as you see how God's judgment at
Babel was reversed at Pentecost.

J UST one more push and he was out. And a moment later, the noise began as the world's first baby announced his arrival on the scene. His mother had no midwife. She had only her husband to help her, and he didn't have the faintest idea of what to do.

Come to think of it, neither did she; but somehow in the mercy of God, they both got through, and now she could hold their little son, Cain, in her arms and say what Adam had said about her, "Here is bone of my bones and flesh of my flesh." I wonder what they said to each other. What would it have been like for the first couple to have the first baby?

Eve must have seen the blessing of God in the birth of her child. After all, God had said that it would be through the offspring of the woman that the head of the serpent would be crushed. Perhaps as she looked into her son's eyes, she pondered how he might reverse the tide of evil and restore them to paradise.

If those were her thoughts, she must have been very disappointed, because the baby into whose seemingly innocent eyes she stared turned out to be the world's first murderer. Far from being the one who would deliver the family from evil, Cain was the one who introduced new depths of evil to the world and new depths of pain to his parents' hearts.

The early chapters of Genesis chart the growing power of sin in the world. This "knowledge of evil" that seemed so attractive at the beginning turned out to be a destroying power and a bitter enemy.

THE GROWING POWER OF SIN

In Genesis 3, we read about one act of disobedience to God. It seems a very simple thing, but the point is that sin did not end there. It is almost impossible to commit a single sin, because sin is a power, and once that power is given room, it grows as it attaches itself to you. In Genesis 4, a baby boy arrived, and the sin that was a free choice for his parents was in him when he was born. It was there from the very beginning. Adam became alienated from God, but Cain began his life in that position.

Genesis 4 describes how Cain became an angry young man. An impulse to fight against God was already inside him, and when he saw his brother enjoying the blessing of God, that made his anger even worse. Cain told his brother, "Let's go out to the field." The two of them went out, and while they were there alone, "Cain attacked his brother Abel and killed him" (4:8).

Evil had reached a new depth. Violence had erupted for the first time. But it didn't end there. Sin would continue to mar the human race.

Adam had a third son, Seth, who replaced Abel in his father's mind: " 'God has granted me another child in place of Abel.'...At that time men began to call on the name of the LORD" (4:25–26). It is not surprising that people began to seek God at that time. The effects of sin went much further than making life difficult at work for Adam and making the bearing of children a painful experience for Eve. Sin was now at work even in their own children. Perhaps they had thought at the beginning that if they had just been able to guide their children by teaching them the difference between good and evil, then everything would turn out fine. But now they knew that they were up against the power of sin. And they begin to call out to God, "We thought we could do this on our own, but now we see that unless You help us, this knowledge of evil will destroy us."

PARENTS IN PAIN

It's very easy for us to think that if we provide a loving environment for our kids, give them the best education that we can, feed them and dress them well, and put them into the best youth program we can find, the result will be godly kids. And then we discover that it's not always like that. We discover this mystery of the power of sin that operates inside human nature. And when we see it, we don't really know what to make of it. The problem is many of us never come to terms with the reality of the power of sin.

When Adam and Eve finally grasped that evil really was a growing power, they began to call on the name of the LORD. They prayed when they were faced with pain. They cried out, "Oh, God, this power of evil is destroying our family. We need Your grace." That's where prayer was discovered. Maybe you will discover the reality of prayer in your pain also.

Genesis 5 describes a continuing line of people through many generations who knew that their only hope was in God, and gave themselves to prayer. It couldn't have been easy for them, because with every generation, new kinds of evil were beginning to appear. We saw in the last chapter that man's wickedness on earth became great, and that "every inclination of the thoughts of his heart was only evil all the time" (6:5). The world "was filled with violence" (6:11 NKJV). In a short time the human race had come a long way, from one act of disobedience in the garden to a tide of violence that was sweeping across the earth.

GOD APPLIES THE BRAKES

When God sent the flood, He cut the entire human population back to just one family of eight people. God chose the family of Noah. They were the best family around. With His judgment by water, God applied the brakes to runaway sin.

Noah had a wonderful opportunity. He emerged from the ark like a new Adam. It was a new beginning in a new environment, with no old scores to settle, no enemies, just one family of eight people. But Noah carried the seeds of sin into the new world with him, and it is not long before we find Noah getting drunk (9:20–23) and the seeds of cynicism growing in one of his children. Sin is a power; wherever it is given room, it will grow in strength, and it will take you where you do not want to go.

This is one of the important truths that God teaches us in the Bible. You need to remember that when you read about the wicked acts of Lot's daughters, or the deceit of Abraham's lies, or the lust of Judah with a supposed prostitute (who was really his daughter-in-law; see 38:13–19). The Bible contains some terrible stories. It is a holy book, but it tells us that we live in an unholy world, in which men and women have made wretched choices that have long-term consequences over generations. Far from telling us that man gets better and better, which is what our society likes to believe, the Bible tells us that as man moves away from God, he becomes worse and worse.

BATTLING THE BINDWEED

I grew up in Scotland, but my wife, Karen, and I lived in London for sixteen years. When we came as a newly married couple to our home in north London, the garden was overgrown. The church, having called a new pastor, decided that they should clean the place up. So they sent teens from the high school group to help us. There must have been thirty of us working together. At the end of the day, the place looked magnificent. Pruned roses, a freshly cut lawn, and not a weed in sight. But underneath the line of sight, hidden in the ground, a root system of the bindweed remained.

Bindweed is a fast-growing, climbing weed. Homeowners hardly see it at first. It rises like a little shoot out of the ground, and then twists itself around the stems of the roses.

Once established, bind weed is an absolute nightmare to remove. If you pull it from the top, it will just snap. If you pull it from the bottom, the same thing happens. The weed will reroot every time it touches the ground. Even an inch of it will sprout, and once it attaches itself to the clay soil and gets into the root systems of plants, it's almost impossible to remove. Karen and I battled that stuff for sixteen years, just growing, cutting back, growing, cutting back.

As I look back on it, I think the only thing that I could have done was to uproot all the plants—flowers, bushes, everything—and throw them out. We should have taken out the soil as well, and brought in some new earth. Since we left, I have discovered that my successor has poured concrete over the lot. He's a wise man. I should have thought of that years ago.

Sin is like this. When you choose to violate one of God's commands, you plant a living seed, and it will grow. The devil says, "This one experience of evil will be good for you," but the reality is that it will bind you. The devil tells you, "This experience of evil will broaden your horizons." The reality is that sin will set up terrible battles within your soul. And the deeper you get into the entanglement of sin, the harder the battle you will face in getting free from it.

The devil comes and he says, "Just tell a little lie. Just nurse that grudge for a little while. Just push the sexual boundaries a little way. Just use a little foul language like everyone else does." The reality is that the lie will soon have you caught in a web of deceit; you will tell other lies to cover the first. The grudge will soon encase your heart with a shell of bitterness. The pushing of the sexual boundaries will soon pull you into the power of lust. And that use of foul language will soon drag you into the power of blasphemy.

Jesus said, "Everyone who sins is a slave to sin" (John 8:34). When you make a deliberate choice to do the thing that God has told you not to do, you establish slavery inside your own soul. My heart sometimes breaks when I see young folks honestly believing that they're going to make their future better by experimenting with all kinds of things that God has told them not to touch. You are setting up battles that you will live with for years.

PREVENTION IS BETTER THAN CURE

Author and pastor Chuck Swindoll has a helpful analogy when he talks about a father trying to teach his teenager to drive. There are two possible approaches: the corrective and the preventive. Corrective is you take your keys and you say to your son or your daughter, "Take out the car, and see how you get on. And when you've crashed it, we will sit down and talk. That will be a wonderful opportunity for you to learn from your own personal experience." How many fathers have tried this approach? Not one, because they know that the issues are much too serious. You don't wait until disaster happens and then teach some kind of remedial lesson.

Swindoll, of course, recommends that fathers use the preventive approach. They should sit in the car and tell their daughter, "I want you to learn to drive in such a way that you will never have an accident. I don't want to see that pretty face of yours scarred. I don't want to see you injured, and I don't want you injuring anyone else either. I love you so I want to teach you to drive in the way that will be as safe as possible for you, and for everyone else. If you drive by these rules and regulations …you could very likely go a long period of time without a single scrape."[1]

The first thing that the Bible says to us about sin is "Don't go there." There are some battles that you should never get into, and you can stay clear of them by making wise choices. Flee from evil. Get as far from it as you possibly can, because it is a growing power. Don't set yourself up for wounds and scars and battles that may be with you for years. Don't plant those seeds that years later you wish you had never allowed to get there. Do not give the devil a foothold.

Maybe you're thinking, *I wish I had thought about that years ago, because I've done some things that have formed habits in my life and now they're battles within my soul.* That's a great response. You are being honest about the weed you've allowed to grow. Now is the time to deal with them. Don't let it go one more day.

God will not allow the bindweed to take over His garden, so He cuts it back. That's a good definition of judgment in this world. It is God cutting sin back. And it's a marvelous thing, because if God did not cut sin back, it would destroy everything good that God has made. You see this throughout the book of Genesis. Adam and Eve chose to disobey God, so God checked the progress of their sin by excluding them from the garden. Cain became the first murderer, so God separated him from the family. In the time of Noah, evil multiplied, so God cut it back through the flood. But sin keeps growing, and it was not long before a community of people at Babel found a new way to express their defiance towards God.

THE "NEW" TECHNOLOGY

Men were migrating eastward, and as they did, an idea was born for a magnificent project. They had developed new technology—bricks! They were a marvelous new discovery and opened up a wonderful new world of possibilities. "Now we will be able to build higher than we ever thought possible before. So let's see how far we can go. Let's build a tower right up into the heavens."

The problem with this building was not its height, but its purpose:

> "Let us build ourselves a city, with a tower that reaches to the heavens, so that we may make a name for ourselves and not be scattered over the face of the whole earth." (11:4)

The purpose of this city was to proclaim man's greatness. Man wanted to make a name for himself and to provide for his own security. Once again, man was grasping at the throne of God. "Hey, we can make a name for ourselves. We can be up there." Instead of worshiping God and believing in Him, man wants to worship and believe in himself. This is not glory to God in the highest. This is glory to man in the highest.

So God came down and took a look at what they were doing (v. 5). Just as He came down in the Garden of Eden, God was watching the building of man's city. God allowed it to proceed to a certain point, and then He cut it back.

The LORD said,

> "If as one people speaking the same language they have begun to do this, then nothing they plan to do will be impossible for them. Come, let us go down and confuse their language so they will not understand each other." (v. 6)

CONFUSION ON THE TWENTY-SECOND FLOOR

It's not difficult to imagine what this must have been like. For the last two years, you have been working with the same colleague on the twenty-second floor of the Tower of Babel. At the end of the day, you say good-bye, pack up your tools, and go home to your family. Next morning you ask him if he saw the game on the television last night (or something like that), and he responds to you with these incomprehensible sounds. You ask him if he needs an aspirin, and you get more meaningless sounds. What is wrong with this guy?

You soon discover that the rest of the crew working on the twenty-second floor is also uttering these incomprehensible sounds, and you wonder if this is some kind of joke.

Eventually, to your great relief, you find someone else on the building site who speaks just like you. So you say to him, "The rest of these folks around here are mad. I can't understand a word they're saying." Soon the two of you find some other folks who speak like you. One says, "You know, this town's turning into some kind of madhouse."

"Yeah, I agree."

"Me too. It's hard to get anything done with these guys. They used to talk sense, but now…"

So all of you agree to pack your tools and move off to create a new community somewhere else, a place where everyone speaks the same language.

> *The LORD scattered them over the face of the whole earth.* (v. 9)

As God looked down, Babel was being abandoned by little groups of families going in every direction over the face of the earth. They were all suspicious of one another. They all felt that the others had tried to make fools of them. The seeds of the future conflict were already sown.

Interesting. The very thing they tried to avoid—disunity—is the thing that God caused to happen.

Notice the pattern. God allows man's pursuit of his own greatness to get to a certain point and then He acts. He did it with Sodom and Gomorrah. He did it with Babylon. He did it with Greece. He did it with Rome, and He has done it with every empire in human history.

That's just one reason for us to cry to God for mercy on our nation. We need it. And it's not just true of nations. It's true individually. It is possible to live a double life. Do you have a secret sin that you have cherished, and that no one else knows about? God will allow you to get to a certain point and then He will cut you back. He must do that, because those He loves, He disciplines (see Hebrews 12:6), and the only alternative is to give you up to the weed of sin until it chokes you.

ROOM FOR GOD'S GRACE

God's judgment is never His final word. When God cuts sin back, it is always to create room for His grace. Adam and Eve were excluded from the garden, but there was the promise of a deliverer. Cain murdered his brother, but then Seth was born and there was a new line of hope. The flood destroyed all life, but Noah was saved in the ark. So when God brought His judgment at the Tower of Babel, we are left wondering how grace will take the initiative.

At the end of the story of the Tower of Babel, we read a genealogy beginning with Shem and ending with Terah (11:10–26). This doesn't sound very promising, but one of Terah's three sons was named Abram; he was later renamed Abraham. The New Testament describes him as a man who was looking for a city whose builder and maker is God (Hebrews 11:10). Abraham had a burning passion to be part of a community that would be the opposite of Babel, where people honor God and trust Him for their security.

God appeared to Abraham (see Acts 7:2), just as He had appeared to Adam in the garden. Up to that time Abraham had known nothing about God. His family had worshiped idols (see Joshua 24:2). But when God appeared to Abraham, He promised to bless him and his descendants, and He pledged that through the line of Abraham every nation on the face of the earth would be blessed (Genesis 12:1–3).

God scattered the nations across the face of the earth. But the judgment was not God's last word to the nations. Instead, God promised that His blessing would come through the line of Abraham.

SPOTLIGHT ON CHRIST

The rest of the Old Testament follows this family history. It started with Adam and Seth, then Noah and Shem, then Abraham, Isaac, and Jacob, leading to Judah and David.

Then, in the New Testament, we learn of the birth of a baby in this line. His mother Mary holds Him in her arms and gives Him the name Jesus. For unlike that first baby who brought new depths of evil, this one would "save his people from their sins" (Matthew 1:21). Jesus taught the words of God and did the work of God. And then He was crucified. But on the third day, He rose from the dead. He appeared to many, and forty days later, He ascended back to heaven.

Then on the Day of Pentecost, God reversed Babel. In a unique miracle in the vocal chords of the apostles, God caused them to speak in languages they did not know so visitors from other countries could understand.

Now there were staying in Jerusalem God-fearing Jews from every nation under heaven. When they heard this sound, a crowd came together in bewilderment, because each one heard them speaking in his own language. Utterly amazed, they asked: "Are not all these men who are speaking Galileans? Then how is it that each of us hears them in his own native language?…[W]e hear them declaring the wonders of God in our own tongues!" (ACTS 2:5–8, 11)

Do you see the grace of God here? At Babel, man was lifted up, and God confused their language with the result that they are divided and scattered. At Pentecost, Christ was lifted up, and God spoke to the nations in their individual languages with the result that they were united and gathered.

The Acts of the Apostles goes on to tell us how the gospel spread through the nations. The blessing that God promised to all nations through the line of Abraham had been released to every people through Jesus Christ.

The story runs through the Bible until you get to the very last book, the Revelation to John, where the apostle describes a holy city. At the center of the city, there is not a tower but a throne, and Jesus Christ is sitting there. Around the throne are assembled people from every tribe and nation and language and culture. They are not lifting up their own names; they are lifting up the name of Christ. Together they are worshiping the Lamb of God, and they are shouting: "Salvation belongs to our God, who sits on the throne, and to the Lamb" (Revelation 7:10).

UNLOCKED

It was God who divided mankind into different linguistic groups. He did this in order to put a brake on man's growing rebellion. The brake has been remarkably effective. Throughout human history, leadership has consistently attempted to bring the nations together, but any success has always been limited and short-lived.

But God is bringing people from all nations together through Jesus Christ. In heaven all the barriers that have divided people through history—race, class, language, and gender—will be completely removed. God calls His people to begin expressing that union in the church.

PAUSE FOR PRAYER

Take a moment to be quiet before God, and then answer these questions: Do you see in yourself the rebellious and self-serving attitude of Babel? Will you embrace God's alternative to Babel?

Almighty Father,

I recognize that I am often more interested about the honor of my name than I am in the honor of Your name. I confess that too much of my life is concerned with gratifying myself rather than glorifying You.

Thank You that through Jesus Christ You are creating a new community of people who will honor Your name, and that You are drawing Your people to faith in Your Son from every tribe and nation and language. May Your gospel come to people from every nation. Help me to do my part in making Your name known. In Jesus' name I pray. Amen.

NOTE

1. Adapted from Charles Swindoll, *David: A Man of Destiny and Passion* (Nashville: Word, 1997), 212.

5

Blood

EXODUS 3, 12

Why is there

such a strong

emphasis on

blood in the

Bible story?

5 Blood

EXODUS 3, 12

DISCOVER
the unique name by which God has made Himself known.

LEARN
the true significance of the plagues in Egypt.

WORSHIP
as you see how Christ's blood delivers us from the terrors of God's judgment.

2100 B.C.

CA. 2092 ABRAHAM'S JOURNEY INTO CANAAN

CA. 2092 THE PATRIARCHS
–1875 ABRAHAM–JACOB

2000

1900

CA. 1876 JACOB TO EGYPT

1800

FOUR HUNDRED YEARS OF SLAVERY IN EGYPT

1700

1600

1500

CA. 1447 THE EXODUS

CA. 1407 CONQUEST OF
–1400 CANAAN

1400

1300

1200

HAVE you ever been promised something and it never came? Abraham waited a long time on two promises. God had promised to bless Abraham with a family and a home (Genesis 12:2; 13:15), and Abraham's faith was stretched to the limits as he trusted God for both of these promises. Years passed without any sign of Sarah conceiving a child.

God left it until their old age when all human hopes of conceiving a child were completely finished. Then He intervened, and Isaac was born. God had fulfilled the first promise.

Isaac had two sons, Jacob and Esau, and Jacob had twelve sons, who became the fathers of the twelve tribes of Israel. The promise about the land for these descendants of Abraham was not straightforward either. Abraham had obeyed the call of God and left his home to go to the place that God would show him, but when he came to Canaan, he found that the land was already occupied. It would be some time before God's promise to give the land to his descendants would be fulfilled.

Isaac and Jacob raised their respective families in Canaan, but in Jacob's later years there was a famine, and the whole family moved to Egypt, where they found food. God had brought Jacob's son Joseph, who had been cruelly treated by his brothers, to a prominent position in Egypt, and in this way, God provided for the whole family.

Jacob's descendants remained in Egypt for the next four hundred years, and during that time grew from an extended family of seventy people into a nation of around two million.

INSTEAD OF THE PROMISE…PERSECUTION

At the beginning of the book of Exodus, we find this growing Hebrew nation facing persecution. It was the first example of violent racism, and especially of anti-Semitism, which has been one of the great evils of history. The Egyptians repressed the Hebrews by subjecting them to forced labor, but the greatest evil was that the Pharaoh decreed that all of the male Hebrew babies were to be thrown into the river Nile (Exodus 1:22).

When Moses was born, his mother put him in a basket on the Nile River. Pharaoh's daughter found him and brought him into the palace to care for him. In God's wonderful providence, Moses' mother was appointed to nurse him.

When he became an adult, Moses felt outrage over the way the Egyptians treated his own people. Eventually he took matters into his own hands and killed an Egyptian who was abusing one of the Hebrews. When word of this got out, he had to run for his life. He came to the land of Midian, where he married Zipporah, and settled down to make a living as a shepherd.

On one occasion, he was tending his sheep in the area of Mount Sinai, which is also called Mount Horeb in the Bible. It was here that God appeared to him in the burning bush and told him to go back to Egypt and tell Pharaoh, "Let My people go!"

Moses obeyed this instruction, and the next four books of the Bible tell the story of how over a period of forty years God brought these people out of Egypt and eventually back into the land of Canaan from which their fathers had originally come.

GOD BREAKS HIS SILENCE

It was four hundred years since Jacob and the family moved to Egypt, and in all of that time, God had been silent. No doubt Moses' mother would have taught him about the God of Abraham, Isaac, and Jacob. But by the time of Moses, these stories must have seemed like ancient history. (After all, not many high school students today find stories from the sixteenth or seventeenth centuries compelling or life changing!)

We know that Moses received a secular education in the pharaoh's palace. That meant that just like any student in a secular university today, he would have had to grapple with teaching about God from his professors that was very different from the teaching he had received from his parents.

In the palace he would have learned about the Egyptian Pantheon, about Orisis, Hekt, Apis, and Ra, the gods of Egypt. So Moses would have been in the same position as a student today who knows the stories of the Bible, but has been brought up in a secular society in which the God of the Bible is regarded as one God among many possible options. It would be no surprise if, in the palace of Egypt, they had taught him that any god you worship is really only a reflection of the culture in which you are raised.

So the great question for Moses must have been, "Who is God?" The story of how he discovered the answer is found in Exodus 3. After four hundred years of silence, the God who came down in the Garden of Eden, who called Abraham and wrestled with Jacob, now came down again to speak with Moses.

THE SELF-SUSTAINING FIRE

This is how it happened. Moses saw a fire resting on a bush, but it did not burn the bush on which it rested. In other words, the fire was self-sustaining. It did not depend on the bush for fuel. All other fires go out when they have exhausted the available fuel. A candle only burns until the wax is gone and then the flame goes out. But this fire was unlike any other. It consumed nothing. It sustained its own life.

Moses had never seen anything like it. He drew closer to look at this self-existent, self-sustaining fire. As he did, the God who spoke to Adam in an audible way began to speak out of the fire.

> "I am the God of your father, the God of Abraham, the God
> of Isaac and the God of Jacob." (3:6)

Suddenly, it all fell into place for Moses. The stories he had heard about God were all at least four hundred years old, and at times he may have wondered if this God was confined to the past. But now the God who appeared to his predecessors was speaking to him! This self-existent, self-sustaining God could not be confined to any time or place in history. He revealed Himself to Abraham, Isaac, and Jacob, but He was not dependent on them. "He is," and He exists by the power of His own being.

Then God revealed the wonderful name by which He wanted to be known: "I am who I am" (Exodus 3:14). Almighty God was saying, in effect, "I am the God who called Abraham and appeared to Isaac. I am the God who wrestled with Jacob, and I am speaking to you. I *am*, and because I am, I always will be."

CONFUSION ABOUT GOD

There's a place near Birmingham, England, called *Spaghetti Junction*. It is a maze of motorways and urban roads that come together in a twisted mass of concrete which, when viewed from the air, shows a remarkable resemblance to a plate of spaghetti. When a motorist takes a wrong turn at Spaghetti Junction, he can spend an hour returning to where he started, as I know from bitter experience.

Many people today look at "religion" in the same way motorists often look at Spaghetti Junction. Though God walked onto the stage of human history, created the heavens and the earth, and made us in His image, Satan, our great enemy, wanted to keep us from knowing God. God came down so that our first parents would know Him, but Satan brought confusion by adding a multiplicity of gods. The result is that many people avoid thinking seriously about God. Like drivers who steer clear of Spaghetti Junction, they're convinced that if they go anywhere near, they will become hopelessly lost!

> It is deeply insulting...to reshape God into a more pleasing image.

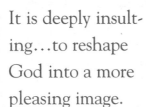

Did you know that there are 900 million gods in India? That's one for every person who lives there. People choose the object of their own devotion. I think we are well on the way to having several million gods in America as well, as we fashion gods to support the lifestyles or values that we choose.

When people say that they don't believe in a God who will judge, or they can't believe in a God who would save people only through Jesus, what they are really saying is that they do not like the God of the Bible, and they have chosen to fashion another god, more to their liking.

If you want to know how offensive that is, imagine a man editing a digital picture of his wife. Imagine him making changes to all the things that he does not like about her in the picture. He deems the nose too large, so he changes its shape. He believes she weighs too much, so he slims her image. Then, when he has the picture as he would want it to be, he goes to his wife and tells her, "I've grown tired of you as you are; here is a picture of what I would like you to be."

Even as I describe the encounter, you can feel the personal insult. The man's wife might well look him straight in the eye and say, with a note of defiance, "I am who I am."

In the same way, it is deeply insulting to God for us to open the Bible, and seeing many things about Him that we do not like, decide to reshape God into a more pleasing image. God is not whoever you want Him to be. He is who He is!

The living God, who introduced Himself as creator of all things on the first page of the Bible, comes down and says, "I am who I am!" Like the fire with no beginning and no end, He depends on nobody and on nothing for His existence. He is subject to no requirement, no restriction, and no obligation.

THE LIVING GOD AND THE OTHER GODS

It is all very well for the God of the Bible to say, "I am," but how do we know that He is, and that the other gods are not? That is the point of the plagues. Pharaoh refused to obey God's command to let the Hebrew people go. He did not recognize the authority of God in his life. Perhaps he took the view that he had his own gods, and that there was no reason for him to obey the God who had spoken to Moses.

As long as Pharaoh continued to believe that he could worship his own gods, he would never submit to the authority of the one true God. So the living God gave proof of who He is by bringing down the powers behind the gods of Egypt. God said,

> "I will bring judgment on all the gods of Egypt. I am the LORD." (12:12)

We noted the many Egyptian gods Moses learned about, including Orisis, the god of the Nile; Hekt, the goddess of birth; and Ra, the sun god. The common wisdom was that each of these gods brought particular blessings to Egypt.

This is very important when we come to the story of the plagues. Much more was at stake than a conflict between Moses and Pharaoh, or between Israel and Egypt. The living God was bringing down the demonic powers that were masquerading behind the false gods of Egypt. Those powers were very real. That is why the magicians were able to produce frogs (though they could not get rid of them!).

We still ask the same question… Does He care enough to act?

God was saying to Pharaoh, "You worship Orisis, saying that the Nile sustains you, but I can turn the Nile into a lifeless swamp. You worship Hekt, the goddess of birth, who is depicted as a frog, but I will give birth to so many frogs that you will wish you had never known her. You worship Ra, saying that the sun will shine on you, but I will turn the sun to darkness. What you have put in My place will become like a plague to you."

Faced with the oppressive Egyptian regime, the defenseless Hebrews cried out to God. What else could they do? They were completely powerless.

The great question at the beginning of the book of Exodus was whether the living God could do anything to rescue these suffering people. And if He was capable of doing something, did He care enough to act? We still ask the same questions of God when we see suffering around us today: Can He do something? Does He care enough to act?

God gives us the answer in the judgment that He brings on Egypt. "I have indeed seen the misery of my people in Egypt. I have heard them crying out because of their slave drivers, and I am concerned about their suffering. So I have come down to rescue them" (3:7–8).

DEFYING THE LIVING GOD
The people could only be saved from oppression if Pharaoh repented of his evil, or if the evil was destroyed. God called Pharaoh to let the people go, but the Egyptian leader refused. So God spoke through one plague, but Pharaoh still refused. Then more plagues followed. Every time Pharaoh defied God, the cost of his defiance became higher for himself and for the people that he led.

The reason that God brings judgment is that He will not allow evil to stand. God made that plain on the day that sin entered the world. If you do not understand that God will destroy all evil, you will never understand the message of the Bible. The modern world does not feel the need of a Savior because it does not believe in a God who will bring judgment, and too often the church responds to that mistaken belief by trying to adapt the message of the Bible. We start hearing that "Christ will make you happy," or "Christ will make you rich," or "Christ will heal your family," or "Christ will fill a God-shaped hole in your life."

There may be some truth in some of these things, but none of them are the gospel. The heart of the gospel is that Christ has come to save us from the judgment of God.

A BLOOD SACRIFICE IN EGYPT
God gave Moses very careful instructions for the people. When the great judgment came on Egypt, God made a way in which all who believed and obeyed could be kept safe. Every family was to choose a lamb. They were to keep it for four days, and then they were to kill it. The lamb's blood was to be painted onto the doorframes of their houses. God said,

"When I see the blood, I will pass over you." (12:13)

Can you imagine the pressure on Moses to communicate this message? He had been in the presence of the living God at the burning bush. He had seen the fire and heard God's voice. He had seen the plagues and he knew that God would strike Egypt with judgment. He knew that God had provided one way in which families could be kept safe through this night of terror. The way of deliverance was by blood. Only blood would save them from death.

I can imagine Moses going around the community asking, "Are you covered by the blood of the lamb? Have you shed that blood yet? Is it over your door? The day of judgment is coming. This is not a hoax; it is absolutely serious. God has said, 'When I see the blood, I will pass over you.' Now, get it on your house. Why haven't you done it yet?"

Notice that God never once said, "If you offer a certain number of prayers, I will pass over you." He did not say, "If you are sincere, I will pass over you." He said only, "When I see the blood, I will pass over you."

When the night of terrors came, I have no doubt that some of the people must have been shaking with fear as they stood by their tables eating the Passover meal. Some of them must have looked up at their doors and wondered if the blood would make any difference when the storm of God's judgment broke.

All they had to go on was the Word of God. There were about two million people who believed and obeyed, and every one of them was kept safe through the judgment of God.

BLOOD IN THE GARDEN

The theme of blood in the Bible story goes back to the beginning. When Adam and Eve sinned in the garden, they knew that they were naked. Then, we are told that "the LORD God made garments of skin for Adam and his wife and clothed them" (Genesis 3:21). That meant that God killed an animal on the very day that the first sin was committed. God had told Adam about how disobedience in the Garden of Eden would lead to death. And there was a death in the garden that day. Adam's life was spared. An animal died instead.

We find the same pattern in the story of Abraham and Isaac. God told Abraham to take his son up the mountain, and God provided an animal, which was killed in Isaac's place. The animal's blood was shed and Isaac's life was spared.

Now, a lamb would be killed for every family in Egypt. God was teaching the same message to a new generation. He was saying, "The way in which you will be saved from judgment is through the death of another. It will involve the shedding of blood. It was like that for Adam and for Abraham, and that is how it will be for you."

Some of Abraham's descendants no doubt found this hard to take that night in Egypt. The kids would certainly have objected to killing the lamb! It took an act of faith to believe God's word and do what He said.

SPOTLIGHT ON CHRIST

Animal sacrifices continued for centuries in the Old Testament story until one day a prophet named John saw Jesus and said, "Look, the Lamb of God, who takes away the sin of the world!" (John 1:29). To all who would listen, John was declaring, "Jesus is the one who's going to take away the sin, not just of Adam or Abraham, and not just of Israel; He is the Lamb of God who will take away the sin of the world!"

Fifteen hundred years after the Exodus from Egypt, Jesus celebrated the Passover, as faithful Jewish people did then and still do today. He told his disciples that He had eagerly looked forward to sharing this Passover with them. They ate the lamb and continued the great traditions of the Passover throughout the meal. At one point in the Passover, a cup is raised and words are said about how God saved His people by the blood of the lamb. During the Passover meal with His disciples, Christ took the cup and said,

> "This cup is the new covenant in my blood, which is poured
> out for you." (LUKE 22:20)

He was telling His disciples that just as the blood of the lamb delivered the Hebrews from the night of terrors in Egypt, so Christ's own blood would deliver the people who were covered by it from the judgment of God on the last day.

As we roll forward to the end of the Bible story, God gave the apostle John a glimpse of the scene in heaven as it will be at the end of time. John saw a great crowd, much larger than he was able to count, standing in the presence of God. They were full of joy. John wanted to know who they were, and he was told that these were people who had "washed their robes and made them white in the blood of the Lamb" (Revelation 7:14).

This story of God letting death pass over His people takes us right to the heart of the message of the Bible. God says, "I am who I am…[and I will destroy all evil, but] when I see the blood, I will pass over you" (Exodus 3:14; 12:13).

UNLOCKED

The repeated slaughter of animals is one of the hardest themes for us to understand in the Old Testament story, but it is also one of the most important. Through these animal sacrifices, God was preparing His people to understand the need for, and the significance of, the sacrifice of Jesus Christ.

"Christ, our Passover lamb, has been sacrificed" (1 Corinthians 5:7). Christ is "the Lamb of God, who takes away the sin of the world." Like the lamb, He died in the place of Adam and in the place of Isaac and in the place of the Hebrews, and in your place too. He bore the judgment of the living God so that it will not fall on you.

But as in the Passover, the blood must not only be shed, it must also be applied.

Just as there had to be an act of faith and obedience in which the Hebrews applied the blood to the doorframes of their own houses, so there must be an act of faith in which Christ's blood is applied to your life.

Since the blood of Christ has been shed, why would you not, in an act of faith, ask that His blood cover you? Then you can rest on God's promise, and God will bring you safely through the day of judgment.

PAUSE FOR PRAYER

Father in heaven,

I bow before You and acknowledge that You are the living God. You are the God of Abraham, Isaac, and Jacob, the God who spoke to Moses; You are the God and Father of our LORD Jesus Christ. Thank You that You have not left Your world in the grip of evil, but have determined that no evil will stand. I acknowledge that if You judged everything that was touched by evil, I would come under that judgment.

Thank You for providing a way for me to be kept safe on the day when You will judge all evil through the blood of Jesus.

I praise You that the sacrificial death of Jesus Christ saves me. I believe Your promise that just as the people of Israel were kept safe through judgment by the blood of the lamb, so I will be safe on the last day through the blood of the LORD Jesus Christ.

Thank You for this incredible gift, which is mine through faith in the Son of God who loved me and gave Himself for me. Amen.

Law

EXODUS 20

What is the

role of the

Law in the

life of a

Christian?

6 Law

EXODUS 20

DISCOVER
life's ten greatest struggles and
the way to prevail in them.

LEARN
how the Law brings us to
Jesus Christ.

WORSHIP
as you see how Christ turns God's
commands into promises.

IT must have been a strange feeling for Moses to return to the place where God had spoken to him out of the burning bush. On his first visit, a flock of sheep had surrounded Moses. Now, two million people surrounded him. God had been faithful and the seemingly impossible had happened: In one of the greatest miracles in the Old Testament, God had parted the waters of the Red Sea. Now, a couple of months later, the Hebrews had arrived at Mount Sinai. Here they set up camp.

Barriers or "limits" were set up as a kind of exclusion zone at the base of the mountain. When the people looked up, they could see "Mount Sinai...covered with smoke, because the LORD descended on it in fire. The whole mountain trembled violently, and the sound of the trumpet grew louder and louder" (Exodus 19:18–19). The God who came down to speak with Adam, Abraham, Isaac, and Jacob was coming down to give His laws to the people.

The Law of God was never a ladder for unsaved people to climb up to heaven. It was always a pattern of life for God's people who had been saved from judgment by the blood of the Lamb.

A NEW DIMENSION OF GOD'S GRACE

God was not saying, "I'm giving you these commandments, so that by keeping them you may become My people." He was saying, "I am giving you these commandments because you are My people." The message of the Law to us today is not that we must keep these laws in order to be saved, but rather that because we are saved, we should keep these laws. The Law tells us how people who belong to God ought to live.

This is important, because some people have the idea that in the Old Testament, God tried to save people by getting them to keep the Law. But then He found that people couldn't do this, and so He came up with a better way of saving people through Jesus Christ. If this were true, the natural conclusion would be that the Old Testament is a book of law, and the New Testament is a book of grace, and that the Old Testament has nothing to do with us because we're not under law, we're under grace.

That is a complete misunderstanding of the Bible. The whole Bible is a book of grace. God has one plan from beginning to end, and it all fits together. God promised the Redeemer on the very day that sin entered the world. God has always saved His people by grace and through faith. We've seen this in the story of Noah, and in the story of the Exodus. There is one God and there is one story.

The Law is specifically given to people who have experienced the grace of God and have become His people, and for this reason it speaks to us today.

GET A GLIMPSE OF THE GLORY OF GOD!

In the New Testament, sin is defined as "fall(ing) short of the glory of God" and as "break(ing) the law" (Romans 3:23; 1 John 3:4). Put these two truths together, and you make an interesting discovery. If sin is falling short of the glory of God and breaking the Law, then we may reasonably conclude that the Law is an expression of God's glory. Every one of the Ten Commandments (listed in Exodus 20:3–17) reflects some aspect of the character of God.

When God declared, "You shall have no other gods before me" (v. 3), it was because He is the only God. There is no one like Him.

God tells us that we must not make any images of Him because when we attempt to shape physical representations of Him, we only succeed in detracting from His greatness and His glory.

The reason you should honor your father and mother is that all fatherhood derives from God, and all authority, even within family life, derives from Him.

Why should you not commit adultery? Because God is faithful.

Why should you not steal? Because God is trustworthy.

Why should you not lie? Because God is truth.

Why should you not covet? Because God is at peace and content in Himself.

God was speaking to His own people at Mount Sinai, telling them, "You are My people. And since you are My people, your lives must be modeled on who I am. And if your lives are to be modeled on who I am, then this is what your lives will look like."

The Ten Commandments are not an arbitrary set of rules. They are a direct reflection of the character of God. The greatest challenge for God's people is to reflect God's character in the world. When we obey His Law, we reflect something of His glory.

The Law reflects the glory of God. So as you think about the Law, let it lead you to worship.

THE GREATEST BATTLES OF YOUR HEART

A second reason for God giving these Ten Commandments is that they speak to the ten most significant struggles of human experience.

Parents know all about this. They always give rules to their children to target areas of struggle. Mom and Dad gave instructions like, "Eat your dinner!" or "Do your homework!" or "Clean your room!" to help us overcome our struggles.

Of course, today's parents do not often find themselves having to give instructions like, "Watch television!" or "Go on-line!" or "Practice your free throws!" The reason that we do not need to give these instructions is that these things come naturally to our children! Every parent knows that you target your instructions to a child's particular areas of struggle. When God gave the Ten Commandments, He spoke directly to the primary struggles that all of us experience.

Jesus gave a wonderful summary of the Law when He said that the most important commandment is, " 'Love the LORD your God with all your heart and with all your soul and with all your mind and with all your strength.' The second is this: 'Love your neighbor as yourself'" (Mark 12:30–31). Christ identified our greatest struggles in life. He was saying, "You will struggle to love God with all your heart, and you will not find it easy to love your neighbor as much as you love yourself."

The first four commandments address the struggle to love God with our whole heart. In the first commandment, God wrote, "You shall have no other gods before me." He was telling us that we're not going to find it as easy as we think to love Him with all our being. You will not find it easy to let God be God. You will keep finding, as Adam and Eve found, that you want to be God yourself. It will be the biggest battle of your life.

In the second commandment, God was saying, "You will struggle to offer authentic worship. You will not find it easy to lift your mind to Me with faith and to worship Me as I really am." In the third commandment, God wrote, "You shall not misuse the name of the LORD your God." He was saying, "You will struggle to speak about Me in a way that truly honors Me." In the fourth commandment, God wrote, "Remember the Sabbath day by keeping it holy." He was saying, "You will find that there is a battle over giving Me your time."

The last six commandments speak to our struggle to love our neighbor as ourselves. When God wrote "Honor your father and your mother," He was telling us that we will have some real battles in life over submitting to authority. Our parents were the first authority figures God put in our lives, but before you were very old you probably found some impulse within you that wanted to fight against that authority.

We also struggle with issues of ongoing hostility. "You shall not murder" is the sixth commandment. Christ tells us that the issue here goes beyond physical violence and includes anger or resentment toward others (see Matthew 5:21–22). This commandment goes to the root of ongoing hostility that arises from broken relationships, and God is saying, "You'll struggle on this one. It will be a battle for you."

These are the battles of our lives.

You will also find that there is a real battle for sexual purity. "You shall not commit adultery," God warned in the seventh commandment. Again, Christ made it clear that the issue is not simply whether a man or woman has committed an act of adultery. God was saying, "You will have a real battle to keep your thoughts and your mind clean." What you think when you look at other people is a reflection of who you really are.

Then, you'll find that there is a battle for personal integrity. "You shall not steal," God warned in the eighth commandment. There will be opportunities that come to you to gain advantage at the expense of another person, and when that happens, you will discover that you love yourself much more than you love your neighbor.

And there will be a battle for honesty. God identified this struggle when He wrote the ninth commandment, "You shall not give false testimony against your neighbor." You will find an impulse within you to distort the truth, to exaggerate a story, to misrepresent the way things are, to tell a downright barefaced lie.

And you will find that there is a battle over this whole business of contentment. That's why God wrote the tenth commandment: "You shall not covet." In a materialistic world, you will find that when you see what other people have, it will create within you a feeling that you should have it too.

These are the battles of our lives, are they not? They're the great struggles that we all face in some degree or another. The Law is like a light. It shines into our souls, and when we look at what God says to us, we have to admit that He is speaking directly to the primary battles of our own hearts.

AN X RAY OF THE SOUL

I went to see the dentist recently. I'd been putting it off for a long time. *I've had no pain, so why should I go?* But I decided it was now time, and he took several X rays. The experience was not the most encouraging.

It's rather disconcerting, isn't it, as you lie there at an extraordinary angle, looking up at the nose of a person you hardly know? My dentist stood there looking at the X rays, holding them up to the light, and making extraordinary sounds. "Mmmm…Oh dear!…Nasty. Which country did you say you came from?…There's a lot of decay underneath these fillings," he said.

> God speaks to us in His Law, which is like an X ray to the soul.

"I've no pain," I insisted. But he didn't seem impressed. "You're going to need some pretty major work," he said. "And the sooner, the better."

There are many people who go through life with no sense of pain over their spiritual condition. They make the false assumption that things are well with them and that having lived generally respectable lives, they are in good spiritual shape. But then God speaks to us in His Law, which is like an X ray to the soul. God holds the X ray to the light and asks us to look at it. And if you look at the X ray of your own inner condition properly, you will not like what you see. The Law announces our need of Christ by showing us what we are like.

Some lines in the Bible are genuinely amusing. Moses "went back and summoned the elders of the people and set before them all the words the LORD had commanded him to speak." Here's one of the great lines of the Old Testament: "The people all responded together, 'We will do everything the LORD has said'" (19:7–8).

As you read the rest of the Old Testament, that line really seems like a rather sad joke. God proceeded to declare His laws to Moses on Mount Sinai, but He had hardly finished writing down those laws on the tablets of stone before the people had broken virtually every one of them. They indulged themselves in an orgy around the gold calf. It would have been better if they'd fallen down on their faces when Moses told them the laws of God and said, "The only way we can ever do this is if God helps us, because winning all of these struggles consistently is beyond our power!"

That was the response of St. Augustine. He struggled to get free from the power of habits that bound him, and so he offered this prayer: "O, LORD, command what you will, only give what you command." He was really saying, "LORD, You may ask me to do anything You want, but the only way I'll be able to do it is if You give me the power."

LEARNING FROM THE TEACHER

The Law not only affirms the glory of God, it also announces our need of Christ. The apostle Paul wrote that the Law is a good thing, just like X rays are a good thing— even if they may bring us bad news. The Law brings us bad news. Yet the Law is a good thing, for it shows us the truth; it shows us the genuine state of our hearts.

Through the Law of God, I discover that I'm a person who finds it difficult to let God be God, and I am a person who is naturally more interested in myself than in the interests of other people. The Law announces my need of Jesus Christ.

The Law is like a teacher to bring us to Christ (see Galatians 3:24 NLT). When you learn what the Law has to teach, you will, if you've learned its lesson properly, come to Jesus Christ. And if the Law has not brought you to Jesus Christ, then you have missed the greatest purpose God intended for it. This, of course, is the point of Jesus' statement to the Pharisees, "You diligently study the Scriptures…yet you refuse to come to me" (John 5:39–40). They were busy studying the Law, but they had missed the whole point of the Law, which was to show them their need for Jesus, the Christ.

The first reason you need Jesus Christ is not that you'll have a richer, fuller, and more satisfying life. It is that you are a sinner by nature and by practice, and the X ray of God's Law shows it, even if you feel no pain. The Law affirms the glory of God, and the Law announces our need of Jesus Christ.

LAYING TRACK FOR THE TRAIN

God's ultimate purpose is to restore in us a true reflection of His glory. Since God's glory is expressed in His Law, that means that the purpose of the gospel is to bring us to the position where we begin to live according to the Law of God.

So the whole of the Christian life is a process in which we are changed from one degree of glory to another, until the day when we see Him, and then we shall be like Him. This transformation is the work of the Holy Spirit, and it is spoken of in both the Old and the New Testament. God says:

> *"I will give you a new heart and put a new spirit in you; I will remove from you your heart of stone and give you a heart of flesh. And I will put my Spirit in you and move you to follow my decrees and be careful to keep my laws."* (EZEKIEL 36:26–27)

In this new covenant, God will not only tell us what to do, He will also give us the power to move in that direction.

The Law of God is like the rails for a train. The rails give direction, but the train will not go anywhere unless there is power in the engine. It is the special work of the Holy Spirit to give God's people power to move in the direction that is laid out in God's Law.

The Christian life is not a matter of believing in Jesus and then trying your best to live according to God's Law. God's promise is that when you believe in the LORD Jesus Christ, the Holy Spirit will come and reside in your life. You will receive power, and that power will make the difference between a battle in which you are destined for defeat, and a battle in which there will be ultimate victory.

SPOTLIGHT ON CHRIST

In his commentary on Matthew's gospel, Bible teacher Charles Price described a man serving time in prison because he was a thief. Stealing had been his lifestyle, until the long arm of the law eventually caught him. During his time in prison, he heard the good news of Jesus Christ and was wonderfully converted.

When the time came for his release, the man knew that he would enter a new struggle. Most of his old friends were thieves, and it would not be easy to break the patterns of his old way of life. The first thing he wanted to do when he was released from prison was to go to church, and so on the first Sunday morning of his new freedom he slipped into a church building and sat somewhere in the back. As he looked up to the front, he saw the words of the Ten Commandments, inscribed on two plaques. He read the words of the command that seemed to condemn him. "You shall not steal."

That's the last thing that I need, he thought to himself. *I know my weakness. I know my failure, and I know the battle I'm going to have.*

As the service progressed, he kept looking at the plaque. As he read and reread the words, they seemed to take on a new meaning. Previously he had read these words in the tone of a command, "You shall not steal!" But now, it seemed that God was speaking these words to him as a promise. "You shall not steal."

He was a new person in Christ, and God was promising that the Holy Spirit would make it possible for him to overcome the habit of stealing. "You shall not steal, and the reason you won't steal is that I have put my Spirit in you and I move you to follow My decrees and to keep My laws."

What once was a condemning command now seemed like a promise (Ezekiel 36:26) of new possibilities that had been opened to him by Jesus Christ through the power of the Spirit.[1]

Where are the greatest battles of your life? Can you hear God's promise of victory? The Law sets the direction in which we must move to glorify God. The Spirit empowers the believer to move in that direction.

If you have understood the Law of God, it should cause you to fall down in worship, because the Law shows us who God is and what He's like. If you have understood the Law of God, it will make you cling to Jesus Christ because you will be absolutely clear about why you need Him. And when you understand the Law, it will give you direction for a new life in the power of the Holy Spirit, in which you are not destined for defeat, but for victory.

UNLOCKED

The Law is one of God's good gifts to His people, and we should thank Him for it. In the Psalms, David spoke about delighting in God's Law. If he could do that, we should certainly not do less. We will delight in God's Law when we see that it reflects the glory of God's character.

While the Law may be like a mirror that reflects things in our lives that we would rather not see, we can be thankful that God uses the Law to make us aware of our sinfulness. This is how He brings us to Christ and continues to remind us of the power available through "Christ in us." We can also thank God that when the Holy Spirit lives within us, the Law is no longer a list of impossible demands, but a description of new possibilities.

PAUSE FOR PRAYER

Which of the Ten Commandments speaks to the area of your greatest struggles right now? Take a moment to identify the commandment, and then ask God to make this commandment an area of victory for you by the power of His Holy Spirit. As you pray this prayer, remember the promise of Romans 6:14 (NLT): "Sin is no longer your master."

O Holy Father,

Thank You for giving the Law to reveal the extent of my sin and show my need for a Savior. You know I continue at times to struggle with _____ (Name the sin), and in so doing break Your commandment to _____. Give me victory in this area by the power of the Holy Spirit who abides within me.

Thank You that such victory is available through the finished work of the Lord Jesus Christ. It is in His matchless name I pray. Amen.

NOTE

1. Charles Price, *Matthew*. Fearn, Scotland: Christian Focus, 1998), 88.

Atonement

EXODUS 32

What is

atonement,

and why is

it necessary?

7 Atonement

EXODUS 32

DISCOVER

why being sorry is not enough to make us right with God.

LEARN

what an atonement is, why it is necessary, and how God has provided one for us.

WORSHIP

because God reconciles us to Himself through the blood of Jesus Christ.

WHEN God first gave the Ten Commandments, He spoke with an audible voice that was heard by all the people. "The LORD said to Moses, 'I am going to come to you in a dense cloud, so that the people will hear me speaking with you and will always put their trust in you'" (Exodus 19:9).

So Moses came down the mountain and told the people what was going to happen (19:25). Then we read that "God spoke all these words" (20:1). Imagine hearing the audible voice of God!

Notice how the people reacted: "When the people saw the thunder and lightning and heard the trumpet and saw the mountain in smoke, they trembled with fear. They stayed at a distance and said to Moses, 'Speak to us yourself and we will listen. But do not have God speak to us or we will die'" (20:18–19).

THE ABSENT LEADER

So Moses went back up the mountain and remained there for forty days and nights (24:18). That is a couple of days short of six weeks, and by the end of that time the people were tired of waiting.

> When the people saw that Moses was so long in coming down from the mountain, they gathered around Aaron and said, "Come, make us gods who will go before us. As for this fellow Moses…we don't know what has happened to him." (32:1)

Only six weeks had passed since they heard the audible voice of God telling them not to make any idol. Now, within a matter of days, they made a choice that directly contradicted one of God's simplest instructions. The effects of their remarkable experience of God have faded quickly. Here is the mystery of sin and the weakness of human nature.

Six weeks of silence from God and the absence of their spiritual leader, Moses, had put their faith to the test, and now they had decided that if God could not tell them what He wanted to say in six weeks, they would go ahead and develop their own religion.

FELT NEEDS AND MARKET FORCES

So they looked for a man with a recognized ministry and leadership ability. Moses' brother, Aaron, seemed the natural choice, and when they approached him, they found that he was quite ready to fill the gap in the market.

I wonder what motivated Aaron? Did he feel that this was his opportunity to step out of the shadow of Moses? Did he justify what he did by saying that he was meeting a "felt" need—giving the people what they wanted?

Aaron's first move was to raise funds for the launch of the new ministry. People donated their jewelry, and from these gifts Aaron shaped a golden calf. Aaron became the sad father of those who base ministry on the primary question "What do people want?" If we apply the principles of the market to ministry, we will always end up with idolatry.

Of course, Aaron wanted to claim that what he was doing was well within the bounds of orthodoxy, and so he said, "Tomorrow there will be a festival to the LORD" (v. 5). But Aaron's festival was nothing more than an indulgent vehicle of self-expression.

THE MINDLESS PARTY

> The next day the people rose early and sacrificed burnt offerings and presented fellowship offerings. Afterward they sat down to eat and drink and got up to indulge in revelry. (v. 6)

In other words, out came the drinks and off came the clothes. It was a big celebration, but it was worshiping the wrong God, indulging the wrong behavior, and tasting the wrong kind of joy.

It is worth pausing to ask what a contemporary news program would make of this. After all, the golden calf would make a good subject for a journalist reporting on new religious movements around the world. The camera crew could get some great shots in the desert, with a reporter profiled against the backdrop of the dancing crowd.

"Out here in the Sinai Desert, a remarkable new religious movement has been born," our reporter would begin. "The movement bears witness to the extraordinary creativity of these primitive peoples, who have adapted religious practices from neighboring cultures and established a new style of worship that is marked by joy and festivity."

There would then be a couple of interviews with exuberant dancers, who would say that the festival of the golden calf was deeply meaningful to them. They may have thought it was meaningful, but God thought it was abominable.

BREAKING UP THE PARTY

Moses was at the top of the mountain in the presence of God when he received the bad news. "Go down, because your people, whom you brought up out of Egypt, have become corrupt" (v. 7). So Moses faced the uncomfortable task of breaking up the party. His first step was to confront Aaron. "What did these people do to you, that you led them into such great sin?" (v. 21).

Had the people subjected Moses' brother to some horrible torture? In fact, all it took to persuade Aaron to disobey the law of God was public demand and a gap in the market. He led them into sin because he was unable to resist the pressure of felt needs and market forces.

Look at Aaron's attempt to deflect responsibility. We are told in verse 4 that Aaron shaped the gold into the form of an idol "with a tool." But when Moses challenged his brother, Aaron gave a sanitized version of the story:

> "I told them, 'Whoever has gold jewelry, take it off.' Then they
> gave me the gold, and I threw it into the fire, and out came
> this calf!" (V. 24; EMPHASIS ADDED).

It just happened!

After confronting his brother, Moses called the people to a point of decision:

> "Whoever is for the LORD, come to me." (V. 26)

Everybody was given the opportunity to repent. They were all invited to declare their allegiance to the Lord. Given that there were around two million people in the camp, we may assume that 1,997,000 responded to Moses' appeal and took their stand with him. We know this because there were 3,000 people who refused the invitation, and that day was the last day of their lives (v. 28).

The issue that brought such devastating judgment on them was not so much their sin as their refusal to give it up. They had seen the glory of God, heard His voice, and refused to come to Him. Ultimate rejection of God's invitation to repent always leads to devastating consequences. The commandments of God are not a list of suggestions. They are real laws with real penalties for those who break them.

LOOKING FOR FORGIVENESS

Now we come to the really fascinating part of the story. By the end of Exodus 32:29, there are 3,000 people dead, and (presumably from the fact that the rest were still alive), 1,997,000 people who had made some indication of repentance toward God. But notice what happened next:

> The next day Moses said to the people, "You have committed a great sin." (v. 30)

Talk about preaching to the choir! These people already know that they have done wrong. So why does Moses get up the next day and say, "You have committed a great sin"? Whatever happened to forgiveness?

Why doesn't Moses draw a line under it? Isn't it his duty to tell them that they are forgiven? These people are sorry. What more does Moses want from them?

Notice there is no forgiveness offered by God here. Why? Isn't it God's duty to forgive them? No, something must happen before forgiveness can be granted.

THE MEANING OF ATONEMENT

At this point in the story, we discover the biblical word *atonement*. Moses told the people,

> "I will go up to the LORD; perhaps I can make atonement for your sin." (v. 30)

Very simply, *atonement* is what it takes to put something that is wrong right. If you divide the English word *atonement* up into three parts, you get "*at-one-ment*." If two people are divided by a dispute, the atonement is what it takes to bring them to be "at one." Wherever there is an offense, we face the question of atonement. What will it take to make what is wrong right?

BEING SORRY WON'T DO IT

I remember a key soccer match during college. At one moment the other team made a breakthrough. I was one of the last defenders, and in a desperate lunge managed to clear the ball off the goal line. I had saved the day.

Unfortunately, the ball sailed in a magnificent trajectory toward the college president's study. It smashed through his window, landing on the floor. He was remarkably kind about it—but he did require that I replace the window and clear up the mess. That was what it took to put what was wrong right.

The key point about an *atonement* is that what is required to put the wrong right is always determined by the injured party. Standing there in my muddy shorts beside the broken window, I didn't feel that I had a lot of bargaining power!

"I'm very sorry," I said. That was good, but it wasn't enough. Damage had been done, and it had to be repaired. I wanted to say, "I won't do it again," but that would have sounded very trite. There was not much else that I could do but stand there feeling rather shabby and listen to what the president determined it would take to put what was wrong right.

"Here is what I need you to do," he said. "I need you to clear up the mess and replace the window."

That was the atonement. That was the price that had to be paid to put what was wrong right and to restore the relationship. Now this word takes us right to the heart of the Bible. What will it take to put man's wrong against God right? What will it take to bring you and God together, and make you "at one"?

There are many people who think that it all boils down to being sorry. They feel that if we are truly repentant and have genuinely tried to change, then things will be right with God.

But Exodus 32 tells us being sorry won't do it. Here, 1,997,000 people were sorry for what they did, and Moses told them that there was still a problem. Being sorry for what we have done will not remove the guilt of our sin. We need an atonement, and being sorry is not enough.

A GREAT LEADER CAN'T DO IT

Moses began to wonder if making atonement was something that he could do. Of all the great moments in Moses' life, this was his finest hour. God had already made Moses an offer that must have seemed very attractive.

> "Now leave me alone so that my anger may burn against them and that I may destroy them. Then I will make you into a great nation." (v. 10)

That was quite an offer! Try and put yourself in Moses' shoes. He thought about leading a new group of people. God was ready to give him a fresh start, with a clean slate. But then Moses thought about the people God had given him, and he could not give them up.

He began to think about what it would take to make atonement for them. No doubt he thought about the Passover and the death of the lamb. That seemed to indicate that God was prepared to accept the death of a substitute and spare the lives of the people.

Perhaps Moses could be the substitute. The more he thought about it, the more he felt that he would be ready to lay down his life if it would mean that these people could be spared.

> The next day Moses said to the people, "You have committed a great sin. But now I will go up to the LORD; perhaps I can make atonement for your sin." So Moses went back to the LORD and said, "Oh, what a great sin these people have committed! They have made themselves gods of gold. But now, please forgive their sin—but if not, then blot me out of the book you have written." (vv. 30–32, EMPHASIS ADDED)

So we have a volunteer. The greatest spiritual leader in the Old Testament steps up to the plate. He is ready to lay down his life for the people. If he has to enter hell to make atonement for them, he is ready to do it.

But God does not accept the offer. He answers, in effect, "No deal, Moses. Making atonement is out of your league." Moses, of course, had sins of his own—he had a murder on his record—and a man with sins of his own is in no position to atone for the sins of others. So there is no atonement; what is wrong is still not put right.

Life will go on for these people, but without an atonement, they will forfeit the presence of God. Back in the Garden of Eden, Adam and Eve discovered that their sin led to them being sent away from the presence of God. Now here, the nation of Israel discovers that sin causes God to hide and withdraw His presence.

God will still give them the gift of the Promised Land, but without an atonement, He cannot travel with them. God says, "I will not go with you" (33:3). The immediate presence of God would be dangerous for them, because it is a fearful thing to be in the presence of an angry God.

When the people heard that they would have to face the future without the presence of God, "they began to mourn" (33:4). They were now facing the most fundamental question in the most personal way. "What will it take to bring back the presence of God? If being sorry won't do it and Moses can't do it, what will it take to atone for our sins?"

PAINSTAKING OBEDIENCE WON'T DO IT

Some people feel a serious commitment to obeying God's commands will make up for their sins. Some of the people of Israel may have thought, *If we are sincere in our obedience, God's blessing will return.*

> *All the skilled men among the workmen made the tabernacle.* (36:8)

Following this summary statement comes a long and detailed description of how the craftsmen made the ark, the table, the lampstand, the altar of burnt offering, the courtyard, the priestly garments, the ephod, and the breastpiece. The precise instructions for building the tabernacle had already been given (see Exodus 25–30). Now as you read the details of the workmanship in Exodus 36–39, it is like a mirror image of God's instruction in chapters 25–30. All of this detail is given to make a single point: The people did exactly what God told them to do. They followed the commands of God down to the tiniest detail: "The Israelites did everything just as the LORD commanded Moses" (39:32).

When all the work was finished, the pieces were brought together and "the tabernacle was set up on the first day of the first month in the second year" (40:17). They had arrived at Sinai on the first day of the third month after they left Egypt (19:1), so two months had passed. We also know that Moses was away for two periods of six weeks. So the travel time plus Moses' absences total about five months. The tabernacle was set up at the beginning of the second year, and so they must have spent the remaining seven months of the year working on it.

The craftsmen must have come to work every day feeling the heaviness of life without God. Imagine a woman sewing embroidery on the curtains for the tabernacle, and feeling that God was so distant. As she followed exactly the instructions God commanded, she thought, *I've got to be obedient to God. Perhaps this will bring back His presence. How I wish I could know the presence of God in my life.* Picture a man working with bronze and wishing that he had not grieved the LORD. Perhaps if his hands could do what God had commanded, God's blessing might return to the people.

> The people must have held their breath as they watched to see what happened next.

For seven months, the people gave themselves to a daily, detailed obedience to the law of God, but at the end of it all there was still no sign of the presence of God.

By that point they must have been wondering what it would take to put what was wrong right and bring back the presence of God.

This is a key issue to grasp if we are to understand the story of the Bible. Many people feel that if they are sorry enough for long enough, things will become right with God. There are others who think that if they shape up to a more detailed obedience to God's laws by attending church, saying prayers, or reading the Bible, this will make things right with God. But right back in the second book of the Bible, God is teaching us that although these things are good, they are not enough. We need an atonement.

A WORTHY SACRIFICE WILL DO IT

The book of Exodus brings us to the day when a priest would offer the first sacrifice in the newly constructed tabernacle. At the end of the book of Exodus, the great day finally arrives.

The detail of how the tabernacle was set up is given in Exodus 40, but a fuller description is given in Leviticus 9. After seven months in which the people had been longing for the presence of God to return, Moses told them how it could happen: "This is what the LORD has commanded you to do, so that the glory of the LORD may appear to you" (9:6).

There must have been a stunned silence as the people waited to hear what he would say. Moses then turned to Aaron and said,

"Come to the altar and sacrifice your sin offering and your burnt offering and *make atonement* for yourself and the people; sacrifice the offering that is for the people and *make atonement* for them, as the LORD has commanded'" (Leviticus 9:7, italics added).

The priests took an animal and slaughtered it so that the blood of the animal was poured out. The blood was then taken to the altar. The people must have held their breath as they watched to see what happened next. They did not have long to wait: "Moses and Aaron then went into the Tent of Meeting. When they came out, they blessed the people; and the glory of the LORD appeared to all the people" (9:23).

God was back, and that could only mean that what had been wrong for seven months had finally been put right. The LORD gave the clearest evidence of His presence not only in the cloud but also in the fire. "Fire came out from the presence of the LORD and consumed the burnt offering and the fat portions on the altar. And when all the people saw it, they shouted for joy and fell facedown" (9:24). The

If the presence of God is…to invade your life, you need an atonement.

same event is recorded in Exodus 40: "Then the cloud covered the Tent of Meeting, and the glory of the LORD filled the tabernacle. Moses could not enter the Tent of Meeting because the cloud had settled upon it, and the glory of the LORD filled the tabernacle" (vv. 34–35).

Can you imagine the impact of this on the people? Imagine a couple sitting in their tent and talking about what they had seen. "I've never seen anything quite like what happened today. Whoever would have imagined that shedding the blood of an animal would bring back the presence of God?" he says.

"Yes, it's incredible!" the wife agrees. "I can't really understand why the sacrifice did it when all those months of being sorry, and all those months of obedience, and even Moses' offer to lay down his life for us didn't!"

"There must be something very powerful about a sacrifice that involves the shedding of blood. Anyway, we have learned something. Where there is sin, we need a sacrifice. It's the sacrifice and the shedding of blood that makes atonement with God."

Do you think the message could be clearer? Sin causes God to withdraw. Life goes on, but it continues without the presence of God. Being sorry won't bring God back. Painstaking obedience won't bring God back. There is only one thing that will bring God back, and that is the blood of the sacrifice shed on the altar.

SPOTLIGHT ON CHRIST

It must have been clear to the people even then, that it was not the blood of the animal itself that would make the people "at one" with God. Atonement would be achieved *by the person that this sacrifice represented.*

Even at this early stage in the story of the Bible, God is preparing us for the coming of Jesus. The whole purpose of the sacrifices in the Old Testament was to shape our thinking so that we would be able to understand why the Son of God had to come into the world. The sacrifices help us to see that in His death on that cross, He did in reality what the sacrifice of animals only did in symbol. Christ made atonement for our sins, and He brings back the presence of God for all who trust in His sacrifice.

Are you feeling that God is far removed from you? Have you wondered what it would take to restore a right relationship with God? If the presence of God is going to invade your life, you need an atonement.

UNLOCKED

The atonement for sin was offered by Jesus Christ through His death on the cross.

Put your trust in that sacrifice, and the presence of God will come to you. You will be "at one" with God.

PAUSE FOR PRAYER

Before you pray, review the words from verse two (adapted) from the classic hymn "Rock of Ages", by Augustus M. Toplady.

All the labor of my hands
Won't fulfill your laws demands;
Should my efforts always grow,
Should my tears forever flow,
All for sin could not atone;
You must save, and You alone.

Father in heaven,

I realize that I needed an atonement for my sins. I realize that nothing I can do will ever atone for my sins. I thank You today that Jesus Christ has offered the atonement through His death on the cross and that His sacrifice covers my sin.

Having put my trust in the blood of Jesus Christ. I rest in what He has done to make atonement for my sins. On the basis of what Christ has done for me, I ask that Your blessing and Your presence remain on me. I pray in Christ's name. Amen.

Priest

LEVITICUS 16

What does God

do with our

sins when we

confess them?

*8*Priest

LEVITICUS 16

DISCOVER
the great drama of the Day
of Atonement.

LEARN
the gospel from God's greatest
visual aid.

WORSHIP
as you see how Jesus fulfills the
role of our great High Priest.

I f you ever find yourself in a court of law, you probably will want to hire an attorney to present your case. Law courts are intimidating places, and they operate under some fairly complex rules, so you need the help of an attorney to represent you before the judge and to speak on your behalf.

In the Old Testament, the priests did something similar in the presence of God. A priest would represent the people to God and speak to God on their behalf. He operated in a mobile worship center called the tabernacle, which was separated into different areas by a series of curtains and contained various pieces of symbolic furniture.

At the center of the tabernacle was the Most Holy Place, which was screened off from view by a heavy curtain. If you could have gone into the Most Holy Place— nobody but the high priest did—you would have seen the ark of the covenant. It was a wooden chest, carried on poles, with a lid over the chest.

Rising from the lid were two golden statues of cherubim. These were angelic figures whose work was especially associated with the judgment of God. At the beginning of the Bible story, the cherubim were placed at the entrance to the Garden of Eden to prevent sinful men and women from entering the presence of God. (Remember chapter 2?) So the golden statues of the cherubim on top of the ark of the covenant were a visual reminder that you can't come near God without coming close to judgment.

MEETING WITH GOD

Between the cherubim was a flat area called *the atonement cover*, or *the mercy seat*. As God had told Moses, "There, above the cover between the two cherubim that are over the ark of the Testimony, I will meet with you" (Exodus 25:22).

Once every year, on the Day of Atonement, the high priest would go behind the curtain into the Most Holy Place. God would come down, just as He had done on Mount Sinai. He did not make Himself visible, but He appeared "in the cloud" (Leviticus 16:2). God met with the high priest at a place that spoke of mercy and judgment.

The Day of Atonement was like a great drama in five acts. Today it remains the most visual presentation of the gospel in the Bible. The whole day was filled with symbolism that points us forward to Jesus Christ and helps us to understand the significance of His death on the cross.

Act 1: The Priest Appears

The high priest was one of the most important people in the whole of the nation. If the people did not know that, they would have got the message just by looking at his clothes.

The high priest's clothing displayed the dignity of his office. Rich in symbolism, his breastplate contained twelve precious stones representing the twelve tribes of Israel. Blue cord joined the breastplate to the underlying ephod, a sleeveless tunic of fine linen, decorated with gold, blue, purple, and scarlet trim. If you saw the high priest, it would be like seeing royalty on a state occasion. The dignity of the high priest's office and the importance of his work were clear.

But on the Day of Atonement, the high priest did not wear his uniform. He discarded his magnificent clothes and appeared in the streets wearing a simple white cloth instead. This was the sort of clothing that the lowest servant would wear.

Now imagine the scene; it is an amazing sight: the man who holds the most digni-fied office in the land, dressed as a common slave! The people come out to watch the spectacle themselves. Imagine the onlookers lining the route along which he walks. He makes his way toward the tabernacle like a boxer entering the ring, the vast crowd pressing round in anticipation of what is about to happen.

Act 2: The Priest Prepares

The first thing that the high priest does is to prepare himself for the special work of the Day of Atonement. Let's look at Aaron, the first high priest. Like his brother, Moses, he has his own sins. He had led the people to worship idols at the time of the golden calf, so this high priest is far from perfect. No doubt Aaron had tried to honor God and live by the commandments, but he had his faults like everybody else. Before he could enter the presence of God to deal with the sins of the people, his first priority was to deal with his own sins.

A bull is brought forward and slaughtered in public view. Then Aaron takes some of the blood behind the curtain into the Most Holy Place where God had said He would come. There, Aaron sprinkles the bull's blood as a sacrifice for his own sins.

This must have made a powerful impression on the people. The high priest, holding one of the most dignified positions in the land, is saying, "Before we get to offering a sacrifice for the people, I want to recognize publicly that I stand in need of a sacrifice myself." The high priest was saying, as every other priest, pastor, or religious leader of any denomination would always have to say, "I have sins of my own, and therefore I am in no position to deal with yours."

Act 3: Atonement Is Made
The high priest now comes back out of the tabernacle, and all the people see him again. Two goats are brought forward, and the first goat is slaughtered. The high priest takes the blood behind the curtain and sprinkles the goat's blood on the mercy seat.

Remember that the mercy seat is the flat surface between the huge golden figures of the cherubim. It is a powerful picture. God's agents of judgment are looking down at the mercy seat where the blood will be sprinkled. When Aaron sprinkles the goat's blood on the mercy seat, it is as if judgment and mercy are meeting together. Judgment, which demands death as the penalty for sin, is satisfied; mercy, which demands forgiveness for the sinner, is sustained. Mercy is released in the place of judgment as the blood of the sacrifice is sprinkled.

Back in the Garden of Eden, God made it clear to Adam that the consequence of sin is death (Genesis 2:17; cf. Romans 6:23). That is why blood had to be sprinkled on the mercy seat. The blood demonstrated that a death had taken place. As we have seen from the beginning of the Bible's story, God was ready to allow the death sentence to be passed on an animal instead of the sinner, but atonement could only come through a death that would satisfy the justice of God in relation to sin.

It is worth remembering that the high priest is never invited to bring a test tube of tears (representing the repentance of the people) to the mercy seat. Nor is he invited to bring rags soaked in sweat (representing the effort of the people). God's justice is not satisfied by our tears of repentance or by the strength of our effort. Atonement is made as blood is sprinkled on the mercy seat.

The high priest had to make atonement not only for himself and for the people, but even for the Most Holy Place itself. God says,

> "He shall then slaughter the goat for the sin offering for the people and take its blood behind the curtain and do with it as he did with the bull's blood: He shall sprinkle it on the atonement cover and in front of it. In this way he will make atonement for the Most Holy Place because of the uncleanness and rebellion of the Israelites, whatever their sins have been."
> (16:15–16, EMPHASIS ADDED)

The point here is that the presence of God has been removed from the people. God is outside the camp. The people are longing for God to come among them, but how can God come into a sinful community? How can God's holy fire come into an unclean place? How can the Spirit of God enter an unholy life? The answer is that the atonement clears the way for God to come among His people.

Act 4: Sin Is Confessed

Imagine you are standing in the crowd. The next act without doubt will be the most dramatic part of the whole day: the appearance of a living sacrifice and a public confession for all the people. Remember, the people have not actually seen the atonement being made. That has remained hidden behind the curtain. They have seen the goat slaughtered, but after that, all the people could do was wait as the high priest went into the Most Holy Place to sprinkle the blood on the mercy seat.

But now the high priest comes out, and the second goat is brought to him. Here's what happens:

> "When Aaron has finished making atonement for the Most Holy Place, the Tent of Meeting and the altar, he shall bring forward the live goat. He is to lay both hands on the head of the live goat and confess over it all the wickedness and rebellion of the Israelites—all their sins—and put them on the goat's head
> (vv. 20–21)

In many churches, when there is a service of dedication for an infant, the pastor will hold the child while he says a prayer. This can cause some problems with struggling children who understandably do not want to be separated from their parents and thrust into the arms of a stranger with a loud voice and a microphone. I have often struggled to offer a coherent prayer as a wriggling two-year-old tried desperately to escape my clutches. On one occasion, my prayer was cut short as a small child became sick over my shoulder!

But such problems are nothing compared with what the high priest had to do here. He was charged with the responsibility of confessing *all* the sins of Israel while laying both hands on the head of the live goat!

I don't suppose for a moment that the live goat was particularly cooperative as the high priest tried to offer his prayer. There must have been a great deal of noise, and perhaps some kicking of hooves as the high priest struggled to keep control of the animal and at the same time to confess the sins of the people.

If you had been in the crowd, you might have heard a prayer similar to this: "Almighty God, we confess our idolatry. We have loved Your gifts more than we have loved You. We confess our envy. We have seen what You have given to others, and we have coveted that for ourselves. We confess our adultery; in our minds and for some with our bodies we have sinned against You. We also confess our anger. We have been determined to have our own way. We have been short-tempered and unkind to others. We confess our stealing. We have not lived up to the trust that has been placed in us, and we confess our lies. We have evaded the truth; we have exaggerated, deceived, embellished, and distorted."

> "We have evaded the truth; we have exaggerated, deceived, embellished, and distorted."

Since the high priest had to confess all the sins of the people, this would have been a long prayer. While he was unable to confess the details of every individual sin, the high priest prayed in such a way that the people recognized that there were specific sins that needed to be dealt with. If you had been standing in the crowd listening to the prayer, eventually you would have thought, *Yes, that sin is one of mine.*

When the high priest confessed the sins of the people with his hands laid on the head of the goat, an act of transfer took place. God moved the guilt of these sins onto the goat. God regarded these sins as being placed on the head of the goat, and being carried by the goat.

Act 5: Guilt Is Removed

What happens next on the Day of Atonement is a marvelous picture of how God deals with our sins when they have been confessed and atonement has been made.

God is using this wonderful visual aid to help us picture how He deals with our sins. As atonement is made and sin is confessed, it is as if that sin is transferred onto the goat's head. It is removed from the person and laid on the goat. So at the end of the prayer you have one very guilty goat!

Then the high priest sends the guilty goat into the desert:

> *"He shall send the goat away into the desert in the care of a man appointed for the task. The goat will carry on itself all their sins to a solitary place; and the man shall release it in the desert."* (vv. 21–22)

I cannot imagine a more powerful visual presentation of the gospel.

Again, picture yourself in the crowd watching this act. The high priest has finished confessing your sins. Your guilt has been transferred to the goat, and now someone comes forward and leads the goat away. You watch him go between the tents and then beyond them outside the camp and into the desert. You watch until the man and the goat are only a dot on the horizon, and then you cannot see them at all.

The entire Day of Atonement was a series of visual aids in which God was teaching the basic truths that we need to grasp:

- We need a priest, who will lay aside his dignity and honor and come as a servant to make atonement for the people.

- That priest needs to be prepared, because a man with his own sins cannot atone for the sins of others.

- Atonement can only be made by the shedding of blood. In this way the justice of God will be satisfied, and mercy will be released to the people.

- Sin must be confessed, and when it is, its guilt will be transferred.

- When atonement has been made and sin has been confessed, then your guilt will be removed. It will be taken out of your sight.

I cannot imagine a more powerful visual presentation of the gospel. This five-act drama was like a dress rehearsal for the real performance that took place when Jesus

Christ came into the world. It was a like a preview, telling us what to look for and what to expect when He came.

Run forward through fifteen hundred years of history and you move from the dress rehearsal to the opening night, from the preview to the main event. The main event features Jesus Christ in the role of the High Priest.

SPOTLIGHT ON CHRIST

As we indicated, the events of the Day of Atonement are a preview of the main action when Christ appeared to the people of Israel. Let's look at the five-act drama that unfolds with His coming.

ACT 1: CHRIST APPEARS

In the New Testament another High Priest appears. He is not another son of Aaron (all high priests had descended from Aaron). This Priest is the Son of God! His glory is much greater than the splendid clothes worn by the high priest. He shared the glory of the Father before the world began.

However, just as the high priest discarded his magnificent clothing on the Day of Atonement, Christ laid aside His glory. He took on Himself the form of a servant (see Philippians 2:6–7). He was wrapped in strips of cloth and laid in a manger. When Christ was born, the real drama of atonement was about to begin.

ACT 2: CHRIST IS PREPARED

As we read through the Gospels, we find that Jesus Christ lived a life that was different from any other life that has ever been lived. He did the will of the Father and fulfilled all the work that the Father had given Him to do.

He could ask His enemies if any of them were able to accuse Him of sin, and they responded only with name-calling (see John 8:46–48). This High Priest was unlike any other. He did not need to offer a sacrifice for His own sin. He committed no sin (2 Corinthians 5:21; 1 Peter 2:22).

He was what every other priest wished he could be. He lived the life that no other high priest was able to live. His perfect life qualified Him to achieve what all the other high priests could only illustrate.

ACT 3: CHRIST MAKES ATONEMENT

After three years of His public ministry, Jesus was arrested and sentenced to be crucified. As He was nailed to the cross, His blood was shed, and His life was poured out. The judgment of God represented by the cherubim fell on Him. Darkness covered the face of the earth, and He cried out from His agony, "My God, my God, why have you forsaken me?" At the end, He cried out in a loud voice, "It is finished," and the inner curtain in the temple that surrounded the Most Holy Place was ripped from top to bottom (Mark 15:34, 37–38; John 19:30). Atonement was made by our great High Priest, and a new and living way was opened into the presence of God.

ACT 4: WE CONFESS OUR SINS

This is where you have a part to play in the drama. Remember that there were two goats on the Day of Atonement. One was sacrificed, and the other was led into the desert. Both of these animals help us to understand what Christ does for His people. He is one who sacrificed His life as the atonement for our sins, but He is also the one who is able to take away our guilt. The work of Christ is so rich that it cannot be fully represented in any one picture.

The high priest laid both hands on the head of the animal and confessed the sins of the people. Now God says to us, "That is what I want you to do. I want you, in an act of faith, to lay hold of the LORD Jesus Christ. I want you to confess your sins, and when you do, this is what will happen: Your guilt will be transferred to Christ. It will be laid on Him, and included in the sin for which He died."

Have you done that? Remember, Christ, the perfect High Priest, has appeared. Atonement has been accomplished in His death. His atonement is sufficient to cover the sins of the whole world. The question is whether that atonement has been applied to your sins in particular. That happens when you lay hold of Jesus Christ in faith and confess your sin to Him. As the hymn "Not All the Blood of Beasts" declared,

> Not all the blood of beasts on ancient altars slain
> Could give the guilty conscience peace or wash away the stain.

> But Christ the heavenly lamb bears all our sin away
> A sacrifice of nobler name and richer blood than they.

> My faith would lay her hand on that dear head of Thine
> While like a penitent I stand, and there confess my sin.

—ISAAC WATTS [ADAPTED]

When faith has laid its hand on Christ and confession has been made, then guilt is transferred and you can look back to the Cross and know that your guilt and your sin were dealt with there.

ACT 5: OUR SINS ARE REMOVED

Try to imagine a person who has been struggling with a troubled conscience. Let's call her Sarah. She has made a foolish choice, and her sin troubles her deeply. She feels that what she has done is always with her and she wonders if God can ever forgive her. Perhaps you know somebody like Sarah.

Now imagine Sarah in the crowd watching the great drama of the Day of Atonement. The following day, she is still struggling with her troubled conscience, when a friend comes to talk with her.

"Sarah, think about what you saw yesterday. What happened when the high priest grabbed that goat by the head?"

"He confessed our sins."

"And did he confess your sin?"

"Yes, he did, and when he spoke about it, I felt so ashamed."

"What happened to the sins that he confessed?"

"They were laid on the goat's head."

"And what happened to the goat?" her friend asks.

"It was taken away."

"How far was it taken, Sarah?"

"Farther than I could see."

Take that picture and apply it to your own life. Can you see your sins lain on Jesus as you lay hold of Him in faith and confess your sins to Him? Can you picture those specific sins being taken away into the distance and out of sight? Can you believe that through the finished work of Christ your sin is not only forgiven but your guilt is also removed? Remember Scripture's promise: "As high as the heavens are above the earth, so great is his love for those who fear him; as far as the east is from the west, so far has He removed our transgressions from us" (Psalm 103:11–12).

UNLOCKED

The Day of Atonement illustrates how Christ has made atonement for our sins. When His blood was shed, God's judgment was poured out, and mercy was released for sinners. The atonement is applied to your sins in particular when by faith you "lay hold of Christ," believing in Him and confessing your sins to Him. Just as the sins of God's people in the Old Testament were symbolically transferred to the goat as the priest laid hold of the animal and prayed, so God will transfer the guilt of your sin to Christ as you lay hold of Him with faith. And when God transfers your guilt, He also removes it from you, so that you can look up to God with the joy and freedom of someone who is truly forgiven.

PAUSE FOR PRAYER

If you have not asked Jesus, the Great High Priest, to be your Savior, now is a good time to do so. Here is a prayer of thanksgiving and confession that will help you to "lay hold" of Jesus, who takes away our sins. into your life.

Gracious Father,

Thank You that the LORD Jesus Christ has come into the world to be my High Priest. Thank You that He was willing to lay aside His glory and to be born in a manger. Thank You for His perfect life that qualified Him to make atonement. Thank You that He has made atonement by laying down His life and shedding His blood.

I believe in the LORD Jesus Christ and, right now, trust in Him as my Savior and LORD. I want to confess my sins to You…[Take time to confess your sins to the LORD.]

Thank You that Christ died for these sins. Thank You for taking these sins from me. Help me now to enjoy the peace of knowing that You have taken them as far from me as the east is from the west, through Jesus Christ our LORD. Amen.

Blessing

LEVITICUS 26

If God's love

is unconditional,

why does obedi-

ence matter?

9 Blessing

LEVITICUS 26

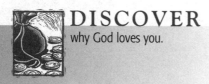

DISCOVER
why God loves you.

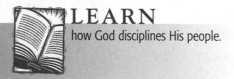

LEARN
how God disciplines His people.

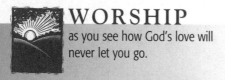

WORSHIP
as you see how God's love will never let you go.

THE popular children's song says it very well:

> *Jesus loves me! This I know,*
> *For the Bible tells me so.*
> *Little ones to Him belong;*
> *They are weak but He is strong.*

Have you ever wondered why God loves you? Indeed, why did God choose someone like Abraham? As one who had been worshiping idols in Mesopotamia (Joshua 24:2), Abraham probably didn't receive God's love because of some great spiritual commitment or insight. Indeed, Abraham did not even know who God was!

On one occasion God seemed almost to tease His people with the prospect of an explanation of why He loves them. "The LORD did not set his affection on you and choose you because you were more numerous than other peoples, for you were the fewest of all peoples" (Deuteronomy 7:7). Our appetite for an answer is aroused. "Yes, Lord, we understand that the explanation of Your love for us does not lie in the strength of our numbers, but now tell us why You love us."

God gave His people the final answer: "It was because the Lord loved you" (Deuteronomy 7:8).

The reason God loves you is simply "because the Lord loves you," and you will never get a deeper answer than that! The explanation of the love of God for you lies in God alone. It lies in the source and not in the object. "He loves you because He loves you."

GOD'S UNCONDITIONAL LOVE

This is quite beyond the range of our experience. It is very easy for me to explain why I love my wife. She captivated my heart; it was love at first sight. I "fell in love" with her. If we look for reasoned explanations of this phenomena, they are not hard to find. Her charming character, striking appearance, her unusual gifts, and warm personality evoked a response from me. It was like that when we met and it is still like that today. I am drawn to things that I see in her, and they evoke a response.

But God's love is very different. The reason God loves you is not because He was smitten with your appearance, bowled over by your personality, knocked out by your good works, or swept away by the sheer genius of your talent. The explanation of God's love for you does not lie in anything within you; it lies in God alone. God is love. He loves you…because He loves you!

The love of God has its explanation in its source. Only God is able to love the unlovely, the unskilled, the wounded, the inhibited, and even the rebel. Only God could love Abraham while he was still worshiping other gods. Only God still loves you in your worst moments.

Over the years I have had the opportunity of trying to help people who have been struggling with the question, "How can God love me?" The problem is that the question focuses all the attention on "me," and when someone is depressed, or if he is struggling to come to terms with a personal failure, then thinking about "me" is not very encouraging. Thankfully, the reason God loves me has nothing to do with me at all. The explanation lies in God. So if we can get our attention away from ourselves and focus our thoughts on God, it will not be long before we are rejoicing in His love rather than deprecating ourselves.

WHY OBEDIENCE MATTERS

Now, at this point in the story of the Bible, we come up against a very important question. If it is true that God loves you unconditionally, why does obedience matter?

Toward the end of his life, Moses was clearly concerned that some of the people might already have been turning away from the living God. "When such a person hears the words of this oath [that is, God's oath and promise to go on loving them unconditionally], he invokes a blessing on himself and therefore thinks, 'I will be safe, even though I persist in going my own way'" (Deuteronomy 29:19).

Can you see how one of God's people might reach this kind of conclusion? "We're God's people, and God has given us the sacrifices to cover our sins. We have a High Priest who goes into the holy place on our behalf, and we have the Day of Atonement. Since God loves us unconditionally, all we need to do is to go through this religious ritual, and then for the rest of the week we can cut ourselves some slack. We can make room for some things that we know God forbids but that we happen to like doing."

Moses saw some people who were beginning to think like that, and it has been the same ever since. How do we answer the person who says, "If God is committed to forgive me through the shed blood of Jesus, then I may live as I choose, in the knowledge that no matter what I do God will never stop blessing me. Why does obedience matter?"

God addressed this issue directly in Leviticus 26. He gave a long list of promises, but they were all conditional on the little word *if*.

> "If you follow my decrees and are careful to obey my commands, I will send…" (vv. 3–4)

And then God listed the blessings that would follow obedience. They included a strong economy (abundant harvests) and national security (victory over overwhelming enemies). In fact, God promised that five of His people would be able to overpower a hundred of their enemies (v. 8). That would cut the American defense budget a little bit if we had that blessing, wouldn't it?

The greatest blessing that would follow obedience is the presence of God among His people. "I will put my dwelling place among you," God said (v. 11). But all of this was conditional upon the massive "if" of obedience. "If you follow my decrees."

Then God spoke about the consequences of disobedience.

> "If you will not listen to me and carry out all these commands, and if you reject my decrees and abhor my laws and fail to carry out all my commands and so violate my covenant, then I will do this to you." (vv. 14–16)

God then gave a list of the consequences of disobedience, some of which could make your hair stand on end. They included ill health, bad harvests, and defeat at the hands of enemies. In fact, God will go so far as to actually bring enemies against His people as a means of disciplining them in order to bring them back to Himself.

SIN AND SUFFERING

The Bible never suggests that *all* painful experiences are a result of sin. Jesus spoke with some folks who were asking why a certain man was born blind. They believed that all suffering was a direct result of sin, and so they assumed that the man's blindness was either the result of his own sin or perhaps a consequence of his parents' sin. Christ cut right through their assumption. The blind man's suffering was not a direct consequence of anybody's sin. On the contrary, the man's blindness was an opportunity for the glory of God to be revealed (see John 9:1–3).

Job's three friends operated on the same false assumption that all suffering is a direct result of personal sin. So when Job suffered, they thought that it was their job to help him identify the particular sin that was at the root of his suffering. They were like detectives looking for evidence, and they became more and more frustrated when they could not find any. At the end of the story, God stepped in and revealed that the purpose of Job's suffering was quite different. Job was a man of integrity, and the supposed sin that his friends were looking for did not exist (see Job 4; 8; 11; 42:7–8). It is a great mistake to think that *all* suffering is a direct consequence of personal sin.

But it is equally mistaken to think that *no* suffering is a consequence of personal sin. Jonah sinned against the LORD, and God sent a great storm. God had called this successful preacher to go to a rather unattractive location, but Jonah did not want to go. He had a good crowd where he was, and frankly he did not care a whole lot about the people in Nineveh. So he found a ship heading in the opposite direction to the call of God and moved out in deliberate disobedience to the will of God.

Would God let him go or would God go after him? God loved this man far too much to let him go, and so God sent a storm, with the single purpose of bringing this man back to his senses and restoring him to the place where he could again be useful to God.

We will see later in the Bible story that for decades the nation of Israel lived in rebellion against God. God loved them, so He sent the prophets. The people would not listen; so God sent an invading army. They still would not change their ways, so finally God brought enemies who flattened the city of Jerusalem. It was a terrible devastation, the city lay in ruins for seventy years, and in the end the most able people were taken as exiles to Babylon.

While they were there, God began to work in the hearts of a new generation of men and women, and out of all this suffering came a group of people who loved the

LORD. Then under Nehemiah they were able to come back and begin again. God brought His people back.

THE LOVE THAT WON'T LET GO

God's unrelenting discipline is an aspect of His blessing for which we should be profoundly thankful. The only alternative would be for God to give us up.

Let's take an imaginary couple, whom we'll call Graham and Sheila. They fall very deeply in love and are married, and for ten years they share a good life together.

Then Sheila begins to notice some disturbing patterns in Graham's behavior. He says he is at the office, but then when she calls the office, he is not there, and his colleague who answers the phone seems strangely evasive about where Graham has gone.

[The angels] must wonder why. The only explanation is the unprovoked, unrelenting, irrepressible love of God.

Then one day when she is sorting through some clothing, she finds a hotel receipt in his pocket, and suddenly some things that she has feared begin to fall into place in her mind. There is a reason for Graham's coldness and distance. He is being unfaithful to her.

Sheila is no longer able to trust him, and the relationship that was once warm and intimate now becomes cold and distant. Sheila has three choices.

1. She can accept things as they are and carry on with the relationship.
2. She can leave the relationship and end her commitment to Graham.
3. She can fight for the relationship to be restored.

It does not take her long to decide. She loves this man and has committed her life to him. They have built a life together, and she is not about to let that go. So she chooses to confront him. But when she does, Graham is unwilling to address the issue. She is met with denials and evasions; soon he ends the conversation.

So now she has to face the same choice again. The thought of carrying on in this situation is incredibly painful. Her love is being given to a man who is unworthy of it and unresponsive to it. But how can she give him up?

She makes her choice. She will fight for Graham. She will fight for however long it takes, and however costly or painful it becomes. The same love that was once expressed in intimate union is now expressed in relentless determination.

That is a small picture of the love of God for us. God has committed Himself to an unconditional covenant. That means that God is committed to do whatever it takes to bring His people out of sin and into His blessing. The same love that caused Him to make an unconditional covenant causes God to be relentless in His pursuit of His people.

As the angels look at this, they must wonder why. The only explanation is the unprovoked, unrelenting, irrepressible love of God. The only alternative would be that He might give us up, and that is the one thing God cannot do with His people. God will not turn a blind eye when His people sin. He will fight to win them back.

God has set His love on His people. He has done it by grace, through faith, and in Jesus Christ at the cost of His shed blood. This relationship is infinitely precious to God, and He will go to any lengths to protect it and defend it. The problem for a woman in Sheila's position is that she may not have a great deal of ammunition to turn Graham around. But what if God should decide to fight for the relationship He has with you?

When you enter a covenant with God, you need to know that He will never give you up and He will never let you go. He is not content to have a relationship with you in name only. He wants to walk with you and to make you a channel of His blessing in the world. He cannot do that while you are distant from Him, and so He will fight to bring you back.

AGREEING WITH GOD'S CURSES

Shortly before God's people came into the land of Canaan, God used a powerful visual aid to teach His people the priority of obedience. He brought them to a place where there were two hills, with a valley between them. The two hills were called Mount Ebal and Mount Gerizim. (See map on opposite page.) When the people came to the pass between the mountains, Moses sent representatives from each of the tribes to the top of these two hills. The story is recorded in Deuteronomy 27–28.

The Levites on the top of Mount Ebal were to shout out the curses from the law of God as the people passed through the valley beneath them. Picture this in your mind: You are one of a vast crowd of people walking along a country path, and high on a rock above you are a group of men shouting, "Cursed is the man who carves an image or casts an idol" (Deuteronomy 27:15). When you hear this threat of a curse being shouted over your head, you have to join with all the other people on the path by saying, "Amen!"

You walk another few yards, and you hear somebody else shouting, "Cursed is the man who dishonors his father or his mother," and again you say, "Amen."

The word *amen* means "so be it," and when you say "Amen," you are saying, "That's exactly what I want to happen. That's what I am asking God to do."

This must have been an unforgettable experience! When they said "Amen" to the curses, the people were really saying, "LORD, I know my own heart. I know that when I am surrounded by the pressure of an unbelieving culture it is very easy for me to cave in, and I do not want You to let me do that. I want to be accountable to You, LORD.

"If, at any time in the future, I am stupid enough to choose a path of disobedience, I want You to intercept me and bring that plan to nothing. [That's what the word *curse* means.] If I use deception, expose me. If I sin in secret, bring it out into the open. If I start living for myself and for my pleasure, take pleasure from me until I find pleasure in You. If I begin to live for money, let the value of my shares fall and go on falling until I love You more than I love money."

[The] way into God's blessing... goes past Mount Ebal, where you renounce sin.

How do you feel about making that kind of commitment to God? It seems demanding, doesn't it? And the response of your heart is a register of where your heart is.

Suppose in your heart you are not so sure that you want to pursue this life of loyalty to God. You want at least to keep your options open. If you had been at Mount Ebal, you might have mumbled your response and tried to mask the fact that you never said "Amen" at all. Are there sins that you would not want God to curse? Are there issues you would like God not to touch? There is only one way into God's blessing, and it goes past Mount Ebal, where you renounce sin and call on God to keep you from it.

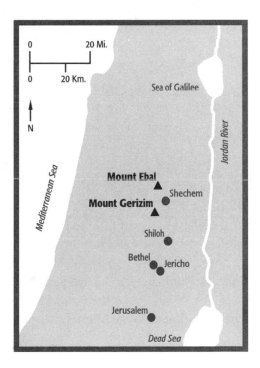

ENTERING INTO THE BLESSING OF GOD

But beyond Mount Ebal lies Mount Gerizim, the mountain of God's blessing. Having passed Ebal, where they renounced sin, God's people now walked under Mount Gerizim where another group of Levites shouted out the blessings of God.

"You will be blessed in the city and blessed in the country....You will be blessed when you come in and blessed when you go out" (28:3, 6).

God was saying, "I will be with you. My hand will be upon you. Though enemies come against you, I will protect you. I'm going to bless you. You will know My presence and I will give you My peace."

Whenever the people looked up to the hills, these two mountains would have reminded them that there are two ways to live and that they lead to two entirely different experiences of the love of God. The path of disobedience leads us to experience the discipline of God's love as He does whatever it takes to bring us back to Himself. The path of obedience leads us to experience the blessing of His love as He continues to shower good gifts upon His people.

Moses set out these choices for the people, and then with all the passion of an aging leader he spoke some of his final words to the people:

> "This day I call heaven and earth as witnesses against you that I have set before you life and death, blessings and curses. Now choose life, so that you and your children may live and that you may love the LORD your God, listen to his voice, and hold fast to him. For the LORD is your life, and he will give you many years in the land he swore to give to your fathers, Abraham, Isaac and Jacob." (30:19–20)

SPOTLIGHT ON CHRIST

This is why Jesus Christ came into the world. "I have come that they may have life, and have it to the full," He said (John 10:10). It is the evil one who comes to kill and to steal and destroy. Christ made it very clear that the two paths—one of obedience, the other of disobedience—lead not only to different experiences in this life, but ultimately to two different destinations. (See His warning in Matthew 7:13–14.) Christ bore the curse for us so that it would be possible for us to get off the road that leads to destruction and onto the road that leads to life.

Look back on the last ten years of your life. What do you see? Is there a pattern of your pressing against the laws of God and pushing outside the boundaries of His commandments? Are those years a story of you resisting God, and then God confronting the problem to bring you back? Have you been wearing yourself out by resisting His will and His truth?

What will the next ten years look like? Choose life! Choose the path of His blessing.

UNLOCKED

God's love for His people is unconditional. But the love that blesses is also the love that disciplines. King David discovered this when he tried to cover up his sin of adultery. He wrote about it in Psalm 32, where he described the pain of a double life. "My bones wasted away,…Day and night your hand was heavy upon me; my [energy] was sapped as in the heat of summer." That's what he experienced from the God who loved him. God's hand was heavy upon him. But when he confessed his sin, he was able to say, "Blessed is the man whose transgressions are forgiven, whose sins are covered."

God wanted to restore His blessing to David, and He was ready to do whatever it would take. That's unconditional love.

PAUSE FOR PRAYER

Almighty God,

I praise You because You will never let me go. But I also thank You that You will never leave me as I am. Thank You for Your unbreakable covenant and thank You for Your unrelenting discipline.

Sometimes I want to hold on to things that You have cursed. Have mercy on me, oh God. Help me to say "amen" to Your curse on every sin so that I may enter into Your blessing.

Bring me back from foolish ways and restore me to the path of intentional obedience. Hear my prayer for the sake of Jesus Christ who came to bring me into life. Amen.

10

Courage

NUMBERS 13–14

How can we

contribute to

advancing

God's purpose

in the world?

10Courage

NUMBERS 13–14

DISCOVER
the key to costly commitment.

LEARN
how God's people lost their way and how we can avoid their disastrous mistake.

WORSHIP
as you see the courage of Christ, who held nothing back in His pursuit of the will of God.

TEN months is a long time to spend at one campsite, but that is how long the Israelites were camped at the foot of Mount Sinai. It took them two months to get from the Red Sea to Sinai (Exodus 19:1), and by the time the tabernacle was set up, a full year had passed.

God used that time to turn a confused crowd into a disciplined nation. By the end of the year, the people had an ordered way of worship, a functioning legal system, and, through leadership in each of the tribes, a system of government and communication that worked reasonably well.

The book of Numbers takes up the story where Exodus left off, "on the first day of the second month of the second year" after their deliverance from Egypt (Numbers 1:1). God told Moses to "take a census of...all the men in Israel twenty years old or more who are able to serve in the army" (1:2–3). That gives us the clue as to what this book is about; God was leading these people into warfare. He was preparing them for a military campaign in which they would enter the land God had promised to them. Costly battles and ultimate victory lay before them.

The book of Genesis tells us that God chooses His people; Exodus tells us that He redeems His people; Leviticus tells us God is among His people; Deuteronomy (which comes next in chronological order) tells us that God loves His people; and Numbers tells us that God commissions His people. God's chosen, redeemed, holy, and dearly loved people were now being sent to war.

The early chapters of Numbers describe their preparation for breaking camp and moving on from Sinai. The twelve tribes were camped around the tabernacle, three to the north, three to the south, three to the east, and three to the west. If you could have looked at these two million people from the air, the traveling nation would have resembled a giant cross, moving across the desert floor. It must have been quite a sight: nearly two million people, ordered, disciplined, with each one knowing his own place and with the presence of God at the center. It is little wonder that the sight would soon strike fear into their enemies.

"On the twentieth day of the second month of the second year, the cloud [of God's presence] lifted from above the tabernacle" and began to move (Numbers 10:11). And so we come to the best-known story in the book of Numbers, the story of the spies in Canaan.

> The LORD said to Moses, "Send some men to explore the land
> of Canaan, which I am giving to the Israelites." (13:1–2)

Moses obeyed and sent them off, and they traveled through the land for forty days gathering information. But when they got back, things began to go badly wrong. The majority took the view that the land couldn't be conquered. Their pessimism spread, and the people lost heart. They were unwilling to press forward in obedience to God's command. Instead, they complained (see 13:31–14:4).

Twelve Tribes Camped Around the Tabernacle

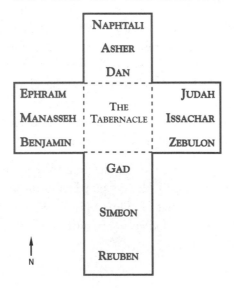

God determined that this generation of grumblers and complainers would not enter the land. They spent the next thirty-eight years in the desert until that whole generation had died and their children had taken their place.

In a sense, Numbers is a book that need never have been written. It is the story of an unnecessary detour, of a group of God's people who were faced with an open door of opportunity but held back when they should have pressed forward. God recorded this sad experience of His people to warn us about the long-term consequences of cowardly choices. Even though we belong to God, there is still the danger that we may miss our calling and become a group of wandering, aimless people who mark time for a generation.

The prospect is frightening, and that is why the book of Numbers is so valuable to us. If we can understand where these people went wrong, it will help us to avoid repeating their mistakes.

GRUMBLING AND COMPLAINING

According to Numbers 11:1, "The people complained about their hardships in the hearing of the LORD." They began by complaining about their food, and then Miriam and Aaron began to complain against Moses (Numbers 12). It is always dangerous to complain about God's gifts, and it is quite clear that the spirit of grumbling was displeasing to God.

God gave them their food, and God gave them their leader, but somehow at the very point where great things lay ahead of them, a negative spirit emerged, and this group of people who had been uniquely blessed by God became deeply dissatisfied with what God had given them.

It is very difficult to make good decisions when you have a bad attitude. If in your heart you feel deeply dissatisfied with what God has given to you, be very careful! That's where God's people were when they made the mistake of a lifetime.

This critical spirit drained strength from their spiritual convictions. It sapped the passion of their commitment to the Lord and left them spiritually limp, so that when the moment of decision came, they moved in the wrong direction. Critical, complaining people usually end up choosing the wrong path. Behind a bad decision you will usually find a bad attitude.

COMPLACENT LEADERS

When the twelve spies were sent out, there was one representative from each of the tribes. All of them are described as "leaders of the Israelites" (Numbers 13:3). They were sent out to gather information that would help Moses form a plan to accomplish the will of God. After a forty-day trip behind enemy lines, they returned to tell Moses that, in effect, the plan of God was not practical!

> "We can't attack those people; they are stronger than we
> are." (13:31)

They were saying, "We can't do it. The land is good, but it is already occupied by powerful forces. This whole project is beyond us."

Notice that they made no reference to God in their report. They simply announced the view that "on the basis of data available we are unable to progress further with the purposes of God at the present time."

Here were leaders who had stopped asking, "What does God want us to do?" and had begun asking, "What seems manageable?" Whenever leadership makes that shift, it will be costly for the people of God. It is a powerful lesson for all who are trusted with the responsibility of leadership. We dare not ask the question "What is manageable?" We must focus our attention on what God is calling us to do. If we lose that proper focus, we will operate at a purely pragmatic level. That often is the beginning of years of aimless wandering in ineffective ministry.

Only two members of the team took a different view. Joshua and Caleb presented a minority report focusing on the fact that God was with them, but by the time they were given the opportunity to speak, the people had already made up their minds.

> [We] must see beyond the data and trust in God.

The Canaan report was a catalog of disasters. The research team made their report in the wrong place: They were commissioned by Moses, but they made their report to all the people. They exceeded their authority: They were asked to bring back information, but they went beyond that and made a recommendation. The result was that the people ended up discussing an issue that never should have been brought before them. The question to be decided was not if they should go into Canaan, but how they should go into Canaan.

Moses allowed the situation to get out of control, and the people ended up making a bad decision over an issue that should never have been brought before them in the first place. It brought the whole community to the verge of disaster.

There are some very important lessons for us here. If the people of God are to advance God's purpose, they must be thankful, and their leaders must be people of faith. They must see beyond the data and trust in God. Here are two critical tests of the health of any church. Is there a grateful and unified spirit among the people? Is there a spirit of faith among the leaders?

CASTING YOUR VOTE FOR COSTLY OBEDIENCE

It is very easy for us to sit in comfortable surroundings and imagine that if we had been asked to vote on entering the land of Canaan, we would have shouted "Yes!" I wonder if you would.

Before we judge them for their feeble choice, let's take a moment to try and stand in their shoes. True, God had done more for them than they had ever asked or thought. He had led them out of Egypt, forgiven their sins, and provided them with food every day in the desert. But they recognized that now the LORD was asking them to do something that would be very costly: to enter a pagan land, Canaan, and take ground that had become a stronghold of Satan. That would mean war, and people would die in the fighting.

So put yourself in their shoes. If you were one of the women, would you vote for entering Canaan when you knew that it was at least possible that your husband would be one of those whose lives would be taken? If you were one of the men, would you vote for a military campaign that could involve you in up to seven years of military service?

I can understand why, when crunch time came, many people were happy to stay in the desert, offering their sacrifices and enjoying the presence of God. That way they could have all their evenings at home, raise their children in peace, and continue to enjoy the blessing of God that they had known since they left Egypt.

Yet it was God who was calling them forward. This seemed to have carried little weight with these people. Many of them seemed to have lost their first love for the LORD. At one time they had danced for joy after God brought them over the Red Sea, but now they had their questions.

Their leaders, realizing that they were responsible for two million unhappy people, had stopped asking what God wanted them to do and were simply trying to work out what was manageable. "We are sorry to announce that we are at this time unable to do what God has clearly revealed, because having done a careful evaluation, we have decided that the personal cost of obedience to the will of God is too high."

So the people made a choice.

"Let us die in this desert rather than deal with these fierce enemies," they said (see 14:1–2). And that's exactly what God allowed them to do; a whole generation perished because of unbelief shown in their complaints.

OFFENDING GOD
"How long will these people treat me with contempt?" (14:11)

If your commitment to the will of God is conditional on your personal comfort, then you are treating God with contempt. That is, you are glad to receive His good gifts, but care little for Him personally. God saw His people holding out their hands every day for fresh blessings, but they were not willing to serve Him if that involved going outside the boundaries of their own comfort. God found that to be personally insulting, and He said that "not one of [these people] will ever see the land I promised on oath to their forefathers" (14:23).

Now it is important to understand the point of all this. The lesson is not that they were finally lost. God was faithful to them even in the desert. They were still God's people, and God provided food for them every day. He never left them. The point is not that they were saved and then somehow lost. The point is that *this generation of people who had experienced the abundant grace of God contributed nothing to advancing the purpose of God.*

The apostle Paul referred to this story in 1 Corinthians 10 and applied it to a local church where some people had become complacent. He reminded the Corinthian believers that "God was not pleased with [that generation]; their bodies were scattered over the desert" (10:5). In effect, Paul said, "You need to be careful that you don't become unprofitable like the generation in the wilderness." He told the Corinthians that this was why he exercised self-discipline in his own life. Having preached to other people, he did not want to become unprofitable; that is, a saved person who is of little use in advancing the purposes of God. (See his warning in 1 Corinthians 9:26–27.)

It would be very easy for me to live as a redeemed child of God within my own comfort zone, holding services of worship, rejoicing in the love of Christ, and doing nothing significant to advance the purposes of God. Similarly, it's easy for churches that have been greatly blessed to grieve the Spirit and become unprofitable in the purposes of God. Once we see the danger, the great question is, "How are we going to avoid being like that?"

UNDERSTAND YOUR CALLING

Our calling is to a life of unconditional obedience to everything God has told us to do. The clearly revealed will of God for Israel in the book of Numbers was for the people to enter the land of Canaan. The clearly revealed will of God for His people today includes the Great Commandment—"Love the LORD your God with all your heart and with all your soul and with all your mind and with all your strength…[and] love your neighbor as yourself"—and the Great Commission— "Go and make disciples of all nations" (Mark 12:29–31; Matthew 28:19).

Our calling is not that we become sponges soaking up God's blessing. Our calling is to a life of unconditional obedience to everything God has told us to do.

We are to go into cold, dark places in industry and business and love people. We are to go into the nations of the world, where Christ is not known, and where they may haul us before courts, and reclaim lives from the darkness in the name of Jesus Christ. We are to see to it that people are built up in their faith and established in authentic Christian lives. We are not called to a life of convenience.

The more God blesses you, the harder it may be to live a sacrificial life. The more God blesses a church, the easier it is to get the idea that our happiness is the ultimate end of all things. This is not the goal. The church exists to do the work that God has commissioned her to do. She exists to be fully obedient to Christ; to be His body, His hands, His feet in the world. The church exists to do whatever Christ says. We must be absolutely clear about our calling. Our calling is to obey Him.

COUNTING THE COST

It is interesting that in the early days after the Exodus, God shielded His people from the full cost of their calling.

> When Pharaoh let the people go, God did not lead them on the road through the Philistine country, though that was shorter. For God said, "If they face war, they might change their minds and return to Egypt." So God led the people around by the desert road toward the Red Sea. (EXODUS 13:17–18; EMPHASIS ADDED).

But then as time went on, God brought them to a place where obedience was more costly. It was time to face the battle.

I have vivid memories of my father taking me to an auction sale when I was young. He prepared me before we took our seats, telling me not to scratch my nose or make any other movement that could be considered as a bid. Then he added, "When you go into an auction sale, make sure you know your upper price limit." That's great advice for anybody going into an auction sale, but it would be a lousy approach to the Christian life.

Christ will not allow His followers to set an upper price limit. He said, "Whoever wants to save his life will lose it, but whoever loses his life for me and for the gospel will save it" (Mark 8:35). He also compared the kingdom of God to a pearl merchant who finally found a pearl of great value; the merchant sold all he had to buy it (see Matthew 13:45–46). Christ declared, "If anyone would come after me, he must deny himself and take up his cross and follow me" (Mark 8:34).

Our calling is to a life of unconditional obedience; the price...is unknown.

Christ does not tell us what that cross will be, only that we have to be ready to take it up. Our calling is to a life of unconditional obedience; the price of such obedience is unknown. Maybe you feel that you wouldn't go into anything where the price is unknown. Well, then you cannot be His disciple (see Luke 14:27). The starting point in following Christ is that it costs everything.

As followers of Jesus, you and I must be willing to say:

- "My money is Christ's." I don't find it easy to say that, because there are many things that I would like to buy. But when I recognize that fact, the only question is, "What does He want me to do with it?"

- "My time is Christ's." I don't find it easy to say that either, because there are many things that I would like to do. But when I have recognized that fact, the only question is, "What does He want to do with it?"

- "My life is Christ's." I certainly don't find it easy to say that, because I have my own goals and plans. But when I recognize that fact, the only question is, "What does He want me to do with it?"

We must be absolutely clear about our calling. We must be ready to pay any price. To use a word that is in vogue right now, following Christ is extreme. There is no upper price limit.

KEEP YOUR EYES ON THE PRIZE

The Gospels record the revealing story of a wealthy man, a successful entrepreneur who knew in his heart that God was laying claim to his life. He came to Jesus one day and asked Him what he had to do to inherit eternal life (Matthew 19:16–22; Mark 10:17–22; Luke 18:18–23). Christ knew that money was strangling the man's spiritual life, and that the only way he would ever be free was if he gave it away. "Go, sell everything you have," Jesus said, "and give to the poor...Then come, follow me" (Mark 10:21). This man knew the calling, but like God's people on the verge of Canaan, he struggled with the cost, and "he went away sad" (10:22).

If I could talk to this man, I'd say, "Don't you realize that the Son of God just invited you to share life with Him? He gave you a personal invitation to follow Him. There are millions of people who will follow you in history, who would give anything they had to have the opportunity that was opened up to you!"

SPOTLIGHT ON CHRIST

The life of Jesus had a very different outcome from the life of the wealthy man. Christ was crystal clear about His calling. "My food is to do the will of him who sent me" (John 4:34). He was sold out to that single purpose, and He was ready to pay any price. With incredible courage He set His face to go to Jerusalem:

> *"The Son of Man must suffer many things and be rejected by the elders, chief priests and teachers of the law, and he must be killed and on the third day be raised to life."* (LUKE 9:22)

Peter came and said, "Don't do that" (see Matthew 16:21–22), but Jesus set His face to go to Jerusalem. That's courage.

The book of Hebrews gives us a clue about how Christ was able to do this. He endured the cross "for the joy set before him" (Hebrews 12:2). In other words, when God held the cross before Him, Christ did not focus on it. He looked through it to the joy that was before Him on the other side of the cross. He kept his eyes on the prize. He focused on the outcome, and Isaiah tells us that, "After the suffering of his soul, he will see the light of life and be satisfied" (Isaiah 53:11).

So here are two stories about different choices and outcomes. One story ends with a man who is sad; the other with a man who is satisfied. The difference is in their readiness to pursue the call of God, without regard for the cost. *Sad or satisfied*—which of these two words will describe what you feel when you look back on your life?

I will never forget sitting in a meeting in England listening to a great preacher of a previous generation, Dr. Alan Redpath. As I recall, he had already retired, and yet he felt that there was something more that he could do for Christ. He said, "I have asked God to give me ten more years so that I can give them wholly to Him." He is with the LORD now, but I reckon that is just about exactly what happened.

If God gives you ten more years before Christ comes, what will you have done to advance the kingdom of God, to push beyond your own comfort zone, to do more than enjoy worship services and your own personal blessing?

UNLOCKED

Looking back on the history of the church, it is clear that some generations have contributed more to advancing the purposes of God than others. The book of Numbers leads us to expect that this would be the case; not all generations serve willingly. A critical spirit among people and a cowardly spirit among leaders will lead to an aimless wandering, which will contribute little to the purposes of God in the world.

The greatest challenge for the church of Jesus Christ is to grasp her calling, and then to look beyond the cost to the prize of God's commendation.

PAUSE FOR PRAYER

Gracious Father, make me crystal clear about my calling.
Make me ready for any cost.
Keep my eyes focused on the crown that lies beyond the cross.
Let me put obedience to Christ before popularity.
Let me put obedience to Christ before profit.
Let me put obedience to Christ before pleasure.
Let Your purposes be advanced through my life.
Give me the power to do all these things through Jesus Christ our Lord. Amen.

Giving

DEUTERONOMY 14 16

How can you

stay spiritually

healthy in a

materialistic

culture?

11 Giving

DEUTERONOMY 14–16

DISCOVER

how to handle the financial responsibilities that come with God's blessing.

LEARN

God's principles for giving and borrowing.

WORSHIP

as you see how Christ proclaims God's Jubilee.

THE atmosphere was electric as the old man began to speak for the last time. He had been their leader for forty years, and it was hard to imagine life without him. The old man spoke with passion, like a father speaking to his children. His beard had turned white many decades ago, but his memory was still sharp as he recounted the years of their journey together; his vision was still clear as he spoke of critical choices that would shape their future.

Deuteronomy records the last words God spoke through Moses. The people were about to enter the land God gave to their forefathers, but Moses would not go with them. He would die before they entered the land, the mantle of leadership moving onto Joshua's broad shoulders.

Forty years had passed since the people had left Egypt (Deuteronomy 1:3), and Moses reminded the people from where they had come. God had brought their parents to the verge of the Promised Land, but they had lacked the courage to press forward. Now God was giving the same opportunity to the next generation. They were ready for the challenge.

As the new generation stood on the verge of entering their inheritance, the great question was how would they handle the intoxicating effects of sudden prosperity. Financial security has a subtle way of sucking the spiritual life out of you. Success brings its own subtle tests; it can dull your spiritual passion.

Deuteronomy has more to say about the spiritual dangers of living in a prosperous society than any other book in the Bible. It is God's handbook on maintaining spiritual health in a materialistic culture. God called His people to develop a culture of kindness in which they practiced giving, exercised restraint, and demonstrated their love for God and their neighbors in their handling of money.

PRACTICE GIVING

> *"Be sure to set aside a tenth of all that your fields produce each year." (14:22)*

The Old Testament goes into great detail about how each tribe and family was to have a share of the land. The land was God's gift, and from it they were able to earn a living. God says that they were to bring a tenth of all that they produced to the sanctuary as a grateful tithe to God.

In addition, every person in Israel had to attend three festivals. "Three times a year all your men must appear before the LORD your God at the place he will choose: at the Feast of Unleavened Bread [Passover], the Feast of Weeks and the Feast of Tabernacles" (16:16). These festivals were to be marked by joyful giving:

> *"No man should appear before the LORD empty-handed: Each of you must bring a gift in proportion to the way the LORD your God has blessed you." (16:16–17)*

Remember that God was speaking these words through Moses in the desert to a group of people who didn't own an acre of land among them. The land was still in the hands of their enemies. Moses said, "God is going to give you this land. It will be your means of income and it will sustain your life. What God has done for the last forty years with manna from heaven, He will now do through the crops of the land. But you must remember that it is still God who gives you everything that you have. So every year, work out your income, and then divide by ten. Then take that tenth and you give it to God."

God's principles of giving have not changed. In the New Testament, the strongest emphasis is on the spirit in which we give. "God loves a cheerful giver" (2 Corinthians 9:7). When you write that check supporting your local church, let it be an act of worship! Let it be an expression of your joy in what God has given you. The more the LORD prospers you, the larger your tenth will be, and the greater your joy in giving.

Remember that God was teaching His people how to maintain their spiritual health in a materialistic culture. When they went into the land of Canaan, the greatest danger was that they would be swamped by the pursuit of money and that the blessing of God would stifle their spiritual life. So God called them—and He calls us—to develop a habit and a culture of giving.

How is your giving to God? Jesus said, "Where your treasure is, there your heart will be also" (Matthew 6:21). It's not that your treasure follows your heart; it is that your heart follows your treasure. If you keep all your treasure, then God will never have your heart. The first key to maintaining spiritual health in a materialistic culture is *practice giving*.

RESTRAIN GREED

The practice of giving was not limited to money; it also included the giving of time. God had established the principle of the Sabbath in the fourth commandment: "Remember the Sabbath day by keeping it holy. Six days you shall labor and do all your work, but the seventh day is a Sabbath to the LORD your God. On it you shall not do any work" (Exodus 20:8–10).

The Sabbath day was "holy to the LORD." It was a day for worship and for the family; a day to be renewed in body, soul, and spirit. The Sabbath law remains of great importance in our 24-7 culture. I was speaking with a local restaurant owner recently, and he told me that he had only taken one day away from his work in the last ten months. He has a wife and a family, yet that is his lifestyle.

God says that on one day in seven we are to stop working. We are to give this day in a special way to God, and we are to use it to be renewed, restored, and refreshed. People will make different choices about what is appropriate on this day, but whatever we do, we must not make it another day of work.

If you think that is challenging, you ain't heard nothing yet! Not only did God say that the people were to rest one day in seven, but the land was to also lie fallow for one year in seven.

> The LORD said to Moses on Mount Sinai, "Speak to the Israelites and say to them: 'When you enter the land I am going to give you, the land itself must observe a sabbath to the LORD. For six years sow your fields, and for six years prune your vineyards and gather their crops. But in the seventh year the land is to have a sabbath of rest, a sabbath to the LORD. Do not sow your fields or prune your vineyards. Do not reap what grows of itself or harvest the grapes of your untended vines. The land is to have a year of rest.'" (LEVITICUS 25:1–5)

God gave a special promise in connection with this law. He would send a bumper harvest in the sixth year so that there would be enough food to sustain the people through the seventh year and during the planting season of the eighth year (Leviticus 25:20–22).

How would you have reacted to the Sabbath year? Perhaps you would look at your fields and say to yourself, *What a waste! This Sabbath law is costing me a whole year of income. Think of the money I could make if I had planted this out.*

The Sabbath law placed a restraint on greed. God's people were to learn how to say no to something good in order to say yes to something better. Thus, one year in every seven they passed up an opportunity for significant income in order to learn again that there is more to life than work and money. The highest good is not the bottom line.

In a world of greed, *practice restraint.* That's the second key to maintaining spiritual health in a materialistic culture. I struggle with a temperament that wants to say yes to every opportunity. It is in my nature to load the plate twice full. Without the Sabbath principle of restraint, my life would have no margins. I need to take a day off, and I need to take my vacations. These are not luxuries; they are God's principles for maintaining spiritual health.

CANCELING DEBTS

"At the end of every seven years you must cancel debts." (15:1)

Lending was encouraged in Israel. The whole nation was descended from one family, and so God said, "If there is a poor man among your brothers in any of the towns of the land that the LORD your God is giving you, do not be hardhearted or tightfisted toward your poor brother. Rather be openhanded and freely lend him whatever he needs" (15:7–8).

Notice the nature of the loan: We are to be "openhanded," lending freely. In Israel, if you loaned money to another countryman, you could not charge interest (see Leviticus 25:36–37). You could charge reasonable interest to a foreigner, but not to your neighbor. Of course, that also meant that if you received a loan from a neighbor, there was an obligation to repay it as quickly as possible.

Today Christians are under an obligation to repay their debts: "Let no debt remain outstanding" (Romans 13:8). We honor God as we plan on repaying our loans. If you have benefited from someone else's generosity through a loan without interest, do not take advantage of that kindness by failing to repay.

Let's return to the case of granting a loan in ancient Israel. Suppose that after seven years your neighbor has been unable to repay you. There are circumstances of misfortune in which this could easily happen. What are you to do?

God says, "Write off the debt."

God sets out a clear process by which this is to be done. The initiative is with the lender:

> *"Every creditor shall cancel the loan he has made to his fellow Israelite. He shall not require payment from his fellow Israelite or brother, because the LORD's time for canceling debts has been proclaimed."* (15:2)

This law was obviously wide open to abuse. Let's say Jared had been given a $10,000 interest free loan. He has paid back half, and it is the sixth year since the loan was made. He has $7,000 in the bank.

He opens his checkbook, and as he is about to write a check, his hand freezes.

I could give him $5,000, but then again, it's only a few months till the year of canceling debts, Jared reasons. *Maybe I'll just wait. After all, he doesn't need the money half as much as I do.*

It is important to remember that the law was given to the people of God. The law presupposes grace. The whole of the law of God is an exposition of those two foundational principles: (1) We must love God with our whole heart and (2) we must love our neighbor as ourselves. Those principles of love extend into our handling of money. Love means that where I receive a loan through the kindness of my brother, I am under an obligation of love to repay him in full as soon as possible.

A TEST OF OUR HEARTS

The year of canceling debts tested the heart of the borrower and his commitment to repay, but it also tested the heart of the lender and his willingness to be generous. Suppose you have $50,000 in the bank, and your brother has come on hard times and needs a loan of $5,000. You look at the calendar and you notice that it is year six in the cycle, and the year of canceling debts begins in just a few months time! So you think to yourself, *If I give him the money now, I don't have much chance of getting it back before the year of canceling debts begins.* But God said,

> *"Be careful not to harbor this wicked thought: 'The seventh year, the year of canceling debts, is near,' so that you do not show ill will toward your needy brother and give him nothing."* (15:9)

These laws tested the hearts of the lender and the borrower. Am I willing to help my brother even if it proves to be costly? If I receive from my brother, am I the kind of person who will abuse his kindness?

Moses was teaching these principles to a group of people who owned no property and had no means of generating income. But God was about to trust them with significant wealth. When that happened, they were to give generously, practice restraint, and demonstrate grace in the way that they used their money. These laws were given specifically to Israel, but they search our hearts today. Even though we are not bound by these laws, they point to the kind of attitude God calls us to display.

RELEASING WORKERS AND SLAVES

If one of God's people had a loan and was unable to pay it back, one way he could fulfill his responsibility was by working for the lender and paying off the loan in kind. God established very clear laws to protect the dignity of the worker in this situation. God's people had been slaves in Egypt, and they were never to return to slavery again (Deuteronomy 15:15). As a result, the lender was not to become a slave master.

> "If one of your countrymen becomes poor among you and sells himself to you, do not make him work as a slave. He is to be treated as a hired worker." (LEVITICUS 25:39–40)

The obligation of the employer went beyond kind treatment of the worker. The law protected freedom by requiring that a servant had to be released after seven years. If a man was working to repay a debt, he could always look forward to the day when his freedom and independence would be restored.

The releasing of slaves was different from the canceling of debts. The debts were written off for everybody at the same time. But the release of servants happened seven years from the day that the contract was made.

> If a fellow Hebrew, a man or a woman, sells himself to you and serves you six years, in the seventh year you must let him go free. And when you release him, do not send him away empty-handed. Supply him liberally from your flock, your threshing floor and your winepress. Give to him as the LORD your God has blessed you. (15:12–14)

The law to release slaves required a compassionate compensation for workers who must have owned little when they sold themselves (their labor) as servants. The law was intended to prevent the rich from exploiting the poor, and to protect the freedom of all the people.

RETURNING THE LAND

The time of canceling debts came around every seven years. Then, after seven cycles of seven years, there was a "once in a lifetime" festival in Israel called the Year of Jubilee. Once in every fifty years, the trumpet was to sound, and there was to be a great festival of grace.

> *"Consecrate the fiftieth year and proclaim liberty throughout the land to all its inhabitants." (LEVITICUS 25:10)*

In the fiftieth year, all of the land was to be returned to the original owners. So if an Israelite sold land in the fortieth year of the cycle, the price would be low, because the buyer would only have it for ten years, and then ownership would return to the seller. If the same Israelite bought land in the tenth year of the cycle, the price would be high because he would have the use of the land for forty years before he had to return it.

Ownership of the land could never be transferred. The land belonged to the LORD. All that could be bought or sold was the use of the land for a limited period of time.

Imagine the impact this would have on the community. Once in every lifetime, there would be a great restoration. The poor would be given a fresh start with the land that the LORD had given to that family at the beginning. The rich who had prospered would retain the capital they had made, but their children would start with the same amount of land.

The restoring of the land placed a check on the growing power of those who had accumulated wealth, and it meant that their children would have to find their own way in life rather than rely on massive accumulated inheritances of land that were passed on to them.

IGNORING THE LAW

Would you have liked to live under these laws? Your answer to that question will probably depend on whether you would be among the lenders or the borrowers. If your debts were greater than your assets, you would probably think that the year of canceling debts, the year of releasing servants, and the Year of Jubilee were marvelous gifts.

But if you were a potential lender, you would be in a different situation. Imagine Jethro, a man with significant wealth. He has several servants, has acquired a number of fields at a good price, and has been in the happy position of being able to make loans to three of his friends who have come on hard times. One day, Jethro sits down with his accountant to do some financial planning.

"Now, let's see. The Sabbath for the land is coming up, and then it will be the year of canceling debts, followed by the Year of Jubilee. That means that there will be no harvest, then there are three loans to write off, and I am going to lose these fields that I have acquired over the last few years! And the seventh year is up for four of the men who are working off their debts for me, and so that means that I will have to go out and hire more staff. These laws are going to cost me a fortune!" His accountant nods his head in sad agreement.

No doubt about it. The Sabbath laws were great for the debtor, but costly for the creditor!

Moses gave the people these laws shortly before he died. The people went into the Promised Land under the leadership of Joshua, and after a few years they quietly forgot about the Sabbath laws. I can well imagine a committee meeting to discuss it.

"You know, next year is the year of canceling debts. This law of Moses is going to be very expensive. Let's just take a pass on it this time, and we will look at it again if the economy is better in seven years."

It seems to have been the same with the Sabbath for the land. The year of rest for the land was systematically ignored. Over the years that God's people occupied the land, there should have been seventy years without cultivation. God counted the Sabbaths on which the land should have been left fallow. Then when the Babylonians took God's people into exile, the land enjoyed its rest in one massive Sabbath, which lasted for seventy years (2 Chronicles 36:21).

Do you know how often the Jubilee happened? Never! Not once.

In their book on Jewish feasts, Kevin Howard and Marvin Rosenthal noted, "The observance of the Jubilee Year, like that of the Sabbatical Year, was also neglected during Israel's early history. In fact, there is no historical record, biblical or extra-biblical, that Israel ever once observed the Jubilee Year."[1]

The people who had the power to call the Jubilee never had the will to do so, because for them it would have been very costly. So the history of Israel was one of frustration for the poor. This is why the eighth-century prophets Isaiah and Amos were so scathing about those who had accumulated wealth and had no regard for the poor. The laws that God had given to restore the economic structure of the nation were systematically ignored.

SPOTLIGHT ON CHRIST

As the years passed, people must have wondered if the nation would ever have a leader who would have the authority and the will to sound the trumpet and proclaim a Jubilee Year.

There was one king who got close. The prophet Jeremiah wrote that King Zedekiah proclaimed a year of freedom for the captives, but later he changed his mind, and it never happened (Jeremiah 34:8–20). Then after the exile, when Jerusalem was rebuilt, the people establishing the new community made a commitment to observe the Sabbath of the land and cancel all debts on the seventh year (Nehemiah 10:31), but that hardly happened either.

Then Jesus came into the world, and Luke tells us about the day He began His public ministry. Jesus went to Nazareth, where He had been brought up, and on the Sabbath day, He went into the synagogue. The scroll of the prophet Isaiah was handed to Him, and unrolling it, He found the place where it is written, "The Spirit of the LORD is on me, because he has anointed me to preach *good news to the poor*. He has sent me to proclaim *freedom for the prisoners* and recovery of sight for the blind, to *release the oppressed, to proclaim the year of the LORD's favor*" (Luke 4:18–19; italics added).

Jesus rolled up the scroll and gave it back to the attendant and then He sat down. Everybody was watching Him. "Today," He said "this scripture is fulfilled in your hearing" (Luke 4:21). Christ has proclaimed God's year of forgiving debts and God's year of restoring the inheritance that men and women had lost. We are still living in that "year" of the Lord's favor.

The Sabbath laws were great for the debtor but costly for the creditor, and the cost to God of canceling all our debts and restoring our inheritances was incalculable. It cost the death of His Son, Jesus Christ.

The only way to write off a debt is to incur the loss of the amount of the debt personally. If you owe me $1,000, and I write it off, then I incur a loss of $1,000. And if God is to write off all our debts to Him, it will mean that He has to incur the total cost of that debt in Himself. That is why Christ went to the cross. He bore the loss, and in this way canceled our debts and restored the inheritance of everlasting life.

This is good news for the poor! Christ was saying to the people "You've been looking to your political leaders to implement the Jubilee, and it has never happened because it is far too costly. But God is going to do a far greater thing for you. He has anointed Me to come and to preach this good news to the poor: God will cancel all debts; God will restore lost inheritances." Indeed, in Jesus Christ that is what He has done.

UNLOCKED

Money is powerful. It can gain a grip on our hearts. If we do not master our money, then our money will master us. The spiritual disciplines of proportionate giving and exercising restraint will help to break the power that money can so easily hold over us. God calls His people to develop a culture of kindness. Let us give a practical expression of our love for God and each other in the ways that we use our money.

PAUSE FOR PRAYER

Gracious and forgiving Father,

I confess that the more You give me, the more I want to keep. Deliver me from the love of money and give me a generous heart.

Thank You for writing off my debts and absorbing the cost through Your death on the cross.

Pour Your Spirit into my heart that I may be a person who practices giving and exercises restraint. As You have blessed me, help me to bless others.

Through Jesus Christ my LORD I pray. Amen.

Note

1. Kevin Howard and Marvin Rosenthal, *The Feasts of the Lord* (Nashville: Nelson, 1997), 197.

Evil

DEUTERONOMY 19

How can we

create a culture

that is conducive

to holiness?

12 Evil

DEUTERONOMY 19

DISCOVER

why God calls parents to exercise appropriate discipline in the home.

LEARN

God's principles for dealing with personal grievances.

WORSHIP

as you see how Christ delivers us from the full penalty of the Law.

DURING my first visit to northern India, I discovered that adultery was almost unknown amongst married men in villages. When I asked about the reason for this, I was given a very simple explanation. If a man was unfaithful to his wife, the rest of the men in the village would give him "a going-over" down by the river. This brought about a certain restraint amongst the village men and so adultery was rare, and marriages, while not necessarily particularly happy, were at least fairly stable.

On the other hand, I found that corruption was rife in India. The explanation again was simple. "People turn a blind eye to the bribe."

A culture can be defined as "what most people think is acceptable." Whatever a community approves will multiply, and whatever a community opposes will diminish.

As the people of God gathered at the edge of the Promised Land, Moses had one last opportunity to bring the Word of God to them. As they entered the land, God's people faced new challenges.

How would the community apply God's laws? What would they do when one of their number flagrantly broke God's Law? Would God's people confront the problem or would they turn a blind eye and ignore it? Perhaps they'd punish some violations more severely than others. The way in which the community responded to different kinds of evil would determine which ones would multiply and which would diminish.

Moses challenged the people of God to create a culture conducive to holiness—to regard every sin as God does. Moses called them to be a community that would support and foster the life that God had called His people to lead.

A CULTURE THAT ENCOURAGES RIGHTEOUS LIVING

This is still a burning issue for the church today. Churches create their own culture. What most people consider acceptable in a particular church will multiply, and what most people think unacceptable in that church will diminish. A healthy church is a community of people who care enough to encourage each other in the pursuit of a consistent, holy life. It also is a community of people who care enough to confront each other over issues of sin. If a member of Christ's body chooses a pattern of sin and refuses to give it up, that person needs to feel the weight of the whole community's disapproval. Such disapproval is the most powerful statement that can be made this side of the final judgment of God.

God could have given the Ten Commandments and said, "These are the laws, and it will be up to every individual to apply them." But God did not do that. He gave the Law to His people and said, "If these laws were openly flouted, then the community must act. You must be ready to do something about it. You must create a culture in which there is every encouragement to righteousness and every restraint against evil."

If you were an observer in ancient Israel, it would not be long before you got the message: "Around here we live by the Law of God. If you honor God's Law you will be blessed; if you fail God's Law you will be forgiven; if you flout God's Law you will be in trouble."

Our choices are heavily influenced by our nature and our environment, and when we come to Christ, God changes both. He changes our nature through the new birth, and He brings us into a new environment called the church. The church is the environment in which relationships are formed that will encourage us toward obedience and discourage us from sin. We need encouragement because we are often weak, and we need restraint because we are often willful.

As we hear God's words to His people through Moses in Deuteronomy, we will discover the distinctive marks of a culture that is conducive to holiness, and we will learn how these principles apply to us in the family, the nation, and the church.

PROTECTING THE VULNERABLE

God told the people that when they settled in the land, they were to identify three centrally located cities and then build roads to them so that each would be accessible from any part of the country. These towns were to be cities of refuge, places where "anyone who kills a man may flee" for safety (19:2–3).

Moses gave an example of the kind of situation in which these cities will be used. Two men are out in the forest cutting trees, and there is a terrible accident. The head of one man's ax flies off the handle, and it hits his colleague and kills him. When the dead man's family hears about it, they do not believe that it was an accident. They're convinced it was criminal negligence, and they set out after the hapless woodcutter intent on vengeance (vv. 5–6).

The cities of refuge provided a place of protection for a vulnerable person until there could be a proper inquiry into what happened. The incident with the axe may have been criminal negligence, or it may have been a terrible accident, but among God's people there was to be a proper, legal process for determining the truth. The community was to make sure that vulnerable people were protected from those who would take the law into their own hands.

Some time ago our church hosted some tribal people from a remote part of Venezuela. They had not heard the gospel, until some Evangelical Free Church missionaries brought the message of Christ's love to them. Many of the tribal people received Christ. It transformed their whole culture.

One of the tribal leaders explained, through double translation—first to Spanish and then to English—the difference that the gospel had made. "Before the gospel came to our culture, disputes were always resolved with the sword," he told our congregation. "Now we have a council to resolve disputes."

That is a wonderful reflection of how God calls a community to function. God is saying, "You must uphold the rule of law; you must have a proper process for dealing with grievances."

Another crucial principle for protecting the vulnerable is that

> One witness is not enough to convict a man accused of a crime....A matter must be established by the testimony of two or three witnesses. (v. 15)

Suppose someone makes a slanderous accusation in public. It may be completely untrue, but once it is made, people often conclude, "There's no smoke without fire," and it may be extremely difficult for a falsely accused person to defend himself.

Knowing this, an enemy may come forward with false accusations. How does a community protect against such slander? God says that if someone brings accusations that prove to be false, the court should do to him as he intended to do to his brother (vv. 18–19). The effect of this will be that, "The rest of the people will hear of this and be afraid, and never again will such an evil thing be done among you" (v. 20).

AN EYE FOR AN EYE

The whole point of these laws is that the vulnerable must be protected. And it is in this context that God instructed His people:

> Show no pity: life for life, eye for eye, tooth for tooth, hand for hand, foot for foot. (v. 21)

"An eye for an eye"…simply established the principle of fair compensation.

Some people are surprised that this statement is in the Bible, and it is important that we understand it correctly. God never intended that if you knock my tooth out, you should then stand against a wall while I line up my punch to knock yours out as well! "An eye for an eye" is not an invitation to retaliatory violence. His command simply established the principle of fair compensation.

God gave a specific application of this principle in Exodus 21:23–27. Suppose a slave owner struck his slave and blinded him. The Law demanded that the slave should be compensated in some way, "eye for eye, tooth for tooth" (Exodus 21:24). God did not intend the blinded slave to put out his owner's eye! The principle is that there should be compensation, and in this case, God says that the slave should be given his freedom (21:26).

"An eye for an eye" also teaches us that compensation should be in proportion to the damage done. It is an eye for an eye, not two eyes, an arm, and a leg! God's Law places restraints on the injured person who says, "You have made me suffer and so I will make you suffer ten times over."

God's Law puts matters of compensation firmly in the courts. It gives guidance to judges by telling them that they are not to make huge and disproportionate awards, but are to keep a due sense of proportion. "An eye for an eye and a tooth for a tooth." Properly understood, this is a principle that we desperately need today, in a society where a simple injury is sometimes seen as an opportunity to make a fortune. The community must protect the vulnerable.

RESTRAINING THE WICKED

The Bible speaks to life in a fallen world where the sad reality is that some people are simply wicked. God identifies some specific areas in which wickedness must be restrained for the health and safety of the whole community.

Suppose, God said, that "a man hates his neighbor and lies in wait for him, assaults and kills him" (Deuteronomy 19:11). Here is an example of deliberate, premeditated, cold-blooded murder. The first thing that the murderer will do is to run to one of the cities of refuge. But he is not to be protected from the consequences of his actions. The elders of the town are to bring him back, and then his life is to be taken (v. 12). God made the reason for this very clear:

> Show him no pity. You must purge from Israel the guilt of shedding innocent blood, so that it may go well with you. (v. 13)

This theme of "purging evil" is repeated through Deuteronomy almost like a refrain. For example, in a case of perjury, where someone has deliberately lied in order to harm another person, God said, "Do to him as he intended to do to his brother. You must purge the evil from among you" (19:19). Or in a case of adultery, "if a man is found sleeping with another man's wife, both the man who slept with her and the woman must die. You must purge the evil from Israel" (22:22). In a case of kidnapping, "if a man is caught kidnapping one of his brother Israelites and treats him as a slave or sells him, the kidnapper must die. You must purge the evil from among you" (24:7). In the case of a prophet among God's people who comes with signs and wonders but calls the people to follow other gods, "that prophet or dreamer must be put to death, because he preached rebellion against the LORD your God....You must purge the evil from among you" (13:5).

When all of these laws are put together, it might give the impression that God's people were in constant danger of capital punishment! In actual fact, the number of offenses that called for the death penalty were remarkably few, and they related to three primary values: the worship of God ("You shall have no other gods before me"), the sanctity of life ("You shall not murder"), and the sanctity of marriage ("You shall not commit adultery").

These are the central pillars of society, and God called the whole community to pull together and uphold them.

RESTORING THE PENITENT

It is important to remember that at the same time God gave His laws, He also gave the sacrifices to His people. God established the death sentence for idolatry, but He also gave His people the sacrifice as a way to make atonement for their sinful rebellion. After the Israelites made the golden calf in the desert, God provided a sacrifice as a way of deliverance.

Similarly, God's Law called for adulterers to be stoned. But God forgave David when he repented after his sin with Bathsheba. Forgiveness and restoration were always in the mind and heart of God. The sacrifices provided a way out of the full penalties of the Law.

The mercy of God in the sacrifices meant that there was room for restoring grace in the community. This is implicit in the Old Testament and explicit in the New (see, for example, Galatians 6:1; James 5:19–20).

The power of restoration was never more beautifully seen than on the day when some Pharisees, a respected group of religious leaders, dragged a woman who had been caught in the act of adultery before Christ. They wanted Jesus the Teacher to sanction the full implementation of the Law.

Christ responded, "If any one of you is without sin, let him be the first to throw a stone at her" (John 8:7). Then Christ went to the woman and He said to her, "Has no one condemned you?...Then neither do I condemn you....Go now and leave your life of sin" (John 8:10–11). Under the justice of God's Law, she would have been dead, but in the mercy of God she was given a new lease on life. "The wages of sin is death, but the gift of God is eternal life in Christ Jesus our LORD" (Romans 6:23).

PUTTING THE PRINCIPLES INTO PRACTICE

If it is God's purpose to establish a community where the vulnerable are protected, the wicked restrained, and the penitent restored, where are we to look for a model of these principles being put into practice? Where can we hope to find a culture that is conducive to holiness?

If we look for this community in the Old Testament, we will be disappointed. After God's people settled in Canaan, the book of Judges tells us that "everyone did what was right in his own eyes" (Judges 17:6; 21:25 NKJV). The book is filled with appalling stories of violence and injustice that were never dealt with. And when the community failed to deal with evil, wickedness multiplied, until eventually the people cried out to God because the cities were so filled with violence that life became intolerable.

SPOTLIGHT ON CHRIST

Centuries later, the LORD Jesus Christ came into the world. His ministry had hardly begun before the Pharisees and the Herodians (political loyalists of King Herod) were plotting to kill Him. Eventually they arrested Him, and He was brought into the religious court.

This was to be the place where the innocent found protection and where an accusation should be established by two or three witnesses. The Gospels record how false witnesses came forward, but Christ was not given the protection of the law against their accusations.

Christ was taken to Pilate, the Roman governor. Instead of overseeing a proper judicial process, he asked the crowd if they would like to have Christ released, or if they would prefer the release of a criminal called Barabbas. Instead of restraining the wicked, Pilate released Barabbas into the community, and Christ was taken outside the city wall to be crucified.

DON'T BLAME THE GOVERNMENT

That raises a question: To what extent should we look to the government to establish a community that is conducive to holiness? We need to be very careful how we draw lines from the laws of the Old Testament to national governments. Christ distinguished between the final authority of God and the derived authority of the state when He said, "Give to Caesar what is Caesar's and to God what is God's" (Mark 12:17). The problem comes in deciding which evils are to be dealt with by Caesar and which evils are to be left to God.

It is important to remember that there is a difference between a sin and a crime. A sin is an offense against God. A crime is an offense against God, but it is also an offense against another human being. All crimes are sins, but not all sins are crimes. Blasphemy is a sin but not a crime. Idolatry is a sin but not a crime. The state has responsibility for punishing crimes (like murder) against people, but it does not have authority to punish sins (like idolatry) that are uniquely against God.

The state can create a culture that is conducive to peace and safety, but it cannot create a culture that is conducive to holiness. It is the responsibility of the state to restrain crime, but it is beyond the means of the state to promote holiness.

There are just two places where we can hope to find a culture that opposes evil and promotes holiness: the family and the church.

The Culture of a Godly Family

God has given Christian parents the responsibility of creating an environment that will make it difficult for their children when they sin, and that will encourage them to pursue what is right.

Likewise, Christian parents must protect the vulnerable. No child should be at the mercy of a father or a mother's temper. Be very careful that you do not act like the hotheaded avenger of blood! When there has been an incident, you need to be very sure that you have made a proper investigation and established the facts beyond reasonable doubt before exercising appropriate discipline.

> God disciplines those who He loves, but He does not stop loving those He disciplines.

Parents must remember to be merciful when something was an accident. I will never forget an occasion when, as a young child, I dropped a pot of black paint on an orange carpet in my parents' home. I remember thinking, *I'm really going to get it,* and being totally surprised that "it" never came. I am still surprised by the fact that I was not punished for it. My father realized that, like the flying ax head, it was an accident and there is all the difference in the world between intentional disobedience and an accident.

That is an important distinction. But when little eyes look at you with defiance, it is time for discipline, because "foolishness is bound up in the heart of a child" (Proverbs 22:15 NKJV), and God has given parents the responsibility of communicating the message that sin leads to painful consequences. In a proportionate and measured way, Christian parents need to communicate to their children that the way of the sinner is hard. If we fail to do this, we will raise children who are unable to make the connection between sin and its consequences.

Are you a parent? Remember, whenever you exercise discipline, you must always make the way of restoration clear. God disciplines those who He loves, but He does not stop loving those He disciplines. I thank God for the privilege of being raised in a godly family where there was every encouragement toward good, and every restraint against evil. God calls Christian parents to establish homes where the way of the sinner is hard but the path of righteousness is filled with encouragement. The Christian family can be a counterculture. It can be a place where a different set of values can be established and fostered.

THE CULTURE OF AN AUTHENTIC CHURCH

The church is at the heart of God's plan to promote righteousness. Most Christians spend the whole week in an environment where sin is joked about, praised, or even actively promoted. The unrelenting pressure of a godless environment can make the Christian life extremely difficult. Christian believers are to help each other in this whole business of living a holy life. The church is to be a place where the encouragement is in the opposite direction.

That means that when your brother is vulnerable, you must protect him. Stand with him in the storm and don't back off. He needs you. And when your brother is being drawn toward sin and you know it, restrain him. Don't look the other way. Powerful forces are pulling him, and your honesty may be the very means that God uses to save him from disaster. Your silence, however, may be the very thing that causes him to stumble.

And what if your brother has fallen into sin? Then restore him. "If someone is caught in a sin, you who are spiritual should restore him gently" (Galatians 6:1). The picture is of someone caught in a trap or tangled in a net. He needs the help of someone who will cut him loose. Don't give up on your Christian brother or sister. Help the person to get out of the mess he's in and back to the path of pursuing righteousness.

Are you a teenager? Imagine being in a youth meeting at church, and someone uses foul language. Instead of ignoring it or sniggering, you can say, "Let's not use that kind of language around here." Or imagine being in a high school group where your friends care about you enough to challenge you when you are losing your spiritual passion, and will confront you when you are flirting with temptation. Imagine a group of friends who will care enough to restore you when you have blown it.

Imagine a congregation where there are relationships deep enough to challenge patterns of deception, where friends will increase your resistance to sin and strengthen your desire for righteousness. The church is not a place we come for one hour on a Sunday to sing a few songs, listen to a sermon, and go home. The church in the New Testament is a community of people who are committed together to pursue a godly life!

We are not being the church, as it is described in the New Testament, until we learn to stand together in times of trouble, hold each other accountable in times of temptation, and help one another escape the entanglement of sin so that we can be free for the pursuit of a godly life.

UNLOCKED

We live in a highly individualistic culture, but God places great importance on the community. He calls His people to create a culture that is conducive to holiness.

The Old Testament Law describes a community where the vulnerable are protected, the wicked restrained, and the penitent restored. These principles are fundamental to the safety and well-being of any nation. But governments cannot create a culture that is conducive to holiness. Parents have the responsibility of building that culture in the home, and believers have the responsibility of building that culture in the church.

PAUSE FOR PRAYER

Heavenly Father,

Show me those with whom I need to stand at this time because they are vulnerable. Prompt me by Your Spirit to say a word that will keep a brother or sister from error and disaster. Show me how I can help to restore someone who is caught in a trap. Show me what You would have me to do and make me what You would have me to be, through Jesus Christ my Lord. Amen.

Covenant

JOSHUA 24

How can

we keep

our covenants

with God?

13 Covenant

JOSHUA 24

DISCOVER
how to renew your
spiritual commitment.

LEARN
the place of accountability in
the Christian life.

WORSHIP
as you see God's faithfulness
to His people.

2100 B.C.	**CA. 2092** ABRAHAM ENTERS CANAAN
2000	
1900	
	CA. 1876 JACOB ENTERS EGYPT
1800	FOUR HUNDRED YEARS OF SLAVERY IN EGYPT
1700	
1600	
1500	
	CA. 1447 THE EXODUS FROM EGYPT
1400	**CA. 1407 –1400** CONQUEST OF CANAAN
1300	
1200	
1100	

ONE of the most moving services of worship I have ever experienced did not take place in a church or a cathedral. It occurred in the living room of our home in London. About thirty adults were there, half of them sitting on the floor. These folks had all been invited because they were friends of a couple who had asked that we meet together.

The couple had been married for about fifteen years and had three children, but most of those years had been pretty unhappy. Steve (not his real name) had become addicted to pornography and abused alcohol. As time passed, he had also become increasingly dependent on drugs. He was abusive at home and unreliable at work.

Gradually, those of us who cared for this couple saw their family life unravel. Lisa's health broke down, their finances were in a mess, and finally, when Lisa discovered a pattern of unfaithfulness that had gone on for some time, she could take no more and threw him out.

It was like that for some time. He was living with a friend; she struggled on with the children. But then at the lowest point, God worked what I can only describe as a miracle. There was a softening in Steve's heart. He began to take responsibility for what had happened, and there was evidence of genuine repentance. He began to spend time regularly with the children. There were some times when they were all together and everyone realized that they were happy. Lisa told me that was scary!

As I had opportunity to talk with Steve, he revealed a new honesty in facing the habitual sins and patterns of behavior that had gripped his life and were eating his soul. At first when he came to speak with me, he wore sunglasses. Then one day he took them off. It seemed almost to be a symbol of the opening up of his soul.

Lisa was very wise and rightly cautious. She did not let him return home, but gradually they began a process of rebuilding trust. Then one day she came to see me. "I feel that I am ready to have him back," she said. "I believe the change has been real, and I think both of us are ready to make a fresh start. But we need to draw a line under the past. We need to know that we are making a new start with the help of God. Is there some kind of service that we could have?"

THE COVENANT MEETING

I said I didn't know of any such service, but I was sure that we could invent one, and so we decided that we would plan it together. They wanted it to be in our home, and so it was arranged. They invited their friends. Now thirty people huddled into our living room, all dressed for the occasion, along with this couple and their three children.

We called it "a renewal of the covenant." I'll never forget that covenant meeting.

"We have come here," I began, "to help our friends make a new start in their marriage. Their marriage never ended, but the covenant between them was vio-lated many times in different ways. They have experienced great pain, and so have their children. But God is gracious, and even when we rebel against Him, He will not let us go. He touches our hearts and makes us want to go in a different direction. Both of our friends were heading away from each other, but God has turned them both around and brought them back together. So this is a time for confession, a time for forgiveness, a time for new commitment, and a time of great hope."

I'll never forget the atmosphere in the room as Steve told us his story, confessed his sins, and then broke down in tears as he tried to thank the friends who had never stopped praying for him. Together we gathered around him and, as many of us as could, laid hands on him thanking God and praying for God's strength in his life.

Then it was Lisa's turn. She spoke about her anger, her hardness of heart, and the bitterness she had harbored. She spoke about how the problems were not all on one side; about things that she might have done differently. She thanked God for what He had done in her life and for showing her that it cost more for God to forgive her than for her to forgive anybody else. We gathered around her and prayed.

Then we came to the vows. We had worked on some appropriate words together. This was not a marriage service, because the marriage had never ended. It was a *renewing of the covenant*. It was a way of affirming that even though promises made yesterday had been broken, they still stood firm today, and that with the help of God, they would be kept in the future. In the goodness of God, that is exactly what happened.

GOD'S BINDING AGREEMENTS

"Renewing the covenant" is one of the main themes of the book of Joshua. A covenant is simply a binding promise. The whole Bible is the story of how God has committed Himself by making a covenant with His people.

The first time we read about a covenant in the Bible is when God said to Noah, "I will establish my covenant with you, and you will enter the ark," (Genesis 6:18). God made a binding commitment to save Noah and his family from the flood, and afterwards He made another covenant that He would never cover the whole earth with floodwaters again (Genesis 9:11–15).

Then, "The LORD made a covenant with Abram and said, 'To your descendants I give this land'" (Genesis 15:18). God made a promise, and this time it was sealed with the blood of a sacrifice. The books of Exodus, Leviticus, and Deuteronomy are all about God's covenant with the nation of Israel. "I will…be your God, and you will be my people" (Leviticus 26:12). Then God gave the Ten Commandments. That covenant was engraved in stone.

In the ancient world, it was common for the terms of a covenant to be written out. Two copies would be made. This is probably the significance of the two tablets of stone, on which the Ten Commandments were written. It is often assumed that God wrote five commandments on one stone, and then ran out of space and had to use another stone for the rest. But it is more likely that God wrote all of the Ten Commandments on one stone and gave Moses two sets. Moses put them in the ark of the covenant. These were the terms of the covenant between God and His people, and just as with any legal contract today there was a copy for both parties: one for God and one for the people.

RENEWING YOUR SPIRITUAL COMMITMENT

We have followed the story of how God brought His people to the verge of the Promised Land, and how Moses, in his parting words, challenged the people about the kind of community they should establish when they entered the land.

The book of Joshua tells us how God gave His people remarkable success in driving out their enemies. The people gathered, full of joy from their victories. Now Joshua challenged them to renew their commitment to the LORD.

For the first time in their lives, God's people were facing the test of prosperity. As they settled into their comfortable homes, Joshua was concerned that they might lose their passion for serving the LORD. So he exhorted the people to "fear the LORD and serve him with all faithfulness" (Joshua 24:14). When Joshua spoke about serving the Lord, he was not talking about volunteering to get involved in some specific program or ministry. Serving the Lord meant then—as it does now—making sure that the first commitment of one's life is to do what God wants done.

This is never easy. We can talk about God being first in our lives, but there is a daily battle to work that out in practice. So Joshua gave the people four strategies (listed in Joshua 24) that would help them to reignite their spiritual passion and keep their covenant with God. They were to (1) remember God's faithfulness, (2) make a decisive commitment, (3) throw out any idols, and (4) hold each other accountable.

REMEMBER GOD'S FAITHFULNESS

Joshua assembled all the tribes of Israel at Shechem.
(JOSHUA 24:1)

Shechem was a place of great significance. Abraham had come there when he arrived in the land, more than five hundred years earlier. It was a small town in the valley between the two mountains of Ebal and Gerizim, where the Levites had shouted out God's blessings and curses. When Abraham (then called Abram) arrived at "the great tree of Moreh at Shechem…the LORD appeared to [him] and said, 'To your offspring I will give this land.' So he built an altar there to the LORD, who had appeared to him" (Genesis 12:6–7).

Now two million descendants of Abraham were gathered at that same town. Imagine the emotion and excitement as these people came over the brow of the hill and looked down into the valley and saw the great trees at Shechem! Moms and Dads would be saying to their children, "You see these trees down there? That's where God appeared to our father Abraham more than five hundred years ago. God said to Abraham that his descendants would live in this land, and here we are! God is as good as His Word."

The value of a promise depends on the character of the person who makes it. What you do with your promises is a defining point of your character. God's character is reflected in His faithfulness to His promises. When the people got to the great trees at Shechem, many must have felt that they were standing on holy ground.

Our commitment is always a response to God's grace.

Then God, through His servant leader Joshua, began to remind the people of His faithfulness.

> *"This is what the LORD, the God of Israel, says:...'I took your father Abraham from the land beyond the River...I sent Moses and Aaron...and I brought you out....I brought you to the land of the Amorites....I gave them into your hands.'"* (vv. 2–3, 5, 8)

God summarized all he that He had done in bringing the people of Israel to the Promised Land. "So I gave you land on which you did not toil and cities you did not build" (v. 13).

Joshua recalled the faithful acts of God. If you want to restore your commitment to the Lord, come back to the great trees at Shechem. Take some time to think about God's love and faithfulness to you. Our commitment is always a response to God's grace. Spiritual passion begins with a mind that has been gripped by the fact that God is faithful.

MAKE A DECISIVE COMMITMENT

> *"But if serving the LORD seems undesirable to you, then choose for yourselves this day whom you will serve, whether the gods your forefathers served beyond the River, or the gods of the Amorites."* (v. 15)

Joshua then directed his attention towards the people who were struggling to make a wholehearted commitment to the LORD. If they didn't want to serve the LORD, they needed to be clear about who they would serve, he argued.

If I ask you the question, "Will you serve the Lord?" you could answer by saying "Maybe" or "I might do that some time in the future" or "I'm not sure if I am ready to make that commitment." But that is not the question that God asks you. The issue is not *whether* you will serve the Lord, it is, *"Which* God are you serving?" The point of the question is that if you are not serving the Lord, you have put something or someone else in the place that belongs to God. It is of the greatest importance that you be clear and honest about who or what that is.

Just in case the people were struggling to think of alternative gods, Joshua gave them some suggestions. "If you are finding it difficult to make a full commitment to serve the Lord, then you could, for example, return to the gods your forefathers worshiped beyond the river!"

Before Abraham knew the living God, he was worshiping idols in Mesopotamia. At that time very few people would have heard of Abraham; his life did not count for anything of great significance. Then God appeared and promised to bless him and make him a channel of blessing to the nations. "Now if you don't want to serve the Lord, who has blessed you and wants to use you to bring blessing to others," Joshua is saying, "then perhaps you would like to go back to these gods who did nothing whatsoever for Abraham!"

> Identify what you have put in God's place...[and] where that substitute will lead you.

Then Joshua had another suggestion. "If you are finding it difficult to give yourself fully to serving the Lord, then why not consider the gods of the Amorites?" That really was laying it on a bit thick, because Israel had just driven the Amorites out of the land! It was quite clear that the gods of the Amorites were unable to do anything to save their people from defeat.

Nobody in the twenty-first century is likely to follow the gods of the Amorites, but Joshua's question is still important for us. If we are not serving the Lord, what have we put in His place? There are times when I am strongly tempted to put myself or success or pleasure there.

There may have been times when you faced a decision, and the issue that determined your choice was not "What does God want" but "What will make me happy?" Or were there occasions when the real question wasn't "What pleases God?" but "What will make more money?"

Maybe at times you answered the question, "What does God want?" with "Who cares? This is what I want to do, and I am going to do it anyway."

There is nothing new in this struggle, and Joshua's question gives us some real help. When you are finding it difficult to serve the Lord, try to identify what you have put in God's place. Then take an honest look at where that substitute will lead you.

The false gods of the twenty-first century are easy to identify. Popularity, money, pleasure. It's worth thinking about the kind of epitaph that these gods could offer.

Colin S. Smith, born, 1958, died, 20__(?)

> *People really liked him…*
> *He left a pile of money…*
> *He had a lot of fun…*

Which of these epitaphs would you settle for? Isn't there something within you that desires something better? Wouldn't you rather stand with the apostle Paul and be able to say, "For to me, to live is Christ and to die is gain" (Philippians 1:21)?

Joshua confronted the people with a radical choice. "If you are not going to serve the LORD with all your heart and soul and mind and strength, then tell me who or what are you going to put in His place?" Then he led the way in saying, "As for me and my household, we will serve the LORD" (24:15b). When you have taken an honest look at the alternatives, it won't be long before you say the same.

THROW OUT YOUR IDOLS

When Joshua gave this challenge to choose whether they would serve the LORD or some other god, the people responded rightly by saying:

> *"Far be it from us to forsake the LORD to serve other gods! It was the LORD our God himself who brought us and our fathers up out Egypt….And the LORD drove out before us all the nations, including the Amorites. We too will serve the LORD, because he is our God." (vv. 16–18)*

So they got the point! Then Joshua made an extraordinary statement: "You are not able to serve the LORD" (v. 19). This is astonishing: The people had responded to the challenge of serving the LORD, and then Joshua told them that they couldn't do it! The people seem to have been offended by this and they insisted that they could (v. 21).

Then Joshua told them that if they were going to follow through on this commitment, they would have to "throw away the foreign gods that [were] among [them]" (v. 23). Evidently, God's people had held on to some of the idols that the Canaanites had left when they abandoned their homes. The idols were offensive to God, and He called His people to toss them.

Suppose Jesus Christ came into your house. Is there anything you would not want Him to find? What if He went through the desk in your office? Joshua spoke with the authority of a prophet here. "You say to me that you want to serve the Lord, but let me tell you, that isn't going to happen until you deal with the stuff that is offensive to Him. Get rid of it!" As long as the idols remained, their commitment to serve the Lord was only words.

It's noteworthy that God had blessed them despite these things in the past. God is incredibly gracious, and sometimes He overlooks inconsistencies in our lives for a long time. But there comes a time when God puts His finger on a particular issue, and when He does, you have to deal with it.

When Joshua said that God "will not forgive your rebellion and your sins" (v. 19), he was not telling the people that they had committed an unforgivable sin. But he was making it clear that God would not forgive a sin that they were not willing to forsake. God would not forgive the sin of following other gods while the people were still holding on to these gods. You cannot ask God to forgive you for a sin that you have no intention of abandoning.

What are you holding on to that keeps you from serving the Lord? Joshua would not allow the people to renew the covenant with words only. Commitment to the covenant involved a clear and decisive rejection of all that displeases God.

Remember God's faithfulness; make a decisive commitment; throw out your idols.

HOLD EACH OTHER ACCOUNTABLE

"You are witnesses against yourselves that you have chosen to serve the LORD." (v. 22)

The witnesses to a covenant had a responsibility to see that the covenant was honored. A good example of this would be a wedding. A young couple are getting married, and all their friends come for the service followed by a free meal and a piece of cake. What is the role of the friends who witness the wedding?

In the ancient world, the witnesses had a responsibility of making sure that the covenant was kept. So if a man was unhappy at home, he would go to his friend, who might have been best man or one of the other friends at the wedding, and talk. He might pour out all the reasons why his marriage was a big disappointment and explain why he was thinking of getting a divorce. His friend would say, "Well, wait a minute; there's a covenant involved here. You took some solemn vows and I am a witness. So let me stand with you as a friend and help you work this through."

Joshua told the people that they were witnesses against themselves that they had chosen to serve the LORD. In other words, they were to hold each other accountable. If you see your brother or sister with an idol, don't turn a blind eye. Help him; you are his witness!

SPOTLIGHT ON CHRIST

"On that day Joshua made a covenant for the people...at Shechem" (v. 25). The place where we renew our covenant is not Shechem with those few trees where God first made His promise to Abraham. It is at another tree, where Jesus Christ gave His life for us. The trees at Shechem spoke to the people of God's faithfulness and love, but the cross proclaims that same truth more clearly.

When we come to the Cross, God calls us to give up our idols, as we make that decisive commitment to Jesus Christ our LORD.

UNLOCKED

God is faithful to all His promises, and one of the first signs of spiritual maturity will be that we are faithful to our promises too. Keeping promises to God or to another person will involve choices that are sometimes costly, so God has given us four strategies that will help us to make covenant-keeping choices.

First, recollect what God has done for you. A lively sense of God's grace in your life will help to strengthen your loyalty to Him.

Second, look at the alternatives to serving the LORD. Take a long-term view of where other choices will lead you.

Third, throw out all that you know is displeasing to God in your life. That will be the evidence that your commitment to Christ is more than words.

Fourth, ask a friend to hold you accountable for the promises you have made. That accountability is one way in which God will give you strength and encouragement.

PAUSE FOR PRAYER

Almighty God,

Thank You for Your faithfulness and love demonstrated beyond contradiction by the Lord Jesus Christ at the cross.

I face a daily battle to let You be God, but nothing else is worthy of the full devotion of my life.

I admit that I have often said words about my commitment to serve You but they have been undermined by hidden idols. Today I want to say with Joshua, "As for me and my household, we will serve the Lord." Help me to throw out the idols and to become a person who is truly committed to serving You.

Through Jesus Christ my Lord, I pray. Amen.

Deliverer

JUDGES 2

What is idolatry,

and how is it

practiced in

America today?

14 Deliverer

JUDGES 2

1900

CA. 1876 JACOB ENTERS EGYPT

1800   FOUR HUNDRED
        YEARS OF SLAVERY
        IN EGYPT

1700

1600

1500

CA. 1447 THE EXODUS FROM
          EGYPT

CA. 1407 CONQUEST OF
1400 −1400 CANAAN

CA. 1360 TRANSITION PERIOD
     −1350 BETWEEN JOSHUA
            AND THE JUDGES
CA. 1350 THE PERIOD OF
     −1084 THE JUDGES

1300

ON April 21, 2000, the *Wall Street Journal* published an article entitled "Redefining God." In her story, reporter Lisa Miller summarized the phenomenon of newly imagined, highly personalized definitions of God.

> Across the country, the faithful are redefining God. Dissatisfied with conventional images of an authoritarian or paternalistic deity, people are embracing quirky, individualistic conceptions of God to suit their own spiritual needs...

> They are cobbling together a spiritual life from a variety of religious influences, along with a dash of yoga and psychotherapy or whatever else moves them.

> "People seek out these new gods the way they seek out new products in the marketplace," says Randall Styers, assistant professor at Union Theological Seminary in New York. "It's the ultimate form of individualism."

Miller then gave an example from America's Heartland.

> Take Ken Zweygardt, a 43-year-old lawyer in Oskaloosa, Kan. Growing up in a strict, Lutheran household, he says he used to imagine God as a "Santa Claus type," a provider and a judge. But as he matured, Mr. Zweygardt became frustrated with the church, and started waking early Sunday mornings to go fishing instead.

> Today, for him, God is being alone "on a lake, seeing the fog lift up at sunrise

and hearing the water bell." When he teaches his children, now two and three years old, about God, "I plan to take them outside and say, 'Here it is.' "[1]

Alongside this article, the *Journal* offered a side panel citing ten people from various backgrounds, offering their response to the question "What is God?" I found it interesting that the question was "What is God?"—rather than "Who is God?" Here are four of the responses.

Rev. James Forbes, senior minister at Riverside Church, New York, said God is "a force field of positive energy." Danny Goldberg, CEO of Artemis Records, who described himself as Jewish, said God is "pure love, intense feelings of love." Bill Joy, cofounder of Sun Microsystems and a self-described Protestant, added, "As scientists we can say God is part of our genes." Dana Buchman, who is a fashion designer and identified herself as a Presbyterian, said, "I don't believe in God, but I think often of close relatives who've had an effect on my life and values. It's like ancestor worship."[2]

The *Wall Street Journal* article brings the book of Judges out of the mists of ancient history and right into the twenty-first century. People do not know the living God.

A GENERATION WHO DID NOT KNOW THE LORD

Joshua had gathered the people together for a great national event where they renewed their covenant with God and pledged to put away the idols. Then the book of Judges takes up the story, telling us that, "after Joshua had dismissed the Israelites, they went to take possession of the land, each to his own inheritance" (Judges 2:6).

When they returned home after renewing the covenant, they followed through on their promise to God.

> The people served the LORD throughout the lifetime of Joshua
> and of the elders who outlived him and who had seen all the
> great things the LORD had done for Israel. (v. 7)

These people had a direct, personal experience of the saving action of God. This was the generation that had grown up in the desert. Some of them would have been small children at the time of the Exodus, and if so, they would have been in their late forties or early fifties when they arrived in Canaan, and by the time the land was conquered, they would have been of retirement age.

Others would have been born in the desert, and would be in their twenties and thirties when Joshua took over leadership from Moses. These folks would have served in the heat of battle during the conquest. They would have seen what the LORD did for Israel on the day the walls of Jericho fell down, or the remarkable day when the sun stood still. As we saw in chapter 13, they recalled what God had done for them and made a commitment to serve the LORD.

But eventually, "that whole generation had been gathered to their fathers" (a rather touching way of saying they died; v. 10). The next generation was different:

> *Another generation grew up, who knew neither the LORD nor*
> *what he had done for Israel.* (v. 10)

This is one of the saddest verses in the Bible, and it sets the scene for the whole book of Judges. This book tells us what happens to a nation when a generation grows up not knowing God and not knowing what He has done for His people. It is not very pleasant reading.

Judges introduces a whole new chapter in the Bible story that is of great importance for the church today. Out in the desert, everybody knew who God is and what He had done for Israel. So if the *Wall Street Journal* reporter had asked these folks "What is God?" they would immediately have said, "Wrong question.

What can be lost in one generation can also be restored in one generation.

You should ask, 'Who is God?' and we can give you the answer to that question. He is the God of Abraham, Isaac, and Jacob. He is the God who appeared to Moses and said, 'I am who I am.' He is the God who came down on Mount Sinai and gave the Ten Commandments."

They would have declared His character. "He is the Creator of all things, and He is our Savior and Judge. He is holy, righteous, loving, gracious, and good. He is to be worshiped and feared; He is to be loved and adored. He is the living God.'"

These people did not always obey the Lord. That generation wandered in the wilderness because of their parents' disobedience, but at least they knew who God is and what He had done. But now a new generation had arisen, and they were in an entirely different situation. Their problem was not that they failed to believe in God; it was that they did not know God.

HOW DID IT HAPPEN?

How could that have happened in one generation? Perhaps it was simply that their parents were busy in a prosperous land. These people had seen God do wonderful things in their own lives, but they clearly neglected the systematic teaching of their children, and within one generation the knowledge of God was lost!

So here in Judges we have a generation exactly like our postmodern society. Born in prosperity, fascinated with the search for spiritual meaning, but not knowing the Lord or what He has done for Israel.

PRIORITIES FOR PARENTS

This crisis in Israel reminds us of the priorities for parents, Sunday school teachers, small group leaders, and every Christian who is concerned about the spiritual life of our nation. We are to teach our children who God is, and we are to teach our children what God has done. These are the essentials.

We are not called to teach that "Johnny must be a good boy" or "Mary should be a good girl." Johnny and Mary must know who God is and what He has done. Without this knowledge, faith is impossible. As the apostle Paul puts it, "How can they believe in the one of whom they have not heard?" (Romans 10:14). So this must be the core of our curriculum. When Johnny and Mary know who God is and what He has done, then they will be in a position to make a meaningful response of faith and obedience.

It is not the job of Christian parents to bring their children to faith. Only the Holy Spirit can do that. But God gives all believing parents the task of teaching their children what the faith is. Our children are growing up surrounded by peers who think that God is "a force field of positive energy," or like Ken Zweygardt's children, that God is, "seeing the fog lift up at sunrise and hearing the water bell." Our great need today is for homes, churches, and seminaries where parents, pastors, and professors will teach who God is and what He has done for Israel.

It only took one generation for that knowledge to be lost. And what can be lost in one generation can also be restored in one generation. In fact, that is exactly what happened some time later in Israel. God spoke to Samuel, and through him, the Word of God came to all of Israel (1 Samuel 3:21).

GOING AROUND IN CIRCLES

The book of Judges records a cycle of events that recurred many times over a period of several hundred years. It began when people forsook the LORD and turned to idols. "Then the Israelites did evil in the eyes of the LORD and served the Baals. They forsook the LORD...They followed and worshiped various gods of the peoples around them" (vv. 11–12).

Then God became angry and gave His people into the hands of their enemies. "They provoked the LORD to anger....In his anger against Israel the LORD handed them over to raiders who plundered them" (vv. 12, 14).

In response, the people cried for God's help, and God raised up a leader, or a judge, to deliver them. "Then the LORD raised up judges, who saved them out of the hands of these raiders" (v. 16). These judges were not like magistrates; they were more like military leaders.

But upon the judge's death, the people returned to their previous ways, and the whole cycle started over again. The people were going around in circles: idolatry, judgment, cries to God, deliverance, and then idolatry again. As Judges 2 summarizes it:

> Whenever the LORD raised up a judge for them, he was with the judge and saved them out of the hands of their enemies as long as the judge lived; for the LORD had compassion on them as they groaned under those who oppressed and afflicted them. But when the judge died, the people returned to ways even more corrupt than those of their fathers, following other gods and serving and worshiping them. They refused to give up their evil practices and stubborn ways. (vv. 18–19)

IDENTIFYING THE IDOLS

As you read through the Old Testament, you will keep coming across this business of idolatry. Every few pages there seems to be something about one of the idols: the Baals, the Asherahs, Molech, or Dagon. It all seems rather remote to us, but it comes up so often that it is obviously important. The *Wall Street Journal* article provides a solid definition of idolatry: "Across the country, the faithful are redefining God....[They] are embracing quirky, individualistic conceptions of God to suit their own spiritual needs."

You will never get a clearer definition of idolatry than that. The *Journal* could equally well have entitled their article "Idolatry in America," and according to the paper, our country is full of such idolatry. Of course, we do not hear about Baal, the Asherahs, Dagon, or Molech; we have replaced them with "a force field of positive energy," or "pure intense feelings of love," or "seeing the fog lift up at sunrise, and hearing the water bell." Redefining God is pure idolatry.

THE ATTRACTION OF IDOLS

Idolatry is powerfully attractive, because it puts you in a position of absolute control. Have you ever thought that you would like to write a novel? You could start with a blank sheet of paper, and you could create a story and take it in any direction you wanted it to go.

Suppose you invent a fictional character and call him Wayne Ford, a sort of mixture of John Wayne and Harrison Ford. You decide that Wayne will be a pioneer, and you sit down at the computer and begin to write about him. "Wayne is rugged and muscular. He has a black mustache."…No, wait! You press the delete key. "He has a brown mustache."

God responds, "I am who I am. You cannot redefine me."

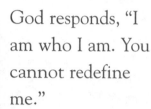

You describe Wayne's encounter with a bear in the Rocky Mountains. But then you need a bit of romance in the story, so you give Wayne a sensitive side. "Underneath that rough exterior, all his life Wayne has been looking for true love."

As you build the story, you are absolutely in control. Wayne is under your total power. The only existence he has is the existence you give him in the pages of your book. You can make Wayne whoever you want him to be, and he will do whatever you want him to do. That is the attraction of idolatry. Instead of worshiping the living God who says, "I am who I am," many people have preferred to create a god that suits their own spiritual needs.

Inventing a character is all very well in writing a novel, but try doing this with a real person and you will find yourself in court for libel or defamation of character! Idolatry is powerfully attractive, but it is also deeply offensive. Suppose that there were some folks in the church that I serve who said, "We like the idea of having a sort of 'Colin figure' around here, but we don't like who you are and we don't like what you do." I think I'd find that moderately offensive. But that is exactly what idolatry does in relation to God. Idolatry says to God, "We like the idea of some kind of God, but we don't like You. We don't like what You say, and we don't like what You do! So we'll redefine You. We'll determine who You are."

God responds by saying, "I am who I am. You cannot redefine Me. But I hear you clearly, and I will withdraw. I will take away My hand of protection, and I will deliver you into the hands of your enemies."

God creates a crisis in order to bring His people back to Himself. He withdraws His protection and allows them to live with the consequences of their own choices. This is the way in which God most often deals with persistent sin.

THE SIN OF THE AMORITES

When God promised Abraham that His descendants would return to the land of Canaan, He indicated that it would not happen until the fourth generation because "the sin of *the Amorites* has not yet reached its full measure" (Genesis 15:16, italics added). This is a very important statement for our understanding of the conquest of Canaan. The Amorites was a general term used to describe the various tribal groups that inhabited the land of Canaan. Evidently these people were sinning,against God. But God is patient. He is slow to anger, and He often overlooks sin for a long time. But at a certain point, God will move to act in judgment. When the sin of the Amorites had reached its full measure, God would bring judgment on them.

At the same time, God was working with Israel. God had allowed them to go through the experience of suffering in Egypt. He brought them to the borders of Canaan, but they lacked the faith and the courage to go forward. So God led them in the desert for almost forty years, until a new generation was ready to trust Him. Then under the leadership of Joshua they were ready to invade the land and drive out the Amorites.

By that time, the sin of the Amorites had reached its full measure. God's time of judgment had come, and so He brought the two together and fulfilled His purposes of blessing for Israel and judgment for the Amorites at the same time.

Now, some years later, we find God's own people turning to the very idols that the Amorites had worshiped. They adopted the very evils for which God had judged the Amorites. So God gave His own people into the hands of the Amorites! "Whenever Israel went out to fight, the hand of the LORD was against them" (v. 15). But that was not the end of the story.

THE GOD WHO DELIVERS

> Then the LORD raised up judges, who saved them out of the hands of these raiders. (v. 16)

Throughout the book of Judges we read about these military leaders and their heroic achievements. There was Othniel, Ehud, Shamgar, Deborah, Barak, Gideon, and, of course, Samson. The Spirit of the Lord came on these judges and enabled them to achieve remarkable victories for God's people.

I was fascinated to read Ms. Miller's conclusion to her article in the *Wall Street Journal*. She wrote,

> These gentler, almost mystical forms of theology [that's a good euphemism for the idols!] have found a receptive audience in today's affluent society…These are relatively peaceful and prosperous times. So even as many Americans search for deeper connections with God, they aren't facing the kinds of crises that often prompt people to seek protection or salvation from above.…

> Tough times or sudden hardships could change all this in a hurry…no matter how broad or far flung people's conceptions of God, they revert to God the Father when the going gets tough.[3]

That is very perceptive. It's exactly what Judges tells us. When the going gets tough, the question becomes very simple: "Is there a God who is able to do something to help you?

When that is the question, the idols don't seem so attractive any more, for the simple reason that they cannot do anything! They may be very convenient in peaceful and prosperous times, because they do not make any moral demands upon us, but how in all the world when you face a crisis in your life can you call on the mist rising from the lake to help you? What can a force field of positive energy do for you when you are on your deathbed?

But there is a God in heaven, and you can call on Him to deliver you. This is what we are to teach the new generation that does not know God. We are to say to them, "There is one living and true God. He says, 'I am who I am.' He is not whoever we want Him to be. We cannot redefine Him; in fact, any attempt to do so is idolatry. God will judge idolatry, so we dare not go down that pathway.

"But remember, God is gracious to all who call upon Him. If you turn to Him in faith, He will deliver you."

SPOTLIGHT ON CHRIST

As you read through the book of Judges, it is clear that while these rather individualistic military leaders achieved remarkable things, they also had significant limitations.

Most of them were seriously lacking in character, and it is difficult to admire them. Ehud seems like a cowardly assassin (3:12–23). Gideon was so lacking in faith that he needed multiple confirmations of what God was telling him to do before he would do anything (6:36–40)! Jephthah made a disastrous choice that involved sacrificing his daughter (11:30–40). Samson's failures are legendary (14, 16) and qualify him as the weakest strong man who ever lived.

As you follow the story, it is difficult to escape the conclusion that after all the activity of the judges, nothing seemed to have really changed. The judges brought about a change in the people's circumstances, but they were never able to bring about a change in the people's hearts.

So the achievements of the judges were short lived. As soon as a judge died, the people returned to the idols, and the whole cycle started all over again. The book leaves you wondering how long this pattern could continue. You rightly conclude that God's people needed a better deliverer than any of these judges; someone who could bring a change of heart, not just a change of circumstances. They needed a savior who could bring change that would last.

Roll the Bible story on another 1,400 years, and you find the people of God under another oppressor. This time it is the Romans. They pay taxes to Caesar, and justice is in the hands of a foreign political pragmatist called Pontius Pilate.

During this time there were riots and attempts to overthrow the might of Rome, and people were hoping that God would raise up a deliverer. Some wanted God to raise up another Ehud or Samson, a strong, aggressive guy who could take out Pontius Pilate and a few others like him. Others, like Simeon and Anna, saw a deeper need. They were praying for a deliverer who could touch the issues of the heart. As they cried out, God did an new thing; He sent His Son into the world.

Jesus' ministry focused on the heart. The angel said to Joseph "You are to give Him the name Jesus, because he will save his people from their sins" (Matthew 1:21). When Judas Iscariot saw what Jesus could do, he knew He could be the deliverer from the power of Rome. But Christ refused to follow that agenda. God could change the external circumstances of your life a thousand times, but if He does not change your heart, your life will go round in circles just like the book of judges.

Then at the height of His ministry, Jesus was nailed to the cross. All hopes of deliverance seemed shattered. On the third day after His death, however, Jesus rose from the dead. Here, for the first time in human history, was a deliverer who would never die. Today He continues to deliver us from our greatest enemies—sin, death, and hell.

A god who only exists in your mind cannot deliver you. The living God invites you to turn from idols and call on Him, and He promises that "everyone who calls on the name of the Lord will be saved" (Romans 10:13).

UNLOCKED

Idolatry is redefining God, and across the centuries people have often chosen to invent their own gods rather than bow before the living God. The gods we create are attractive because we control them, but they are powerless to help us, and they are deeply offensive to God.

The living God is able to deliver us. He has sent His Son Jesus Christ into the world to save us from sin, death, and hell. People today still face a choice between the gods of their own imagination and the living God of the Bible. Only the living God can deliver.

PAUSE FOR PRAYER

Almighty God,

Thank You that You are the living God, and that You are able to save Your people. Forgive me for my reluctance to love and worship You as You are. Help me to trust what You say more than what I think. Let my faith life be built on Your truth rather than on my imagination.

May parents and pastors, with the help of Your Spirit, teach Your Word, so that a new generation may know who You are and what You have done. May Your name be known and honored in our nation. In the name of Jesus Christ our Lord I pray. Amen.

NOTES

1. Lisa Miller, "Redefining God," *The Wall Street Journal,* 21 April 2000, W4.

2. "When We Talk About God," *The Wall Street Journal,* 21 April 2000, W4.

3. Miller, "Redefining God," W4.

Redeemer

RUTH

Why do we need

a redeemer?

15 Redeemer

RUTH

DISCOVER

the most beautiful love story
in the Old Testament.

LEARN

how true love is always
ready to pay a price.

WORSHIP

as you see how Christ has
become our Redeemer.

Wᴴᴬᵀ do you do if you have a wife and two children to support and the amount you make won't buy the food you need? No doubt some husbands would talk about "trusting God," but that isn't easy when the kids are saying that they are hungry. Elimelech watched his family suffer through famine and finally felt that he had waited on God long enough. He and the family packed what they could from the farm in Bethlehem and headed to Moab.

Moab wasn't the kind of place any self-respecting Jew would want to live. There was a sense in which the Moabites were a nation who should never have existed. Their ancestry went back to a rather sordid story of incest with Lot and his eldest daughter (Genesis 19:36–37). They were known for worshiping idols, and the Moabites had been enemies of Israel for years.

Some years earlier, a Moabite king named Eglon had invaded Israel and oppressed the people for eighteen years. Then God raised up a judge by the name of Ehud, who delivered God's people when he assassinated Eglon with a left-handed thrust of his dagger. So Moab was hardly a first choice for Israelites planning a vacation. It was hostile territory. But desperate situations sometimes call for desperate measures, and Elimelech decided that Moab was his best option.

Besides, things were pretty grim in Israel as well. The book of Judges is so full of sordid stories of gang violence and especially violence towards women that you wonder whether some of this should really be in the Bible. But the Bible records what life was like in Israel in those days when there was no king. Everyone did what was right in his own eyes. The rule of law and order had often broken down, and Israel was not a safe place to bring up children. So Elimelech decided to go. He left the people of God and the land God had chosen to bless to make a new beginning.

The whole family moved to Moab, and soon after they arrived there, Elimelech died. So now we have a mother whose name is Naomi, with two sons, probably in their teenage years, trying to make a life in a foreign land.

ALONE AGAIN

In the course of time the two boys married local Moabite girls, named Orpah and Ruth. Naomi was left alone in her empty nest.

Another ten years passed, and then tragedy struck the family again. Naomi's two sons died as well. Naomi was now absolutely alone in a foreign land. She had come to Moab because of her husband, she had stayed in Moab because of her sons; and now she felt like a lost soul in an alien place.

Despite this tragic beginning, the story of Ruth is one of the most beautiful and moving stories in the entire Bible. In the end, both Naomi and her daughter-in-law Ruth would play a key role in God's plan of salvation. They lived during the distressing days of the judges and their story is like an oasis of joy in a rather bleak time for the people of God.

Soon Naomi heard news that the famine in Israel was over and there was food in Bethlehem. She knew that as an aging single woman without family members she could no longer run the farm. But the farm was still home, so she decided that it was time to return. At least she could generate some income by selling the land.

The old lady didn't want to be a burden to her two daughters-in-law, though they seemed willing to go with her. She knew that if they came with her to Israel, they would face the same problems she had endured in Moab; they would become lonely foreign women in an alien culture, with no means of support. Without a husband or a father, two foreign women in Israel would be vulnerable and defenseless. Better that they stay in Moab, where there was hope that they would marry again. So Naomi gave her daughters-in-law sound advice when she urged them to remain in Moab (Ruth 1:11).

CALL ME "MISS BITTER"

But Naomi was struggling with a deeper problem. She had become convinced that

God was against her (1:13). She believed in God, like a good Jewish woman should, but as she grew older, the experiences of life had led her to the conclusion that God must be against her.

When Naomi arrived back in Bethlehem, we're told that "the whole town was stirred." Women asked, "Can this be Naomi?" (1:19). That somewhat insensitive remark can only be an indication of how bad she looked. She had left Bethlehem as a bright-faced mother with two healthy sons; she returned as a rather sad and haggard-looking woman. Suffering had taken its toll.

When Naomi returned to Bethlehem, she asked her friends to call her Mara, which means *bitter* (1:20). That tells us a lot about what was going on inside her. How would you like to live with an aging lady who says, "I want to be known as 'Miss Bitter'"?

Clearly, Naomi had sunk into a deep depression. "The Almighty has made my life very bitter," she told the townspeople (1:20). If God was against her, then it would do her daughters-in-law no good to stay with her. "You don't want to hang around with me. Leave me with my grief. Go and see what you can make of life for yourselves." When Naomi told the two women, "Return home, my daughters," all three cried together. Then Naomi's daughter-in-law Orpah went back to Moab (1:12–14).

But Ruth wouldn't go, and that was when she said some of the most beautiful words of commitment that have ever been spoken:

> *"Where you go I will go, and where you stay I will stay. Your people will be my people and your God my God. Where you die I will die, and there I will be buried. May the LORD deal with me, be it ever so severely, if anything but death separates you and me." (1:16–17)*

LOVE THAT CHOOSES TO PAY A PRICE

Here was a young lady making a costly commitment of love and loyalty to a rather difficult, bitter older woman. At the same time she was making a costly commitment to the God of Israel, who had allowed great pain and disappointment in her own life. Love proves itself when it chooses to pay a price.

I sometimes reflect on this when a young couple tells me how much they are in love. I remember one couple who wanted me to do their wedding. Perhaps they were anxious to let me know that they really were a perfect match, as they each said, "We really love each other, and we have an amazing relationship." After listening to their praise for each other, I decided to ask a few questions.

"Have you ever had an argument or disagreement?" I asked with a smile. They looked shocked at the impertinence of the question!

"No, never," they said.

"Have either of you ever been disappointed in each other?" Their faces were a register of astonished surprise.

"Tell me about some problems you have faced together." By now they were seriously wondering if they were talking to the right pastor.

"We told you that we love each other," the woman said.

Real love proves itself in the face of overwhelming obstacles.

"But how do you know that you love each other if that love has never been tested, never been disappointed, and you have never had anything to forgive?"

Real love proves itself in the face of overwhelming obstacles, and Ruth gives us a marvelous model of what true love is all about. She looked Naomi in the eye, knowing her mother-in-law was rather bitter and that life with her would not be easy, yet she made a commitment to care for her anyway. "Where you go I will go, and where you stay I will stay."

LOVE DESPITE DISAPPOINTMENT AND PAIN

Then she made the same commitment to Naomi's God. "Your God will be my God." Think of it! Ruth was saying, "I do not know why my husband died or why I never had children. But You will be my God. My love for You will not depend on You answering every question, or on You meeting all of my hopes and dreams. I will not be a fair-weather disciple. I am committed to You. I love You." That is just about the highest worship that anyone could offer.

You don't know what it means to love another person until you have been disappointed or it begins to cost. You don't know what it means to love God until you have experienced pain and you love Him still. That is exactly how God loves us. "God demonstrates his own love us in this: While we were still sinners, Christ died for us" (Romans 5:8). That is the love that God pours into our hearts by the Holy Spirit so that we may be able to love in an unlovely world.

LIFE ON THE BREADLINE

It could not have been easy for the two women when they arrived back at Naomi's farm. The fields had not been cultivated for at least ten years, and the whole area would have been overgrown. Even if they had a workforce, it would be weeks before they cleared the fields for planting and months before they could raise a harvest. So the women had no source of income. They were poor.

One way in which the poor could get food was through *gleaning*. The poor were permitted to pick the corn from the edge of any field; they would follow the harvesters to pick up any grain left on the ground. It was like sorting through the trash, and it was not the kind of thing that most people would have wanted to do. Sometimes the gleaners were viewed as pests, and landowners could be abusive or threatening.

Boaz felt that it was the least he could do for a woman who… loved his God.

Yet Ruth went out, willing to glean in the fields, behind anyone "in whose eyes I find favor" (2:2). What she meant was that if anyone would allow her to gather the leftover grain, that was what she would do.

The field she chose belonged to a man named Boaz, amazingly (or to be more accurate, providentially) a distant relative of Elimelech. Boaz had a considerable estate and ran a large farming operation. He was supervising the harvest when he noticed a foreign woman picking up the grain behind the harvesters.

"Who is she?" he asked.

"She is the Moabitess, a foreigner. She came back with Naomi."

Boaz had heard about Ruth's kindness to Naomi, and he told her to stay in his fields. He also made sure that the harvesters showed kindness to her. Ruth was surprised that a complete stranger should treat her with such kindness, but Boaz felt that it was the least he could do for a woman who would support a grieving relative and loved his God. "May the LORD repay you for what you have done. May you be richly rewarded by the LORD, the God of Israel, under whose wings you have come to take refuge" (2:12).

THE INFECTIOUS POWER OF KINDNESS

Ruth had shown great kindness to Naomi. Now Boaz was showing great kindness to Ruth. Kindness is the fruit of the Spirit (Galatians 5:22). It is an evidence of the grace of God in our lives. God has a wonderful way of making sure that kindness given leads to kindness received. The woman, who showed such great kindness, now received kindness that she did not expect.

Notice that Boaz offered protection to someone of another race, who had put her trust in God. I have no doubt that there would be others who thought that God's covenant meant His love was limited to Israel, and that God cared nothing for the rest. But that has never been the case. God's promise was that He would bless Abraham, and that through Abraham all the nations of the earth would be blessed. Even in the Old Testament, God was ready to receive all who would take refuge under His wings.

Boaz recognized that this penniless foreigner was every bit as important to God as a wealthy landlord like himself. He treated Ruth with all the dignity and respect that he would have given to her if she had been born among the people of Israel.

The kindness of Boaz is a powerful challenge for the church today. Christ has broken down the dividing walls of society so that people from every background can find a place in the family of God. Whoever wants to come and take refuge under the wings of the Almighty may do so, and all who take refuge in God are to be received by the people of God with kindness.

TAKING AN INITIATIVE OF FAITH

Now we come to the best part of the story. First, though, a short legal briefing so you can understand what's about to happen. Two laws in ancient Israel apply here. The first is the *law of redemption* (Leviticus 25:25). This law said that if a person became poor and had to sell land, the first right of purchase was given to the nearest relative in their family. If the relative purchased the land, then it would remain within the family, and when the Year of Jubilee came, the land would be returned to its original owner.

The second law is the *law of levirate marriage* (Deuteronomy 25:5–10). This law said that if a man died without children, his brother should take responsibility for the support of the dead man's widow, including marrying her and raising children together. The law especially applied to a situation where an extended family was living together. It seems that the closer the relationship, the greater the obligation.

In this story, Boaz was not even the nearest relative, and it had not occurred to him that he would have any greater role in the lives of these women than the kindness he had already shown. He was rather slow, as men sometimes are, and so it fell to Ruth to take an initiative of faith.

Naomi came up with the plan, but it was Ruth who took the risky initiative of faith. Boaz was working around the clock on the harvest. During the day he would be harvesting, and in the evening he went to the threshing floor, and when he was through, he would lie down and sleep by the corn.

One night Ruth went over to the threshing floor and lay down by his feet. During the night, Boaz stirred, and as he wakened, he realized that somebody else was there.

"Who are you?" he asked.

"I am your servant Ruth," she said. "Spread the corner of your garment over me, since you are a kinsman-redeemer" (3:9).

If you want that in plain English, she said, "Marry me." That's what the phrase "Spread the corner of your garment over me" means.

Remember, Boaz had prayed that God would bless Ruth as she had taken refuge under His wings (2:12). The word Boaz used for *wings* and the word Ruth used for *garment* are the same in Hebrew. So there is a beau-

[Ruth] was not afraid to take an initiative of faith.

tiful double meaning in the words. Ruth was saying, "Boaz, you prayed that God's wings would be spread over me. But I think that the way this should happen is for you to spread your wings over me too! Marry me."

This was one sharp lady! She placed her trust in God, but she was not afraid to take an initiative of faith. She was willing to take a risk in order to see the fulfillment of God's purpose for her life. Faith trusts, but it also acts.

Boaz did not think twice. Of course he would marry her, but there was one problem. There was another relative who was closer to the family than he. We may wonder why this closer relative had not done anything to help Naomi and Ruth before, but now he appears in the story, and it seems that he might spoil the party.

AT THE CITY GATE

Boaz went to the city gate where legal contracts were struck and where the elders of the town hung out. He sat there until this unnamed relative came by. Boaz persuaded him to sit down, and then he gathered ten elders of the town as legal witnesses of the conversation (4:2). To paraphrase Ruth 4:3–5, the dialogue went like this:

"Naomi is selling the Elimelech farm," Boaz said, "and you have the first right to buy it."

"Oh yes," he said, "I'll buy. It's a good farm at a nice price. I'll cover my costs in a few years, and it will be a nice little earner!"

"Of course, you realize that when you acquire the property, you will also assume responsibility for the support of two women," said Boaz. "There are two laws to consider here. One gives you the right to buy the land; the other gives you the responsibility of supporting the widows. You can't claim the privileges of the one and deny the responsibilities of the other!"

This was a masterpiece of negotiation! The price of redeeming was going to be higher than the unnamed relative thought. It would not be a one-time payment; it would be a lifelong commitment!

The close relative didn't like that idea. "Then I cannot redeem it because I might endanger my own estate. You redeem it yourself. I cannot do it" (4:6).

"If you don't want to redeem," Boaz answered, as the witness listened to the transaction, "I will. I am ready to pay the price for the farm and assume the support of the women. I will take Ruth the Moabitess as my wife" (paraphrase of 4:9–10).

The nearer relative, who had forgone his right to act as the kinsman-redeemer, breathed a sigh of relief and handed Boaz his sandal. That was the sign of consenting to a legal deal. Then he disappeared off the scene, never to be heard of again.

SPOTLIGHT ON CHRIST

One of the greatest titles given to our LORD Jesus Christ is the name *Redeemer*, and the story of Ruth gives us a wonderful insight into its meaning.

To deliver Ruth from pain and poverty, Boaz acted as a kinsman-redeemer, a blood relative of a person in need, able and willing to pay a price. Likewise, to become our Redeemer, Christ had to take upon Himself our flesh and blood. That is what the Christmas story is all about. When Christ was born at Bethlehem, He entered the human family and became our close relative.

A WILLING REDEEMER

Christ was able and willing to pay the price of buying us out of our spiritual poverty and our alienation from God. That price was the shedding of His own blood. "It was not with perishable things such as silver or gold that you were redeemed from the empty way of life…but with the precious blood of Christ" (1 Peter 1:18–19). When He paid that price, Christ won the right to take redeemed sinners as His bride. That is why the New Testament pictures the church as "the bride of Christ" (see Ephesians 5:22–33).

At the end of the story, the women of Bethlehem said to Naomi, "Praise be to the LORD, who this day has not left you without a kinsman-redeemer" (4:14). Since Christ has come, God has not left us without a Redeemer, either!

Once again, if you have never done so, I invite you to follow the example of Ruth and take a risky initiative of faith. You can come to Christ in faith and say, "Under Your wings I take refuge. Spread Your garment over me for protection. I ask You to be my Redeemer." Christ has the right, the ability, and the will to redeem you. If you come to Him, He will not turn you away.

A TWIST IN THE TALE

Like all the best stories, this one has a fascinating twist at the end. Indeed, that twist is probably the reason God has preserved Ruth's story for us in the Bible.

Following her marriage, Ruth conceived and gave birth to a son, whom she and Boaz named Obed (4:17). The story concludes by saying, "Obed [was] the father of Jesse, and Jesse [was] the father of David" (4:22).

That same David was the second king of Israel, and if you follow the line of David for another thousand years, you will find that it was into this line that Jesus Christ was born. Matthew gives a special mention to Ruth the Moabitess in the human ancestry of Christ (Matthew 1:5).

God was at work through all of this family's tears of disappointment. Through this foreign widow who trusted in God and her mother-in-law who almost gave up hope, King David was eventually born—and the Messiah would appear.

You may sometimes feel that God's plans for the world turn on governments, businesses, kings, and armies. But the book of Ruth reminds us that at one point God's plan of salvation flowed through one woman who decided to trust God and love a rather bitter old lady.

The extraordinary thing is that Naomi, Ruth, and Boaz all died without having any idea of what God would do as a result of their faithfulness. An older lady whose family nest was empty and a younger woman who no doubt thought she would never have children found their lives caught up in God's redeeming plan for the world.

Never underestimate the significance of what God has given you to do. It may be a hidden, costly commitment to a rather difficult person or a simple act of kindness to a foreigner you have never seen before. It may be an initiative of faith to get the will of God done. The most ordinary acts of faith and obedience can lead to most extraordinary results.

UNLOCKED

A redeemer is only needed when an individual finds himself or herself in difficulties beyond their own control. Naomi's poverty illustrates this point. The Bible makes it clear that we need a spiritual redeemer because sin leaves us bankrupt before God with no means of generating the ability to pay.

Christ is willing to redeem you. He is ready to make a lifelong commitment to you and invites you to embrace Him as your Redeemer.

PAUSE FOR PRAYER

Gracious LORD,

Thank You that You are the Redeemer I need. Thank You that You paid the price on the cross and that You never turn back on Your commitments to Your people.

I praise You for Your Son's love that reached out to redeem me from the curse and pain of my sins. Continue to cover me with Your garment, protecting me from harm and keeping me safe in Your great family.

Help me to love You even when that love is costly. Help me to show kindness to those who are in need and especially to those who may be lonely or even bitter.

Help me to reflect Your love in this broken world, through Jesus Christ our Lord. Amen.

King

1 SAMUEL 8

Why did God

not want

His people to

have a king?

*16*King

1 SAMUEL 8

DISCOVER
the qualifications for leadership among God's people.

LEARN
how God is at work even when His people make bad choices.

WORSHIP
Christ, the King of Kings.

1500 B.C.

CA. 1447 THE EXODUS

1400 CA. 1407 CONQUEST OF
      −1400 CANAAN

CA. 1360 THE JUDGES
−1084

1300

1200

1100

CA. 1051 KING SAUL
−1011

CA. 1011 KING DAVID
−971

1000

CA. 971 KING SOLOMON
−931

CA. 931 DIVIDED KINGDOM
UNDER JEROBOAM
AND REHOBOAM

900

800

RETIRED General Norman Schwartzkopf, one of the architects of American victory in the 1991 Persian Gulf War, often is asked about war strategy and his opinion of the U.S. military. Imagine the four-star general being asked to give a military analysis of the battles fought by the Israelite army. I have no doubt he would say, "Well, none of those battles makes any military sense at all."

It was God who gave His people victory in all their battles. God gave the troops courage and specific plans, and at times He even caused confusion among their enemies, so that the people of God prevailed, even when they were hopelessly ill-equipped and outnumbered by their enemies.

The exodus from Egypt was a marvelous example of overcoming a stronger enemy. God's people had no weapons, and the Hebrew men, women, and children were being pursued by a vast, well-ordered army with horses and chariots. They did not have a chance as they stood in front of the Red Sea, except for one thing: God was with them. God opened the sea, and then He closed it over the chariots!

Then they faced a military campaign against the Amalekites (Exodus 17:8–13). As the battle progressed, the initiative seemed to swing one way, then the other, and the people must have wondered what made the difference. The Bible tells us that when Moses held up his hands in prayer, Israel prevailed, and when his hands became tired and dropped, the Amalekites prevailed. So this battle turned on the intervention of God, in response to prayer.

TRUSTING GOD FOR GREAT VICTORIES

You find the same pattern when God's people came to invade the land of Canaan. The town of Jericho was well fortified, and there was no obvious means of taking it. God told Joshua and the Hebrew army to march around the city seven times blowing trumpets, and when they did, the walls of the city fell down. That was one of the most unusual victories in the annals of military history!

The book of Judges tells us about Gideon, who raised an army of 32,000 people to fight the Midianites. God said that was far too many, and so Gideon went through a de-selection process; in the end he had reduced the number to three hundred, who went at night to lay an ambush. They entered the camp of the Midianites with torches, pitchers, and trumpets, making an extraordinary noise as they sounded the trumpets and broke the pitchers. God caused confusion among the Midianites, so that they ran off in panic.

Israel's victories were not by might or by power, but by the intervention of the Spirit of God. At times when they were likely to win because of their overwhelming numbers, God cut their numbers back so that it would be absolutely clear that God had given them the victory.

THE FRUSTRATIONS OF LIVING BY FAITH

The whole story was a pattern of miraculous deliverance by God. For almost four hundred years, from the time of the Exodus to the end of the judges, God led His people Israel. But the people of God were becoming dissatisfied with this.

The obvious weakness was that the judges lacked continuity. God raised up a judge when there was a crisis, but this meant that the people were dependent on God all the time. Other nations did not operate like that. They had kings, standing armies and national defense strategies. When a king died, his successor was crowned immediately, amid chants of "The king is dead; long live the king!"

The people wondered why Israel could not have this kind of stability and continuity. Eventually the elders of the community came to Samuel, who was a judge and a prophet, and asked him to appoint a king (1 Samuel 8:5).

The answer to their question, "Why do we not have a king?" was that God was their king. God led them into battle and into blessing. God did everything that a king would do for his people, and much more. But the people were not satisfied. They did not want to go into battle depending on God alone, and they did not want to wait on God to raise up their leaders. They wanted a system of succession, a "flesh and blood person" to lead them into battle and into blessing.

> *"It is not you they have rejected, but they have rejected me as their king." (v. 7)*

It is quite clear from the LORD's words to Samuel that this was not pleasing to God. When the people asked for a king, they were turning away from a life of faith in which they were directly dependent on the LORD.

But God let them have their way. The LORD said to Samuel, "Listen to them and give them a king" (v. 22). God's people made a decision that was displeasing to Him, but He allowed their decision to stand. God gives us the incredible privilege of making real choices.

THE SIGNIFICANCE OF CHOICES

You have choices of friends, careers, and relationships; choices to spend, borrow, or pay, choices to marry or stay single; and choices to fight, part, or reconcile. These choices matter; they have long-term consequences.

The first book of Samuel tells the story of how God's people made a poor choice. They knew that their desire for a king was displeasing to God, and Samuel had warned them of the consequences of their choice. "If you have a king, you had better know what is going to happen. There will be taxes and conscription, and your sons and daughters will wish that you had never made this choice." In 1 Samuel 8:18 he declared, "You will cry out for relief from the king you have chosen, and the LORD will not answer you in that day." But they were not listening. Their minds were made up, and so God gave them what they asked for. The rest, as they say, is history.

> No choice, however poor, can put us beyond the grace of God.

In the well-known parable of the prodigal son (Luke 15:11–32), a son asked his father for his inheritance. The father granted his son's request to receive his inheritance early. The father loved the son, but the son was free, and the father would not keep him against his will. The father saw the determination in the lad's eyes and knew that the only way to change the boy's will was to let him go. So the son went to pursue his dream, and as a result of his choice, he became absolutely miserable.

Never underestimate the importance of your choices. Poor choices always lead to painful consequences. Experience is a great teacher, but her school fees are very high. God is sovereign, and that means that no choice, however poor, can put us beyond the grace of God. But the Bible also teaches us personal responsibility. That means that each of our life choices has significance. Each choice has consequences.

An earlier generation in Israel had already learned this when the people made the choice of unbelief and refused to go up and take the land of Canaan. Their choice led directly to almost forty years in the wilderness. Where you are today is the result of the grace of God, but it is also related to a series of choices. Where you are tomorrow will be by the grace of God, but it will also be affected by your choices today.

IRREVERSIBLE DECISIONS

The decision to anoint a king was irreversible. Once made, it led to all kinds of trouble. While some kings ruled well, most of them were a great burden to the people. Israel lived with the painful consequences of a poor choice.

We all make poor decisions at some points in our lives, but some people live with the pain of daily regret over a major choice. For some it is a career or marriage choice. Others make a decision that leads to a permanent injury or poor health. Such choices have irreversible consequences, and can leave you looking back in regret and saying, "If only…"

The good news is that God works in hard situations that are brought about by irreversible bad decisions. It may be that if you had not made a poor decision years ago, you would not be dealing with what you are facing now, but it is also true that God will work in the present situation. Just as there is no sin that puts us beyond the grace of God, there is no decision that puts us beyond the help of God.

God does not abandon us when we make faithless choices. God redeems bad decisions. He advances His great purpose for our lives even through circumstances that might never have been. Indeed, the main story of the Bible is about how God has blessed people who are living with the irreversible consequences of a poor decision made by Adam in the Garden of Eden. The story of the kings reminds us that a bad choice cannot put an end either to God's grace or His purpose for our lives.

LEADERSHIP QUALIFICATIONS

Once the decision to appoint a king had been made, the people had to determine the qualifications. God did not ignore His people; He gave guidelines for the leaders they would elect.

The king would have the responsibility of making sure that God's will was done among the people. He was to deliver the people from their enemies and to lead them in right paths. This is a high calling, and God's people needed to be very careful about selecting a person who could be trusted with this kind of authority.

Saul was anointed as the first king of Israel, and when he was crowned, "Samuel explained to the people the regulations of the kingship" (10:25). God had anticipated the time when His people would ask for a king. So back in the book of Deuteronomy, God had already given a profile of the person who should be king among His people. There are seven distinct qualifications, and each one is reflected in the New Testament teaching about qualifications for leadership in the church.

First, the king must be anointed by God. "When you enter the land the LORD your God is giving you and have taken possession of it and settled in it, and you say, 'Let us set a king over us like all the nations around us,' be sure to appoint over you the king the LORD your God chooses" (Deuteronomy 17:14–15). If God did not approve the king, there was no hope whatever of him advancing God's purpose. The New Testament parallel to this is in Acts 6, where the first deacons are appointed, and the church is told to "choose men who are filled with the Holy Spirit" (v.3). There must be the mark of God's presence in their lives. That is the primary qualification.

Second, the king must belong to God's people. "He must be from among your own brothers. Do not place a foreigner over you, one who is not a brother Israelite" (Deuteronomy 17:15). Again in Acts 6, church members are told that they are to choose leadership from among the number of believers (6:3). The church is not to depend on the sponsorship of famous names; it is to find its resources from within the body of believers. God's people should look for leaders who have proved themselves in the local church.

Third, the king must exercise faith. "The king, moreover, must not acquire great numbers of horses for himself or make the people return to Egypt to get more of them" (Deuteronomy 17:16). Chariots and horses were the key to Egypt's military power. Israel had never enjoyed these resources. All of their fighting had been done on foot, and their victories had been given by God. Now God was telling the people, "If you have a king, then I do not want him building personal security by making alliances with My enemies."

The king is to model faith. He is to put his trust in the living God. When the church appointed the first deacons, they chose Stephen because he was "a man full of faith" (Acts 6:5). Leadership among God's people must always be in the hands of people who know how to trust in the living God.

Fourth, the king must be loyal. "He must not take many wives, or his heart will be led astray" (Deuteronomy 17:17). The same principle is reflected in the New Testament: The elder must be "the husband of but one wife" (1 Timothy 3:2). In Old Testament times it was common for kings to seal alliances with marriages. God said, "Don't do that." Today, a Christian leader's loyalty to God will be expressed in his loyalty to his wife.

Fifth, the king must be ready for sacrifice. "He must not accumulate large amounts of silver and gold" (Deuteronomy 17:17). Kings in the ancient world had the opportunity to make a pile of money. But God said that the one who is given leadership responsibility over His people must not use his privileged position to feather his own nest. He must not be greedy, but must use his power for the benefit of the people. In the New Testament, Peter wrote to pastors and elders, instructing them not to be "greedy for money, but eager to serve; not lording it over" the flock (1 Peter 5:2–3).

> The king was to make a hand-written copy of the law for himself.

Sixth, the king must know the Scriptures. "When he takes the throne of his kingdom, he is to write for himself on a scroll a copy of this law, taken from that of the priests, who are Levites. It is to be with him, and he is to read it all the days of his life so that he may learn to revere the LORD his God and follow carefully all the words of this law and these decrees" (Deuteronomy 17:18–19). This is marvelous! The king was to make a handwritten copy of the Law for himself.

Imagine if, when an American president was inaugurated, his first job was to go into the Oval Office and copy out the Law of God by hand, and then keep it beside him so that he would be careful to lead the people into following all these decrees! Again the New Testament reflects this priority for leaders in the church. Deacons must "keep hold of the deep truths of the faith with a clear conscience" (1 Timothy 3:9). Leadership is to be given into the hands of people who know the Word of God and will lead the people in it.

Seventh, the king must be an example of obedience. The king must "not consider himself better than his brothers and turn from the law to the right or to the left" (Deuteronomy 17:20). The king could not say to the people, "Do as I say, not as I do." The most powerful man in the land must be the first to model commitment to the Law of God. Others were looking to him, and they would follow his example. For the Christian church, Peter wrote that pastors and elders are to be "examples to the flock" of God (1 Peter 5:3).

A PROFILE FOR CHRISTIAN LEADERS

This profile for leaders of God's people is of great importance for pastors, elders, lay leaders, and all who participate in appointing them to positions of leadership. It is a profile for students preparing for ministry and for everybody else who wants to see that God's will gets done.

If you want to be used by God, seek the anointing of His Spirit. Be committed to God's people, and learn to trust God for great things. Cultivate loyalty to all your commitments and especially within your marriage; place the pursuit of money on the altar and determine to receive whatever God gives you gladly. Be crystal clear in your convictions regarding the central truths of the gospel, and feed on the Word of God every day. Ask for the grace and help of God to live a life that is worthy of the calling that God has given you in Christ Jesus.

That's the profile of the man or woman God will use to get His will done, and these are the first things that we should be looking for in the process of trying to identify leaders for the church.

WHO FITS THE PROFILE?

As we follow the rest of the Old Testament story, it is interesting to see how the kings who ruled Israel over the next six hundred years measured up against the profile. Which of them fulfilled what God required of a king?

It certainly wasn't Saul, the first king. His self-willed disobedience to God soon became very evident. And it certainly wasn't Solomon, the third king. He did some marvelous things, including writing some Scripture and building the temple. He made some wise choices, but he also made some very foolish ones. He had seven hundred wives, which must have made Valentine's Day a nightmare, and the Bible says when he became old, his wives turned his heart toward other gods (1 Kings 11:4). He failed God's fourth qualification for leadership big time.

The most likely candidate might have been David. However, King David was not the husband of one wife. Still, he came the nearest to God's profile because he had a genuine desire in his heart to follow the Lord.

After Solomon, the story of the kings of Israel was very disappointing. Some were better, some worse, but none were able to fulfill God's mandate for the king of Israel.

Let's roll the Bible story forward another thousand years. Another king is in power in Jerusalem. King Herod has very little interest in obeying the Word of God, however, and he doesn't have much real power, because that lies with a foreigner, whose name is Caesar. The people of God are still waiting for the king who will get God's will done.

God answered their pleas for a flesh-and-blood leader who would deliver them from their enemies. A star shone in the east and an angel announced to shepherds the birth of one who would be "the King of the Jews."

FULFILLING THE ROYAL PROFILE

Christ fulfilled all the qualifications of the king of the Jews. Jesus was born into the line of David, so this king belonged to God's people. At the age of twelve He was in the temple talking about the Scriptures. The Word of God filled His mind, and people who heard Him were amazed at His understanding. This king knew the Scriptures.

At His baptism, the heavens were opened, a dove descended, and God announced, "This is my Son, whom I love; with him I am well pleased" (Matthew 3:17). This King was anointed by God. After that, Jesus went into the wilderness to confront the great enemy of the people of God, who immediately suggested an alliance. "All these kingdoms I will give You if You will only bow down and worship me." But Christ refused any alliance with the enemy. This king was absolutely loyal.

Throughout His life, Jesus modeled absolute faithfulness to the Law of God. He did all the work that the Father had given Him to do. This King was an example of obedience. Christ told His disciples that He had "not come to be served, but to serve, and to give his life as a ransom for many." (Mark 10:45). As the apostle Paul wrote, He did not consider His own interests "but made himself nothing, taking the [form] of a servant" (Philippians 2:7). This king was ready for sacrifice.

Then His enemies came to arrest Him. Peter thought that the King needed some weapons to defend Him, so he reached for his sword. But Christ told him to put the sword away, telling the disciple, "Do you think I cannot call on my Father, and he will at once put at my disposal more than twelve legions of angels?" (Matthew 26:53). This King was ready to live by faith.

When Christ was brought to Pontius Pilate, the procurator had one question. "Are you the king of the Jews?" Jesus replied simply, "Yes, it is as you say" (Matthew 27:11).

THE MOCKED AND HUMBLE KING

As Pilate handed Christ over to be crucified, he said to the people, "Here is your king" (John 19:14). For many in the crowd, that was the ultimate insult. After all, what use is a king who is bound? What help is a disfigured leader whose face is bruised and whose brow is scarred? If He was the one who had been sent to get the will of God done, then what hope was there for God's people now?

Then Christ was given to the Roman soldiers who "stripped him and put a scarlet robe on him, and then twisted together a crown of thorns and set it on his head. They put a staff in his right hand and knelt in front of him and mocked him. 'Hail, king of the Jews!' they said" (Matthew 27:28–29).

The mocking of Christ continued when He was on the cross. A notice above His head proclaimed, "Jesus of Nazareth, the king of the Jews" (John 19:19). The crowd that had gathered to watch saw the sign and shouted, "If you are the king of the Jews, save yourself" (Luke 23:37). The teachers of the Law and the elders shouted, "He saved others...but he can't save himself! He's the King of Israel! Let him come down now from the cross, and we will believe in him" (Matthew 27:42).

Yet it was through this bruised, disfigured, and crucified King that the will of God was done. Through Christ crucified your enemies of sin and death and hell are defeated, and the way is opened for you to enter everlasting life.

God raised Jesus to life and "exalted him...and gave him the name that is above every name" (Philippians 2:9). Indeed, the story of the Bible ends with the announcement of His name: "King of Kings and Lord of Lords" (Revelation 19:16).

UNLOCKED

God did not want His people to have a king because He was already leading them into victory and into blessing Himself. The people of God made a big mistake when they chose to rely on human leadership rather than to exercise faith in the LORD. But God allowed their choice and continued to bless His people.

None of the kings was able to fulfill God's profile, and so God Himself took human flesh in Jesus Christ and became the flesh and blood king that His people had asked for. Christ is the King who leads God's people into victory and into blessing.

PAUSE FOR PRAYER

A prayer for Christian leaders:

Gracious Lord,

Thank You for the leaders You have given to Your church. May Your anointing be upon them, so that they will be able to lead Your people with wisdom and strength. Keep them from temptation, and nourish them with Your truth. May Christ truly be Lord over His church so that Your will may be done and Your people may be blessed.

In Jesus' name I pray. Amen.

Throne

2 SAMUEL 7

Where should we

look for stability

and security?

17 Throne

2 SAMUEL 7

DISCOVER

the challenge of humility in God's service.

LEARN

how disappointment is God's door to promise.

WORSHIP

as you see how Christ will reign forever.

A S David looked back, he could hardly believe what God had done for him. It wasn't so long since he was a shepherd and nobody had heard of him. Then he defeated Goliath, and from that day on, everybody knew who David was. God's people had a hero.

Of course that wasn't the way that King Saul saw it! When the ancient equivalent of cheerleaders started singing, "Saul has slain his thousands, and David his tens of thousands" (1 Samuel 18:7), it just about drove Saul crazy. David had to flee for his life.

Saul spent the last years of his life trying to destroy the future. But God's hand was on David, and eventually King Saul died, a bitter, disillusioned man. The way was opened to crown the king who had a heart to serve the living God.

Of course, resistance emerged to the new leadership. Some of Saul's loyalists fought to defend their turf; they resisted the new thing that God was so obviously doing. During the next two years "the house of David…grew stronger and stronger, while the house of Saul grew weaker and weaker" (2 Samuel 3:1). Eventually everyone accepted David's position as leader of the people of God (see 2 Samuel 5:1–5).

GOD WITH KING DAVID

Then David marched to Jerusalem (5:6). Although God's people had been in the land for around three hundred years, they had still not occupied the great city. But under David's leadership they captured Jerusalem, and when the city was taken, David established his palace and his center of government there.

David wanted the presence of God at the center of national life.

Then, he had to deal with the nearby Philistines. When they heard that David was king over Israel, they sent a special expeditionary force to take him out. They already had good reason to fear him since his extraordinary victory over Goliath, and the news that David was now king provoked them to take desperate action against him, so "they went up in full force to search for him" (2 Samuel 5:17). But God gave David a great victory, and it was a long time before the Philistines attacked Israel again.

Then David brought the ark of the covenant to Jerusalem. Remember that when the people were in the desert, God's presence actually came down to the ark. God met with the high priest at the mercy seat.

We can gauge what had happened to the spiritual life of the nation from the fact that during the reign of Saul the ark had been placed in storage and then forgotten (1 Samuel 7:1–2). Now King David wanted the presence of God at the center of national life; so he brought the ark to Jerusalem. When the ark that symbolized God's presence was brought to the capital city, there was great joy and celebration (2 Samuel 6).

So the new king was settled in his palace and had peace from all his enemies. It had been a long time since God's blessing on His people had been so obvious. The nation was united, prospering, and at peace. David had been more successful than he had ever dreamed. The blessing of God had exceeded all his expectations, and he felt that this was a moment of opportunity to give something back. David was a godly man with a good heart and a great idea.

A KING'S PLAN TO HONOR GOD

So he called his friend Nathan. You can read about their conversation in 2 Samuel 7:1–3. To paraphrase their words, David said: "You know, Nate [that's *my* version!], I have been thinking. It doesn't seem right to me that I get to live in this lavish palace and the ark of God is housed in a tent. The palace is a statement of the greatness of the king. I want to put up a building that will be a statement of the greatness of God."

Nathan liked the idea. "You know, David, everything you touch right now turns to gold. So whatever you have in mind, just go ahead and do it."

But that night, when Nathan went home, he had an uncomfortable time alone with God. Nathan was a prophet, and that meant that God revealed things directly to his mind. In effect, God said, "Nathan, you told your friend David that he should do whatever he has in mind, but that was bad advice. I will honor David my servant and establish a home for him. But tell him that he will not be the one to put up this building. I am going to give that privilege to his son" (7:9, 11–12). Then God added that David's son "will build a house for my Name, and I will establish the throne of his kingdom forever" (v. 13).

Have you ever been in a situation when you wanted to do something good and God closed the door on you? Or maybe a friend encouraged you to pursue some initiative that you thought would be for the glory of God, but it didn't work out. Or perhaps you had a great idea, and the next thing you knew, God gave somebody else the opportunity to develop it! This is the ultimate test of humility. David was humbled, but in accepting this position, he would be honored.

In effect, God was telling the king, "David, you say this building would be for Me. If the temple is really for Me and for My glory alone, then it should make no difference to you who builds it! Your dream will come true, David. There will be a temple, but your son will build it."

David recognized that God's plans, even when not fully understood, are best. And he recognized the final result would honor God. (Just read his prayer of praise after being denied; it's in verses 18–19.)

THE TEST OF HUMILITY
David accepted God's plan with humility. True humility is not a false attempt to deflect praise when you have done something well. If you have played a marvelous game or made a great speech or landed a new position, and somebody praises you for your effort, it is not humility to hang your head and say, "Oh, it was nothing." That's false humility that pretends something God enabled you to do was of no importance or value. Such feigned humility does not glorify God.

What is real humility? C. S. Lewis described humility as "a state of mind in which (a man) could design the best cathedral in the world, and know it to be the best and rejoice in the fact, without being any more glad at having done it than he would have been if it had been done by another."[1]

Such humility doesn't come naturally. For instance, on a soccer team true humility means that you would have great joy if you scored three goals, but that you would feel the same joy if someone else scored the goals! In music ministry true humility means that you would have great joy in singing a solo to the glory of God, but you would have the same joy if someone else was chosen and sang it equally well. For a pastor genuine humility means that you can have joy in God's blessing on your ministry, but you would experience the same joy in hearing that God had poured out even greater blessing on one of your brothers.

True humility means that you are more concerned that God is glorified, and less concerned about whose name gets on it.

DAVID'S HUMILITY

Thus, while David would have felt great joy in building a temple for God, his joy was no less when that honor was given to his son. That's true humility. David knew history would describe the building as "Solomon's temple," yet he was not jealous—he was joyful.

To David's great credit, he learned humility and counted the glory of God more important than his own name. It would not have been surprising if David had lost all interest in the temple project after God told him that he would not be able to complete it. But David's humility is shown by the fact that he gathered the wood and the stones. He prepared all the materials and then handed the great privilege of building the temple over to his son.

True humility is never easy. None of us is naturally humble. Yet it is the mark of true greatness in God's kingdom. As Jesus told His followers, "Whoever wants to become great among you must be your servant, and whoever wants to be first must be slave of all. For even the Son of Man did not come to be served, but to serve" (Mark 10:43–45).

Sadly, the early church wrestled with this issue. Some preached "Christ out of envy and rivalry...[and] selfish ambition" (Philippians 1:15, 17). Even in the early church, there were ministries that centered on the heavy promotion of a particular personality. Paul was saying, in effect, "I really don't care about any of that, just so long as Jesus Christ is preached. That is all that matters to me. I rejoice that Christ is preached and God's kingdom is being extended. I don't have to have my name on it" (see Philippians 1:18).

DISAPPOINTMENT AND THE DOOR OF PROMISE

When David faced the disappointment of a closed door, God gave him a wonderful promise. "Your idea was to build a house for Me, David. It isn't going to happen, but I have a better idea. I am going to build a house for you."

"The LORD declares to you that the LORD himself will establish a house for you." (7:11)

Then God explained that He was not talking about putting up some brick and mortar. He was making a promise about one of David's descendants: "When your days are over and you rest with your fathers"— that is, when you are dead—"I will raise up your offspring to succeed you, who will come from your own body, and I will establish his kingdom" (v. 12).

God promised He would raise up [a] descendant of David to the position of king.

God promised that He would raise up one particular descendant of David to the position of king. That promise was remarkably similar to the promise given to Eve in the garden, when God said one of her offspring would crush the head of the serpent (Genesis 3:15).

God then gave David three marvelous promises about this special offspring. God said:

"He is the one who will build a house for my Name, and I will establish the throne of his kingdom forever. I will be his father, and he will be my son." (vv. 13–14)

God was saying, "David, here is what I am going to do for you: Your son will build a house for My name, and I will establish His throne forever, and more than that, David, I will be His father and He will be My son. Your son will be My son!"

David was so overwhelmed by the weight and the glory of these promises that he had to go in and sit down (see v. 18). God was promising to do something that was beyond his wildest imagination, and he was struggling to take it in. How could a son of David possibly be the Son of God? How could any king's reign last forever?

These were incredible promises. The question was, which son of David would fulfill them? The first and most obvious candidate was David's immediate son, Solomon. It is a matter of history that Solomon built the temple in Jerusalem. He used materials gathered by his father, and you can read about the construction of this magnificent building in 1 Kings 5–8.

A PROMISE DEFERRED

God allowed Solomon to fulfill David's dream of putting up this magnificent building. And when the temple was dedicated, the cloud of God's glory came down and filled the temple. God filled the building with His presence.

When that happened, no doubt some people thought, "This is it! This is what God promised to David. Solomon is the king who has built the Lord's house. His kingdom will last forever." But a few years later Solomon died, and when he did, the kingdom was divided in two. And a few centuries after that, Solomon's temple was destroyed.

From the time of David onward, the Bible story revolves around a search for a son of David who would build a temple, whose throne would last forever.

SPOTLIGHT ON CHRIST

Fast-forward the Bible story one thousand years, and you come to the opening verse of the New Testament:

> A record of the genealogy of Jesus Christ the son of David.
> (MATTHEW 1:1)

The first thing that we learn about Jesus is that He is the Son of David. From the beginning, Jesus is introduced to us as the person who fulfills God's incredible promise to David.

JESUS, THE SON OF DAVID—AND THE SON OF GOD.

That theme runs all the way though the Christmas story. Luke records the angel's announcement to Mary that God's promise to David would be fulfilled:

> "You will be with child and give birth to a son, and you are to
> give him the name Jesus. He will be great and will be called the
> Son of the Most High. The LORD God will give him the throne
> of his father David." (LUKE 1:31–32)

Jesus is the Son of David. But He is more; He is also, as the angel Gabriel announced, the Son of the Most High—that is, the Son of God.

Later, other angels appeared to the shepherds in the fields and announced that "Today in the town of David a Savior has been born to you; he is Christ the Lord" (Luke 2:11).

When Jesus began His ministry and people saw His miracles, they were so astonished that they said, "Could this be the Son of David?" (Matthew 12:23). Could this be the one that the people of God had been looking for for a thousand years? As the ministry of Jesus continued, more and more people put their hope in Him so that crowds were lining the streets when He arrived in Jerusalem.

They were waving palm branches and shouting, "Hosanna to the Son of David!" (Matthew 21:9). They were convinced that Jesus would fulfill the ancient promise that God had given to David.

Others perceived more deeply; they understood that Jesus was not only the Son of David, but also the Son of God (Matthew 16:16; John 11:27). The demons were the first to recognize this. As soon as Jesus addressed them, they knew who He was (Mark 5:7).

Jesus affirmed that He is indeed the Son of God. Caiaphas, the high priest, asked Him directly, "Tell us if you are the Christ, the Son of God," and Jesus gave him a straight answer, "Yes, it is as you say" (Matthew 26:63–64).

Jesus Christ fulfilled the mystery of God's promise to David. He was God in the flesh, and He took His flesh from the line of David. David's son was also God's Son!

A PLACE FOR MEETING WITH GOD

If Jesus was indeed the promised Son of David, it would follow, from God's promise, that He would be the one to build God's house. So discerning people would listen very carefully to anything that Jesus said about the temple.

And sure enough, John tells us that at the beginning of His ministry, Jesus announced in the temple courts: "Destroy this temple, and I will raise it again in three days" (John 2:19). Those who heard Him thought that He was inviting them to bulldoze the building so that He could reconstruct it. "It has taken forty-six years to build this temple," they reminded him, "and you are going to raise it in three days?"

But when Jesus spoke about the temple that would be destroyed, He was not talking about the building; He was talking about His own body. The magnificent structure that stood around Him as He spoke had at one time been the place where God had met with His people, but it had become a center of commercial enterprise. It was as if Christ was saying, "This building used to be the place where men and women met with God, but from now on, My body is a new temple." The presence of God is found in Jesus Christ. In Christ "all the fullness of the Deity lives in bodily form" (Colossians 2:9).

When Jesus was crucified, the temple of His body was torn down. When He rose three days later, it was built again! A few years later (in 70 A.D.), the temple building in Jerusalem was destroyed by the Romans, and it has never been rebuilt. There is great significance in that. The place where men and women can meet with God is not a building in Jerusalem, or anywhere else. The place where you meet with God is though Jesus Christ.

God promised David that his son would build a house for God's name. Christ never put up any buildings of stone, but He is building a house of people for the glory of God. The writer to the Hebrews told believers in Jesus that they are God's house (Hebrews 3:6), and Peter described believers as "living stones…being built into a spiritual house" (1 Peter 2:5).

The New Testament places very little importance on buildings. God "does not live in temples built by [human] hands" (Acts 17:24). But God's presence is among believers who are built together as a living temple for God's glory (see Ephesians 2:21). That is why the apostle Paul expected when unbelieving people visited the worship service of the Corinthian church, they would respond by saying, "God is really among you!" (1 Corinthians 14:25). God's presence is always among His people gathered together in the name of Jesus.

THE THRONE THAT WILL LAST FOREVER

God's promise of a king whose throne would be established forever was repeated by later prophets in the Old Testament. For example, Isaiah said that a child would be born and a son given, and that the government would be on his shoulders.

> Of the increase of his government and peace there will be no end. He will reign on David's throne and over his kingdom, establishing and upholding it with justice and righteousness from that time on and forever. (ISAIAH 9:7)

Later the angel Gabriel announced the birth of Jesus: "The Lord God will give him the throne of his father David, and he will reign over the house of Jacob forever; *his kingdom will never end*" (Luke 1:32–33; italics added). Two great promises, one from a prophet, the other from an angel: "A government [to which] there will be no end…His kingdom will never end." But a question arises: How can any kingdom last forever? Kings have their time, but eventually each one dies; so how could any king reign forever?

This is the great significance of the resurrection and the ascension. Christ died and rose again. Death no longer has power over this king. As King of kings, Jesus Christ is seated at the right hand of the Father, and no power can ever move Him from the position in which God has placed Him. "He must reign until he has put all His enemies under his feet" (1 Corinthians 15:25). Then "the kingdoms of this world [will] become the kingdom of our Lord and of his Christ, and He will reign for ever and ever" (Revelation 11:15).

The following words were penned by a soldier under siege during the First World War. The soldier knew his source of strength as he wrote these words while in a trench:[2]

> They cannot shell his temple, nor dynamite his throne.
> They cannot bomb his city, nor rob him of his own.
>
> They cannot take him captive, or strike him deaf or blind,
> nor starve him to surrender, nor make him change his mind.
>
> They cannot cause him panic, nor cut off his supplies.
> They cannot take his kingdom, nor hurt him with their lies.
>
> Though all the world be shattered, his truth remains the same;
> His righteous laws still potent, and Father still His name.
>
> Though we face war and hunger and feel their goad and rod,
> we know above confusion there always will be God.

Christ made a wonderful promise about thrones to His disciples. He said, "I confer on you a kingdom, just as my Father conferred one on me, so that you may eat and drink at my table in my kingdom and sit on thrones, judging the twelve tribes of Israel" (Luke 22:29–30). The disciples will participate in Christ's reign, and that is a distinctive promise of the New Testament to Christian believers. "To him who overcomes," Jesus said, "I will give the right to sit with me on my throne, just as I overcame and sat down with my Father on his throne" (Revelation 3:21).

THE BIBLE'S GREATEST MIRACLE

God promised that David's offspring would be God's Son, and this promise points us to the greatest miracle in the Bible. When Jesus was born, he came into the line of David through Joseph's fiancée, Mary. Joseph was a descendant of David (Matthew 1:1, 16). But Jesus was not born as a result of intercourse between Mary and Joseph (Matthew 1:25). He was conceived in the womb of the virgin by a creative miracle of God: "The Holy Spirit will come upon you, and the power of the Most High will overshadow you. So the holy one to be born will be called the Son of God" (Luke 1:35). The Son of David was the Son of God!

When we think of a son, we think about someone who is born twenty or thirty years after his father. But there was never a time when the Son of God was not with the Father. When the Bible tells us that Christ is the Son of God, it is telling us that Christ shares the nature of the Father, and it is the nature of God to have no beginning. If Christ, as the Son of God, shares the nature of

God, it follows that He has no beginning and no ending. Indeed, the apostle John wrote, "In the beginning was the Word, and the Word was with God, and the Word was God" (John 1:1).

This is the central mystery of the whole Bible. It is impossible to comprehend, and yet once this truth is grasped, it begins to make sense of everything else. God became man. The eternal Son took flesh. The One who had always been beside the Father became a son of David and in His own nature brought God and man together. When He appeared in the Bethlehem stable born of Mary, He fulfilled the promise that God had given to David. The incarnation is the Bible's greatest miracle.

CHILDREN OF GOD

When you came to faith in Christ, who is the one and only Son of God by nature, God received you as an adopted child into His family! As John explained, "To all who received him, to those who believed in his name, he gave the right to become children of God" (John 1:12).

I wish I had a dollar for every time I hear or read about the search for self-worth and significance. If you are struggling in this area, let the truth of who Christ is and what He does for His people sink into the very core of your being.

- Christ is the temple, He reigns on the throne of the universe, and He is the Son of God.

- Faith joined you to Christ, so that in Him, you have become God's temple, a place where God's presence will come.

- You are a citizen of God's kingdom living under the benefits of His rule.

- You are a son or a daughter of the living God, and your destiny is to enjoy Him forever.

Take that into your most ordinary day or into your darkest hour. Let it lift you to see the honor that God has bestowed upon you. Let it lift you to praise and glorify His name.

UNLOCKED

The experience of God's people in the Old Testament depended in large degree on the king who was reigning at the time. It must have been a great relief for the people when a bad king died, and when a good king died, there must have been great anxiety about what the future would hold. At the heart of the Old Testament,

God gave a wonderful promise to David that one of his descendants would reign forever. Christ fulfills this promise.

God's people can be confident about the future because Christ is on the throne. This King has many enemies, but they will all be put under His feet (Psalms 110:1). The ultimate destiny of Christ's people is to enjoy the blessing of His everlasting kingdom and to share in it.

PAUSE FOR PRAYER

For our prayer, use these Scriptures (from Revelation 5:9–10, 13) that ascribe the King of Kings praise due His name:

Great King of Kings and Lord of lords,

You are worthy to take the scroll, and to open its seals, because you were slain, and with your blood you purchased men for God from every tribe and language and people and nation.

You have made them to be a kingdom and priests to serve our God, and they will reign on the earth....

To him who sits on the throne and to the Lamb be praise and honor and glory and power, for ever and ever! [Amen].

NOTES

1. C. S. Lewis, *The Screwtape Letters* (New York: Macmillan, 1942), 73.

2. I heard this poem years ago in a recorded message by English Pastor Paul Tucker. I do not know its prior source.

18

Prophet

2 SAMUEL 12

How has God

spoken to us?

18Prophet

DISCOVER
how God spoke to and through the prophets.

LEARN
how we know that the biblical authors were not expressing their own opinions.

WORSHIP
as you see how all that God says is expressed in a person.

A FRIEND of mine, who I'll call Brian, was hired to a position in which his salary quadrupled overnight. I remember being in his home as he talked enthusiastically about his new opportunity. Brian had landed a senior management position; he was only in his early thirties.

At the time, he spoke about how God had given him this opportunity. But within a few months, Brian had blown his faithfulness to God and to his wife.

Beware. People who are given positions of power often begin to feel that they are somehow beyond the rules that apply to others. That's exactly how it was for David. One day, the king saw a married woman by the name of Bathsheba, and when he saw her, he decided that this was the person he wanted. David had the power and, of course, the money to have whatever he desired, so he ignored God's law and took the woman.

THE ULTIMATE COVER-UP

David loved the Lord, even as Brian seemed to love God. But even a heart that loves God can harbor some strange affections. David's feelings for Bathsheba were utterly offensive to God, but they were also very powerful, and he gave way to them. No Christian is ever beyond the power of temptation, and the moment we think we are, is probably our time of greatest danger. "If you think you are standing firm, be careful that you don't fall!" (1 Corinthians 10:12).

As the story develops, we discover that Bathsheba was carrying the king's child. So now, the great king of Israel became involved in a squalid cover-up. The woman's husband, Uriah, was on the battlefield, and David ordered that he be sent home, supposedly to bring news from the battle. David was really hoping that the man would spend a few nights at home with his wife so that he could be identified as the father of the child.

God had seen what was done.

But it didn't work. Uriah was a conscientious soldier, and did not feel that he should be at home with his wife while his colleagues were risking their lives on the field of battle. So David had to resort to even more desperate measures. He ordered that Uriah be put into the front lines of battle, making his death almost inevitable. The field commander obeyed, and Uriah died in fierce fighting (2 Samuel 11:5–17).

A short time later, David took the recently widowed Bathsheba to be his wife. The whole thing happened without a trace of public knowledge. The papers hadn't got hold of it; David's family didn't know about it. Only David and Bathsheba knew what was done. It was the ultimate cover-up, and we can reasonably assume from the way the story is told that David was highly delighted with the outcome of his marriage to Bathsheba.

His marriage to Michal was a great disappointment. She was the daughter of Saul, and from her attitude when the ark was brought to Jerusalem, it seems that she was a sultry cynic. When David was filled with joy because of the blessing of God, Michal "despised him in her heart" (2 Samuel 6:16).

However, the outcome probably pleased Bathsheba as well. There seems to be little doubt that Bathsheba made a play to attract the attention of the king while her husband was away from home. She must have known when she went out to sunbathe on her roof that she was within sight of the palace.

So here we have two rather unhappy and frustrated people who got together. Bathsheba had what she wanted, and the king had what he wanted. End of story…

…Except for one thing. "The thing David had done displeased the LORD" (2 Samuel 11:27).

God had seen what was done. The LORD could have remained silent, in which case David's sin would remain hidden, and he would live as a believing man at a distance from God. Or He could create a situation that would bring what had happened into the open so that forgiveness and restoration would be possible. Guess which choice God made?

THE TERRORS OF HEARING THE VOICE OF GOD

We have already seen from the Old Testament story that hearing the voice of God directly was a terrifying experience. When God spoke to Moses at Mount Sinai, there was thunder and lightning and the sound of trumpets announcing the glory of God's presence. The people saw that the mountain was surrounded in smoke, and then they heard the audible voice of God. God spoke!

You have to imagine yourself in an earthquake or a hurricane to get any sense of what this must have been like. Even Moses was trembling with fear, and when the people heard the voice of God, they begged that no further word be spoken to them, because they could not bear it (see Hebrews 12:18–21). They must have felt something of what it will be like for sinners to stand before almighty God on the last day. As the psalmist wrote, "He lifts his voice, the earth melts" (Psalm 46:6).

When God was present at Mount Sinai, the people said to Moses, "Speak to us yourself and we will listen. But do not have God speak to us or we will die" (Exodus 20:19). So Moses went up onto the mountain, and God spoke to him, and then Moses came down from the presence of God and repeated the words of God to the people. That was the beginning of what we call "prophecy."

God sent prophets to bring His Word so that the people would be saved from the terrors of hearing God speak to them directly. When God sent a prophet, it was always a sign of His grace. Sometimes the prophets could say pretty fierce things, but nothing that any of the prophets said could ever come close to what it would have been like for the people to actually stand in the presence of God and hear His voice directly. That was how David would hear God's Word—through the strong, direct words of a prophet sent by God.

THE ROLE OF A PROPHET

People sometimes say, "I don't want to go to church to hear a preacher talk about my sins." Well, it would be better for the Holy Spirit to convict you through a preacher than having your sins remain hidden until the last day and then have God speak to you about them Himself! Prophecy can be expressed today as preachers proclaim the Word of God, declaring God's counsel for His people. It's not the same as during Old Testament times, because preachers do not bring new revelation. Nonetheless, when God's Word is proclaimed, then God's voice is heard.

In Old Testament times, God spoke through the prophets, who were given the unique privilege of standing in the counsel of God.

Those prophets heard the voice of God directly so that they could repeat the actual words of God to the people. There is a sense in which the role of a prophet was the opposite of the role of a priest. Priests spoke to God on behalf of people; prophets spoke to the people on behalf of God.

In order to understand the Bible, you need to grasp that (1) God speaks, that (2) He has spoken through these prophets (Hebrews 1:1), and that (3) the Old Testament records the Word of God spoken through the prophets from Moses onward.

STANDING IN A PROPHET'S SHOES

What would it have been like to receive the Word of the Lord? And how did God actually speak to the prophets? The apostle Peter tells us about this in the New Testament:

> *Above all, you must understand that no prophecy of Scripture*
> *came about by the prophet's own interpretation. For prophecy*
> *never had its origin in the will of man. (2 PETER 1:20–21)*

In other words, there was always a clear distinction between the prophet's own opinions and the words that God spoke to them.

We have already seen a good example of this in the story of David's desire to build a temple for the Lord. David asked the prophet Nathan what he thought about the idea, and Nathan told him to "go for it." That was Nathan's opinion. But that night, God said to the prophet, "Go and tell my servant David, 'This is what the LORD says: Are you the one to build me a house to dwell in?'" (2 Samuel 7:4–5). The distinction between Nathan's opinion and God's Word is very clear. It is as if God said, "All right, Nathan, David has heard what you have to say, now go and tell him what I have to say!"

So Nathan went to David and, speaking in the first person because he was repeating the actual words of God as he had heard them, he said, "I will raise up your offspring....I will establish the throne of his kingdom forever....I will be his father, and he will be my son" (2 Samuel 7:12–14).

Sometimes in a discussion I have often quoted a statement from the Bible and been told, "That is just somebody's interpretation." But Peter tells us that is not the case. The Bible claims to be the Word of God. It is the record of the words God spoke to the prophets. Christians believe in a God who speaks; we believe that He has spoken through the prophets. And there is a big difference between a prophet's opinion and that prophet speaking the Word of God.

God has spoken through the prophets in order to protect us from the terror of hearing His voice directly. And God spoke to the prophets in such a way that they could record the precise words that God had spoken without elaboration, interpretation, or distortion.

PROPHETIC INSPIRATION

The apostle Peter tells us, "Men spoke from God as they were carried along by the Holy Spirit" (2 Peter 1:21). In what way were these prophets "carried along"? Some months ago, our neighborhood was hit by a severe storm. We lost several trees, one of which was blown onto the roof of our home. In the process of clearing up, we found a chimney pot, a couple of trash can lids, and several other items that had been blown into our garden by the wind. We had no way of telling where they had come from or how far they had traveled. They had been picked up and carried along by the wind.

That is the picture that God uses to describe the way in which He communicated His Word to the prophets. When God spoke to the prophets, it was like the force of a great wind, and they were caught up in it. These men were not in control of the process. They were not applying deductive logic to work out what God might be saying. They were "carried along" by the Spirit of God and accurately recorded God's words.

This does not mean that they were like robots or that Scripture was given by some process of automatic writing. There are different styles in the writing of the prophets. "Men spoke from God." Different men, at different times, with different personalities, but all of them swept up into this gale of the Spirit which blew upon them. The Word of God came to the prophets with such force and clarity that what God said to them and what they wrote is exactly the same thing.

This is how the prophets could speak about things that otherwise could not have been known. Isaiah spoke about a virgin who would conceive and give birth to a son. Zechariah spoke about a king who would come to Jerusalem riding on a donkey. The only way the prophets could have known these things was that God told them.

> The only way the prophets could have known these things was that God told them.

Now how did Nathan know what David had done with Bathsheba? Had he noticed that Bathsheba got married rather quickly after the death of her husband and that the baby was born soon after, and somehow put two and two together and decided to have a word with David about it? No! God told him what had happened. God spoke to Nathan and blew David's cover apart.

A PROPHET IN THE KING'S COURT

So Nathan, God's appointed prophet for this time in the history of Israel, approached the king. David had become convinced that his cover-up of the scandal had been so effective that nobody knew what had happened. But God knew, and He told Nathan to speak to David about it.

I feel sorry for Nathan! God was telling him things that he didn't want to know, let alone have to repeat to the king! But he was being carried along by the Spirit, and he knew that when God spoke, he could not be silent.

No doubt it was with fear and trembling, and yet in the power of the Spirit, that Nathan went to the palace to speak the Word of God to his old friend David. Using a clever parable, Nathan told David about a rich man who stole a poor man's lamb. As David listened to the story, he was filled with anger at what this man had done. He wanted to know who the man was so that he could see him brought to justice. Nathan looked at David and said, "You are the man!" (12:7).

David's defenses were ripped wide open. He had thought that any potential Bathsheba-gate scandal was behind him. But God knew, and God had told Nathan. David had moved into the darkness, so God sent a prophet to expose what has been hidden. David had lost his fellowship with God, so God sent a prophet to bring him back.

This was God's grace in action. The prophets were like prosecuting attorneys sent by God to bring His case against His people. But they were also like wise counselors who helped God's people to face the truth about themselves so that they could return to God and find grace and forgiveness.

SPOTLIGHT ON CHRIST

Down through the centuries, God spoke His Word to the prophets and sent them to His people. They were often hated, despised, brutalized, and sometimes murdered. Then in the fullness of time God sent His Son (Hebrews 1:1–2).

In the Old Testament, the Word of God was given to a man, but in Jesus Christ the Word of God became a man. "The Word became flesh and dwelt...among us" (John 1:14 NKJV).

It was not that Christ heard the Word of God like the prophets. He is the Word of God. Everything that God has to say to you is expressed in Him. This is why we do not need any other prophet today. God spoke in the past by the prophets, but they were all pointing forward to Christ who is the Word of God. There can be no further Word beyond the One who is the Word.

A PROPHET…AND MORE THAN A PROPHET

Jesus exercised the ministry of a prophet. The words He spoke were the words He was given by the Father. "I did not speak of my own accord, but the Father who sent me commanded me what to say and how to say it….So whatever I say is just what the Father has told me to say" (John 12:49–50).

He knew what was in the hearts of people who professed to follow Him (John 2:24–25). He told the Samaritan woman at the well that she had been married five times and that the man she was living with was not her husband (John 4:18). Christ said this so that she would discover who He is and receive new life from Him.

People soon recognized Jesus as a prophet, but it was not long before His disciples realized that He must be more than a prophet because He claimed what no other prophet could ever claim. "I and the Father are one." "Anyone who has seen me has seen the Father" (John 10:30; 14:9).

As His ministry progressed, the plot to discredit Him gained momentum. Eventually Jesus was arrested, and the Scriptures tell us that the guards blindfolded Him, and in a scene of horrible brutality, they circled around Him and took turns striking Him with their fists. Then they said, "Prophesy! Who hit you?" (Luke 22:64). They knew the people called Him a prophet; now they asked that He have God tell Him which of them had dealt the last blow.

HOW DOES GOD SPEAK TODAY?

People often say, "I wish that God would speak to me." He does, yet not as He spoke at Mount Sinai, where His people were so terrified that they begged Him to stop. We can be profoundly grateful that God has spoken through the words of the prophets and Jesus Christ, and that the Scriptures have recorded His words.

The role of a prophet in the Old Testament is fulfilled by the work of the Holy Spirit in the New. Jesus said that when the Holy Spirit came, He would convince the world of sin, righteousness, and judgment (John 16:8). It is the work of the Holy Spirit to bring hidden sin to light through your conscience.

But God's purpose goes far beyond revealing sin. That is simply a means to the end of restoring sinners. Jesus said that the Holy Spirit would take the truth about

Himself and make it known to us (John 16:14). That means that it is the special work of the Holy Spirit to show us that God offers His grace to us in Jesus Christ. Just as David was restored to fellowship with God, and then went on to live for God's glory, so our sins may be forgiven, and we may live a new life.

RESPONDING TO THE WORD OF GOD

The Bible tells us the stories of two kings who received God's word from a prophet and responded in very different ways: David and Herod.

When God spoke to David through Nathan, David said, "I have sinned against the LORD" (12:13). He could have said, "Nathan, you have to understand that the woman threw herself at me," and there may have been some truth in that. He might have said, "Nathan, you don't understand. My marriage has been dead for years," which may also have been true. David could even have said, "Nathan, I know that I did something wrong, but a lot of earlier leaders of this people have done the same or worse." That also would have been true.

But David did not use any of these excuses. He said, "I have sinned against the LORD."

Would you have said that? How you respond to the Word of God when it hurts you is probably one of the most revealing statements about you. It will determine whether you remain on a spiritual casualty list or are restored to living fellowship with God.

The result of David's honest confession was that he found forgiveness. The pain of his suppressed conscience was released, and the joy of his salvation was restored.

One thousand years later, another king, Herod, sat on the throne in Jerusalem. God spoke to him through a prophet whose name was John the Baptist. Herod was very interested in spiritual things, and he liked listening to John's preaching. He felt that there was something authentic about him and he was drawn to that.

One day John the Baptist was taken up in the gale of the Spirit, and God gave him words to speak to Herod about his illicit relationship with his brother's wife. The king didn't want to know, and in the end he ordered that the head of John the Baptist be brought to him on a plate.

It is significant that Herod's sin did not dull his interest in spiritual matters. For some time, Herod had wanted to see Jesus (Luke 23:8). Eventually he had the opportunity, because Christ was sent to him by Pilate, who was trying to avoid the responsibility of making a decision. We're told Herod "plied him with many questions, but Jesus gave him no answer" (Luke 23:9).

Herod had refused God's word to him through John the Baptist. He had hardened his heart, and now the Savior had nothing more to say to Him.

As far as we can tell, the next time God spoke to Herod, it was without a prophet, and without a Savior. The next time he heard the word of God, he was in the presence of God. If you will not hear the word of God through the mediator, there will come a day when He will speak to you without a mediator, and that would be absolutely terrifying. That is why the Bible says, "How shall we escape if we ignore such a great salvation?" (Hebrews 2:3).

God's promise is that, "If we confess our sins, he is faithful and just and will forgive us our sins and purify us from all unrighteousness" (1 John 1:9). That is what happened to David, and it can happen for you.

UNLOCKED

God has spoken to us through the prophets and through His Son Jesus Christ. We should be profoundly grateful that God has not chosen to speak to us directly. Israel discovered something of the terror of that at Sinai. God has graciously chosen to speak to us indirectly, through the prophets and by His Son who is the Mediator.

God speaks to us about our sins so that we may turn from them and be forgiven. He speaks through His Word and by His Spirit.

PAUSE FOR PRAYER

Almighty God,

Thank You that when we have sinned, You have not remained silent.

Thank You that You have spoken Your Word by the prophets and through yYour Son. Thank You that the Word became flesh. May I continue to listen to Your Words through these two sources.

Through Jesus Christ my Lord. Amen.

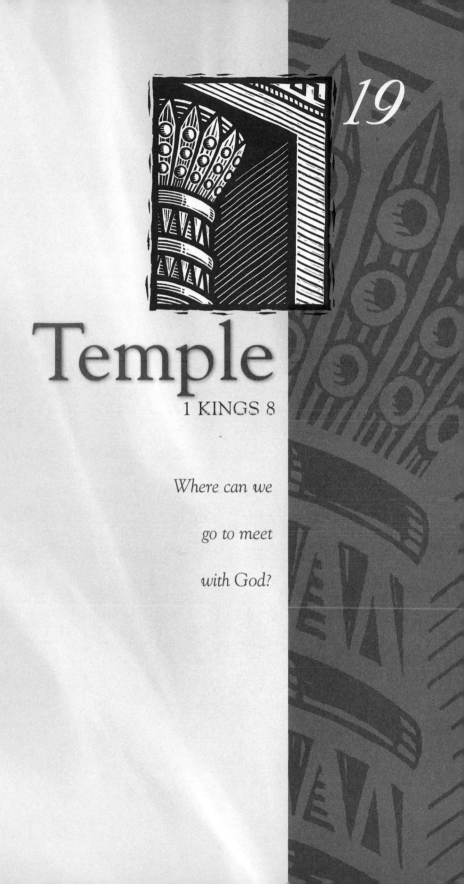

Temple

1 KINGS 8

Where can we

go to meet

with God?

19 Temple

1 KINGS 8

DISCOVER
the significance of the lost ark of the covenant.

LEARN
how God uses trials as stonecutters in your life.

WORSHIP
as you see how God's presence comes to us in Jesus Christ.

THE Bible story is about how men and women can live in the presence of God. It begins with the first man and woman enjoying God's presence in a garden, and ends with a vast crowd enjoying the presence of God in a city. Between these two scenes, we have the story of how God's presence was lost through man's choice of sin and disobedience, and how the presence of God is restored by God's initiative of grace.

So the Bible answers the question, "How can a man or a woman live in the presence of God?" After Adam and Eve were thrown out of the garden and God's presence, they only knew God from a distance. But God wanted His presence to be known, and He revealed Himself through a number of *theophanies*, or divine appearances. He appeared in human form so that He could communicate with His people. But these experiences of the presence of God were very rare. (Abraham experienced four theophanies, Isaac two, and Jacob probably three.)

After that, there was no manifestation of the presence of God for four hundred years. Then God appeared to Moses in a self-sustaining fire, and when Moses led the people out of Egypt, God's presence was with them in a pillar of cloud by day and a pillar of fire by night.

SEEKING GOD'S PRESENCE

When God's people came to Sinai, they saw a new manifestation of the glory of God. The cloud of God's presence came down on the mountain, and the people were filled with fear and awe. It was as if the day of judgment had come.

The people asked Moses to go up the mountain into the presence of God, and while he was there, the people made an idol in the shape of a golden calf. So God said, "Go up to the land flowing with milk and honey. But I will not go with you" (Exodus 33:3).

God was ready to give the people all the blessings of life in the land of Canaan, with the single exception that God Himself would not be with them. Upon hearing His words, God's people recognized that all the prosperity, peace, and freedom in the world would be nothing without the presence of God. So they mourned their actions, and removed their ornaments, as God commanded (see 33:4–5). And they waited for God to act.

But God had already told Moses how His presence could come among the people again. He had given precise specifications for building the ark of the covenant to be placed in the inner court of a tabernacle. The high priest was to enter the Most Holy Place once a year, and there God promised to meet with the priest on behalf of the people (Exodus 25:22).

So now they built the ark, which contained the covenant (or testimony) between God and His people, and the tabernacle to house it. You can read about it in Exodus 35–40:33. When the tabernacle and the ark were complete, "The cloud covered the Tent of Meeting, and the glory of the LORD filled the tabernacle. Moses could not enter the Tent of Meeting because the cloud had settled upon it, and the glory of the LORD filled the tabernacle" (Exodus 40:34–35).

The cloud of the presence of God had returned to His people. This was the sign that their sin was forgiven and that their relationship with God was restored.

THE STORY OF THE ARK

From that time on, the ark was the symbol of the presence of God with His people. When the people traveled, they lined up in formation around the four sides of the ark. When they crossed the Jordan River to enter the land, the priests carried the ark first, and the people followed. Sometimes they took the ark into battle with them as a sign of the presence of God. When God was with His people, nothing was impossible for them.

One day, however, the Philistines captured the ark of God. Many mourned; one woman giving birth that day named her son Ichabod, which means "the glory has departed" (1 Samuel 4:21–22). The loss of the ark was a sign that the presence of God had departed from Israel. Eventually the ark was returned, but for a whole generation in the time of Saul, it was placed in storage and neglected. That tells you something about Saul's sense of priorities!

When David came to the throne and established his center of operations in Jerusalem, his first action was to bring the ark of God to the capital city. He wanted the presence of God to be established at the center of national life.

As noted in chapter 17, David wanted to honor God by building a beautiful temple. The building would shelter the ark of the covenant. It would be a permanent meeting place between man and God. It had always been in the plan of God that such a place should be built. That is why, back in the time of Moses, four hundred years before David, God had spoken about "the place [where] the LORD your God will choose...to put his Name there for his dwelling" (Deuteronomy 12:5).

God would choose a certain place where people could meet with Him, and He would "put his Name" there. When David came to the throne and brought the ark to Jerusalem, he began to think that this might be the place. He was right that it was the place, but it was not yet the time. David's role was to subdue the enemies of Israel. It would fall to his son Solomon to build the temple.

TIME FOR THE TEMPLE

It is hard to think of any other time when God's people were so singularly blessed as when Solomon came to the throne. It seemed that God was giving His people a unique moment of opportunity. He had given them wise and stable leadership and had entrusted them with significant resources.

Right from the start, Solomon knew what God wanted him to do with this moment of opportunity. God had said to his father, David, "Your son will build a house for me." So Solomon knew from the prophecy given to his father that God had work for him to do.

> In the four hundred and eightieth year after the Israelites had come out of Egypt,...[Solomon] began to build the temple of the LORD. (1 KINGS 6:1)

The stones were cut, shaped, and dressed at the quarry, and then delivered to the building site. Then, when all of the materials were assembled, a command was given— "Build!"—and the whole building went up in silence. "No hammer, chisel or any other iron tool was heard at the temple site while it was being built" (1 Kings 6:7).

That picture is taken up in the New Testament, where God's people are described as "living stones" who are being built into a temple that will be for the glory of God (1 Peter 2:5). Every stone has to be shaped for its place in the building.

The pain that God may allow in your life, or the hardships that you struggle with, are like the hammer and chisel in the quarry. God is shaping you as a living stone to take your place in that building that will be for His glory. All the painful preparatory work is done here and now in the quarry, because on the day when Jesus Christ returns, the command to build will be given, and all the people of God will be brought together. In heaven, all the preparation and shaping will allow you to glorify Him together with all His people forever. If you can think of some of the most painful experiences of your life as being like the chiseling in the quarry, you will have a proper perspective.

GOD'S STONECUTTERS

Some years ago, we had the opportunity of welcoming a Romanian pastor, Joseph Ton, into our home for several days. Back home, he had been imprisoned for his faith, and we listened intently as he talked about the cost of commitment to Christ. One night he told us about how some of the prison guards had noticed that Joseph's attitude was very different from that of other prisoners. Nearly every prisoner hated the guards because of their cruelty, but Joseph prayed for the guards and for their families.

A guard once asked Joseph, "Why are you not filled with bitterness toward me?"

"Because to me you are God's stonecutter," Joseph answered.

Who are God's stonecutters in your life? They may have brought you pain, but God will use that pain in His great purpose of shaping you into the likeness of Christ so that you can take your place in the living temple that will be for God's glory in eternity.

I don't know who—or what—God is using in your life to cut you into shape. It may be a challenging problem, such as a health, job, or financial issue. No matter the cutting instrument—a person or a situation—the process can be painful. But when Christ returns, the stones will all be sized and dressed and the command will go up "Build!" and in silence and in wonder, the church will be all that Christ died for it to become, and you will be a part of the place where God's glory is known and enjoyed forevermore.

Solomon paid particular attention to the inner sanctuary of the temple. The old tabernacle had been a series of curtains dividing off different areas, but this flimsy structure was now being upgraded to a permanent building with walls.

The Most Holy Place would now be an unlit room about thirty feet square and thirty feet high; so it was a perfect cube. Solomon had two sculptures of cherubim made from olive wood and overlaid with gold (1 Kings 6:20–28). Their wingspan was fifteen feet, and so when they were positioned side by side, their wings would have spanned the whole room. They were also fifteen feet high, so they were positioned to look down on the ark. We keep coming across these cherubim in the Bible story. They always represent exclusion from the presence of God. These massive carvings positioned so that they were looking down on the ark were symbols of how God above is separated from man below.

This massive construction project took seven years to complete. Fully 30,000 men were conscripted to fell timber in Lebanon, working in shifts of 10,000 men for one month at a time. There were 80,000 stonecutters, 70,000 carriers, and 3,300 foremen working in the quarries.

A SERVICE OF DEDICATION

When the building was complete, the people gathered for a service of dedication. The temple dedication was one of the greatest occasions in the nation's history. Solomon summoned the elders of Israel, the heads of the tribes, and the chiefs of the families to bring up the ark of the covenant (see 1 Kings 8:1). "The priests then brought the ark of the LORD's covenant to its place in the inner sanctuary of the temple, the Most Holy Place, and put it beneath the wings of the cherubim" (8:6).

> When the priests withdrew from the Holy Place, the cloud filled the temple of the LORD. And the priests could not perform their service because of the cloud, for the glory of the LORD filled his temple. (vv. 10–11)

The last time God's glory had shown itself like this was in the desert, more than four hundred years earlier. But now, this same God, whose glory came down and rested on the ark of the covenant in the desert, had come down into the temple!

Solomon had to explain to the people what was happening. They had never experienced the immediate presence of God. They did not even know what the cloud was! So Solomon told them, "The LORD has said that he would dwell in a dark cloud" (v. 12).

We have seen that the Most Holy Place was a darkened room, dominated by two fifteen-foot figures of cherubim. Beneath them was the ark of the covenant, a wooden chest about six feet by two, and on the lid of the ark there were also golden figures of cherubim. If God's presence were to come down into that room and touch the ark of the covenant, then God would have to come down through the cherubim. God breached the wall of separation and judgment, represented by these figures, and came to meet with His people at the mercy seat.

RESPONDING WITH WORSHIP

Solomon's first response was to worship! "Praise be to the LORD, the God of Israel, who with his own hand has fulfilled what he promised with his own mouth to my father David," he began (v. 15; the entire ascription of praise is found in vv. 15–21). Then he turned to God in prayer and expressed the longing of his heart (vv. 22–53). Solomon was a wise man and he knew that no building could ever contain God. He knew that the cloud could leave as quickly as it came. He longed for much more than a once-in-a-lifetime experience of God's presence and wanted the temple to be a place where God's presence could always be found. So he made this request:

> "May your eyes be open toward this temple night and day, this
> place of which you have said, 'My Name shall be there.'" (v. 29)

Solomon knew that heaven is the dwelling place of God, but his desire was that the temple would be the place where God would meet with men and women on earth.

Some people who were living miles from Jerusalem would also want to seek the face of God. So Solomon asked that God would hear them as they directed their prayers toward the temple. "Hear the supplication of your servant and of your people Israel when they pray toward this place. *Hear from heaven, your dwelling place,* and when you hear, forgive" (v. 30, italics added). Then Solomon concluded by rising "from before the altar of the LORD, where he had been kneeling with his hands spread out toward heaven" and began a final praise and benediction for the people:

"Praise be to the LORD, who has given rest to his people Israel just as he promised. Not one word has failed of all the good promises he gave through his servant Moses. May the LORD our God be with us as he was with our fathers" (vv. 54, 56–57).

THE SAD STORY OF THE TEMPLE

For a time, that was how it was. But it was not long before there were some sad changes. A king by the name of Manasseh promoted the worship of other gods and introduced astrology into the temple (2 Kings 21:5). This provoked the LORD to anger, and eventually the pattern of idolatry became so offensive to God that He gave His people into the hands of their enemies. The Babylonian army laid siege to Jerusalem; the city fell, the temple was destroyed, and the most gifted people were deported to Babylon.

Jerusalem was reduced to a pile of rubble, and in the process, the ark of the covenant was lost, so that even when the temple was rebuilt, the place where God said He would meet with the people was gone.

ONLY A SHADOW

That's how it was for seventy years. Then God allowed the people to return under the leadership of Ezra and Nehemiah. They rebuilt the walls of the city and then the temple. But it was only a shadow of Solomon's temple. When the foundations were laid, some of the older people wept. They knew that the new temple would never match the one that had stood there before. And when the new temple was dedicated, the Scripture records no reference to the cloud of God's presence. It was simply a building in which people worshiped.

It wasn't long before the country was overrun again and the second temple destroyed. It was not until the time of Herod that it was rebuilt, and there certainly is no evidence of the cloud of God's presence in the third temple. By that time, God's house of prayer had become a den of thieves and robbers.

SPOTLIGHT ON CHRIST

During the time of the third temple, our LORD Jesus Christ was born. John wrote that "The Word became flesh and dwelt among us" (John 1:14). The word that is used for *dwelt* literally means "tabernacled," or "pitched His tent." John is telling us that when Jesus Christ was born, the presence of God came to His people.

THE TEMPLE WITH US

At the beginning of His ministry, Jesus spoke about His own body as a temple that would be destroyed and rebuilt within three days. In referring to His own body as the temple, Christ was telling us that He is the new meeting place between God and man. "You used to look to the temple as the place where you could meet with God. Don't look there. If you want to meet with God, come to Me."

In the Old Testament, the meeting point between God and man was a place, but in the New Testament, the meeting place between God and man is a person. On one occasion, Jesus spoke with a Samaritan woman who wanted to discuss the best place to worship. Jesus told her that God was seeking people who would worship Him "in spirit and truth" (John 4:23).

Solomon asked that God would listen to all those prayers that were directed toward the temple, but Jesus promises that God will hear prayers that are offered in His name. "Whatever you ask the Father in My name He will give you" (John 16:23 NKJV).

THE SPIRIT IN US

When Jesus began to speak to the disciples about His departure, the thought appalled them because that would mean that the presence of God would be taken from them. But Jesus told them what would happen. "I will ask the Father, and he will give you another Counselor to be with you forever—the Spirit of Truth" (John 14:16–17). The presence of God would not only be *with* them as it had been through Jesus, but God's presence would "be *in* [them]" by the Holy Spirit (John 14:17, italics added).

Then after the resurrection, Christ came to His disciples and He breathed on them. He said, "Receive the Holy Spirit." Jesus was picturing what would happen after His ascension on the Day of Pentecost.

On the Day of Pentecost, the disciples heard the sound of a rushing wind. Now the breath of God was indeed blowing on them. Next they saw a fire—a symbol of God's presence just as it had been when a pillar of fire hovered over His people in the desert. But on the Day of Pentecost, the fire separated into tongues of fire, and the flames rested on each of the disciples. God was showing in a visual and powerful way that His presence was coming upon these people. The breath of God's life had entered them.

Now if the presence of God comes into a man or a woman's own body, that person becomes a place where God is; or to put it another way, that person becomes a living temple!

That is how the New Testament describes Christian believers. "Your body is a temple of the Holy Spirit," the apostle Paul told the Corinthian church (1 Corinthians 6:19). When you come to Christ, your own body becomes a place where God is. God's presence is with you.

AN ONGOING STORY: GOD WITH HIS PEOPLE

Do you see the glorious sweep of this story right through the Bible? The presence of

God remains with His people. God was with two people in the garden. Then God came down in awesome power to speak with Moses on Mount Sinai. Then God's presence came to the mercy seat between the cherubim on top of the ark. Next God's presence shone in the cloud that filled the temple. Later the presence of God became incarnate in the person of our LORD Jesus Christ. Today the presence of God is breathed into all His people by the Holy Spirit.

The whole of human history is leading up to the day when Jesus Christ will return in glory and take His people into the immediate presence of God. Then, we will see Him and we will be like Him (1 John 3:2).

The apostle John was given a glimpse of what this will be like. He saw a great city and a great crowd of people. Then he heard "a loud voice from the throne saying, 'Now the dwelling of God is with men, and he will live with them. They will be his people, and God himself will be with them and be their God'" (Revelation 21:3).

Do you feel something of the glory of this? One of the greatest problems in the Christian church is that Christian people have hardly begun to grasp the glory of their salvation. You are a living stone in the temple of God, and everything that God is doing in your life is shaping you for your eternal destiny with Christ.

Think about the cloud of God's presence filling the temple. Think of that as a picture of God's Spirit filling you. Let it stir your mind and imagination. Paul prayed that Christian believers would be "filled with all the fullness of God" (Ephesians 3:19 NKJV).

Think about the two temples in the Old Testament. God's presence filled Solomon's temple, but the temple of Nehemiah's day was simply a building with God's name on it. We must be careful not to become like the second temple. Many have the name "Christian" but have no observable evidence of the presence of God in their lives. Christ came to change that. He has opened the way for the presence of God to fill us by the power of the Holy Spirit.

UNLOCKED

The Bible story is all about how we can enjoy the presence of God. Since Adam was evicted from the garden, any hope of meeting with God depended on His choosing to come and meet with us. The Bible tells us how God has repeatedly come down to make Himself known and to reach out to men and women. He did this through the theophanies, and then by coming to the mercy seat on the ark, and then by the cloud of His presence filling the temple.

Despite the efforts of Indiana Jones and the fantasies of Hollywood, the truth is that the ark of the covenant has been lost. There was no ark in the second temple, and it has never been found. The fact that the ark is gone is very significant. God no longer meets with us at a particular place but through a particular person.

The manifestations of God's presence at the ark and in the temple were pointing forward to something greater that God would do in Christ. God took human flesh and has made Himself known through Jesus. When we come to Jesus in faith, God's presence enters our lives by the Holy Spirit. Then, either through death or at His second coming, Christ will take us into the immediate presence of God. We will see Him, and we will be like Him.

PAUSE FOR PRAYER

Take a moment to identify God's stonecutters in your life. You may want to tell God how painful they are for you.

Ask God to help you believe that even the stonecutters are part of His purpose. Ask Him to use the trials in your life to shape you for ministry now and prepare you for the place you will take in His presence.

20

Worship

1 KINGS 18

What are the

distinguishing

marks of

authentic

worship?

20Worship

1 KINGS 18

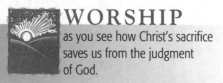
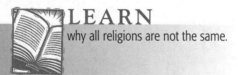
**THE UNITED KINGDOM AND
KINGS OF THE NORTH**

1000 B.C. | CA. 1011 –971 | KING DAVID

971–931 | KING SOLOMON

931–910 | JEROBOAM

910–909 | NADAB
909–886 | BAASHA

900

886–885 | ELAH

885–874 | OMRI

874–853 | AHAB

800

SEVERAL years ago I spent two weeks of ministry in northeast England, having been asked by our denomination to give support and encouragement to the work of some pastors I knew there. The northeast of England is strewn with Methodist chapels. Most of them were started at the time of John Wesley, when revival was sweeping through England. People came to Christ by the hundreds. They were discipled in small groups, and then gathered into local congregations.

Now, more than one hundred years later, many of the chapels are relics of history; those that still function often don't proclaim the gospel. Indeed, the area has become one of the hardest in Britain for the work of the gospel. The experience of working there made me wonder how it was possible for living congregations to die in such a short space of time. How could these beautiful buildings, once filled with worship, now be disused shells that do little more than perpetuate a past tradition? One thing I know: What happened to these buildings can happen to people too.

And that raises another question: What kills worship in your life and what would it take for worship to become a living experience for you? The first book of Kings speaks directly to these issues.

PLANTING THE SEEDS OF DIVISION

When Solomon came to the throne, the people of God had everything going for them. They had wise and godly leadership, peace from their enemies, and strong unity. Under those circumstances, they were able to accomplish remarkable things.

Solomon assembled a workforce of nearly 200,000 people, and after seven years of construction, the temple of God was built. When the building was dedicated, the glory of God filled the temple. It was one of the greatest moments in the history of Israel.

God's people became the envy of the nations. The queen of Sheba came to visit Solomon to learn from his wisdom and marvel at what he had accomplished. Our Lord Jesus Christ referred to "Solomon in all his splendor" (Matthew 6:29).

But there was a very short distance between triumph and disaster. As time passed, we find that Solomon's success began to breed complacency, and the seeds of future disaster were planted in the later years of his reign. Solomon made three mistakes that are a warning for all who are called to leadership among the people of God. He (1) lost touch with hurting people, (2) slid into indulgence, and (3) did the popular (rather than the right) thing.

LOSING TOUCH WITH HURTING PEOPLE

Solomon put all of his attention on the palace and the temple in Jerusalem. While people in the south were prospering, the people in the north were struggling. Solomon had focused his forced labor program in the north. The result was a significant group of people that were feeling increasingly marginalized among the people of God.

Solomon lost touch with hurting people. Perhaps he thought the people in the north were unimportant, but that shortsighted leadership decision had long-term repercussions after his death.

It is always important for leaders to be sensitive to those who are feeling left out among the people of God. Solomon was not hearing the growing discontent among the people, and so when he handed the country over to his son Rehoboam, it was filled with suppressed bitterness and tension. The seeds of disunity were already planted.

SLIDING INTO INDULGENCE

Solomon was in a position where he could do virtually anything he wanted. He had almost unlimited power and great resources of wealth. In his early days, he was a man with a mission. He knew that God had called him to build the temple, and he threw his time, energy, and money into accomplishing something for the glory of God.

But later in his life, he used his position to support his own indulgence. Solomon had 700 wives and 300 concubines (1 Kings 11:3). That's indulgence! And the interesting thing is that his indulgence was the root of his own downfall. "As Solomon grew old, his wives turned his heart after other gods, and his heart was not fully devoted to the LORD his God, as the heart of David his father had been" (1 Kings 11:4).

It is extraordinary that Solomon, who was so wise in his early years, became so foolish in his personal choices. In his later years, the relationships he had chosen became a burden and a snare to him. The constant influence of ungodly people eroded his faith. Be very careful about your choice of significant relationships, friend-ships, and partnerships.

DOING WHAT'S POPULAR

Solomon's third mistake was that he chose what was popular instead of what was right. "On a hill east of Jerusalem, Solomon built a high place for Chemosh the detestable god of Moab" (1 Kings 11:7). It's not hard to imagine the circumstances that led him to do this. One of his wives who was especially in favor at the time probably said, "Solomon, I have one tiny little favor to ask of you, but it's not just for me; it's for a number of us here in your harem. I'm from Moab. I have left my home and family to be your wife. But just sometimes, I feel I would like to have a little taste of home. And I know you wouldn't want me going back to Moab, so what about us having a little bit of Moab here!

"If I had a place where I could go and practice my religion, just a little shrine to Chemosh, that would be so wonderful."

So Solomon built a high place for Chemosh for his Moabite wives. Then you know what would happen next. Another of Solomon's wives came to him, this one from Ammon, asking for similar treatment. So Solomon set up a shrine "for Molech the detestable god of the Ammonites" (1 Kings 11:7).

Then the rest of the harem would all come forward with their petitions, and at some point, Solomon must have become completely fed up with the whole thing. Maybe he said, "To make it fair, the rule is that all of the women may have a shrine of their own choosing." The record reads: "He did the same for all his foreign wives, who burned incense and offered sacrifices to their gods" (1 Kings 11:8).

This was the beginning of a radical transformation that infected God's people. At the start of Solomon's reign, Jerusalem was the place where the living God had put

His name. By the end of Solomon's reign, there was a place near Jerusalem with the name of just about every other god from a surrounding kingdom or culture!

When the queen of Sheba came to Jerusalem, she saw a temple that spoke of the unique glory of the God of Israel. Now the temple of the living God was surrounded by a smorgasbord of shrines to other gods, so that any visitor to Jerusalem would draw the conclusion that the God of Israel was one among many. It was the first step towards becoming a multi-faith society.

Solomon's choices were the beginning of true worship being lost in Israel. Our personal worship may also be stifled by poor choices. The apostle Peter warns husbands to be careful about the way that they treat their wives "so that nothing will hinder [their] prayers" (1 Peter 3:7). King David wrote that "the eyes of the LORD are on the righteous and his ears are attentive to their [prayers]" (Psalm 34:15). If we intentionally hide sin in our hearts, then the LORD will not hear us.

A TURNING OF THE TIDE

After years of peace, prosperity, and the blessing of God, the tide began to turn. "The LORD raised up against Solomon an adversary" (1 Kings 11:14). In fact, Solomon faced three adversaries during a short period (see 11:14, 23, 26). Then after Solomon's death and during his son Rehoboam's early rule, rebellion in the north allowed Jeroboam to usurp part of the kingdom.

Solomon did great things for God in the first half of his life and then reversed much of that good through the indulgence of his later years. He received a kingdom from his father David that was united and at peace, but he handed his son a kingdom that was divided and at war. Thus when Rehoboam took over, he immediately faced rumbling discontent among the people in the north. Eventually those northern tribes found a leader in Jeroboam. They rallied around him and crowned him as their king. That meant that the ten tribes in the north were separating from the line of David that God had promised to bless. The kingdom that was once the envy of the world was now divided and at war—the north (called Israel) against the south (called Judah).

THE STORY IN THE NORTH

Jeroboam was a shrewd leader of the ten northern tribes of Israel, and although he had little personal knowledge of the Lord, he did realize the cohesive power of religion. He saw that if faithful people from the north kept going down to Jerusalem to worship God in the temple, then they would keep being reminded of the powerful unity they shared with the people from the south, as together they worshiped the one living God.

So Jeroboam decided to establish his own centers of worship for the northern tribes using an old image: the golden calf of Mount Sinai. The northern king had two golden calves crafted and told the people: "It is too much for you to go up to Jerusalem. Here are your gods, O Israel, who brought you up out of Egypt" (1 Kings 12:28). That final statement contained the same words that Aaron had used when he made the golden calf in the desert half a millennium earlier (Exodus 32:8)! It was politically shrewd but entirely wrong, and it was deeply offensive to God. Jeroboam was not seeking the presence and the blessing of God on his kingdom. He was merely using religion to strengthen the corporate identity of the people he was leading, and when that is the aim, any religion will do.

After Jeroboam, there was a succession of kings in Israel who followed the same policies over a period of about fifty years. Jeroboam handed the kingdom over to his son Nadab, who followed in the ways of his father until he was murdered by Baasha. He was followed by Elah, who was a drunkard and murderer. Then there was Zimri, who was guilty of treason and only lasted seven days, and then Omri, who "sinned more than those before him" (1 Kings 16:25). Finally there was Ahab, who topped Omri by doing "more evil in the eyes of the LORD than any of those before him" (1 Kings 16:30).

Ahab thought nothing of committing the sins of Jeroboam. He also married the infamous Jezebel and began to serve Baal. Jezebel used the power of the palace to initiate a program of persecution in which the prophets of God were hunted and killed.

In just fifty years after the death of Solomon, Israel had changed beyond recognition. At the beginning of Solomon's reign, the king said, "There is one God." By the time of Jeroboam, the official position was that "there are many gods," and by the time of Ahab, it was unacceptable to say that there is one God, and those who did so were subject to violent persecution.

In half a century, Israel had gone from a people united in worshiping the living God to a nation confused and divided, where people assumed that all religions were essentially the same and therefore that the God you worshiped was a matter of personal choice. As long as you were sincere, it really did not make any difference!

Only a few years earlier the presence of God had filled Solomon's temple; now the knowledge of God was all but lost, even among His own people. If that could happen in Israel around 800 B. C., it can certainly happen in America around 2000

A. D. So how can authentic worship of the living God be restored in the land? That is the theme of the great story of Elijah on Mount Carmel. Here we find several distinctive marks of authentic worship.

AUTHENTIC WORSHIP IS A RESPONSE TO REVEALED TRUTH

> *Elijah went before the people and said, "How long will you waver between two opinions? If the LORD is God, follow him; but if Baal is God, follow him."* (18:21)

The prophet Elijah was on Mount Carmel, facing 450 prophets of Baal, 400 prophets of Asherah, and "people from all over Israel" (v. 19). Even King Ahab was there. But Elijah was honest and direct. In effect, he said: "If Baal is God, then the thing you should do is follow him. If he's not, return to God!" That is like someone saying today, "If Allah is God, then leave the church and go to the mosque! If Siva or Vishnu are God, then adopt Hinduism!"

Elijah did not appeal to tradition. He was not interested in perpetuating a system of vested interests that are used to dominate the culture. He appealed to the truth: The single reason for worshiping the Lord is that He is God.

Nobody has the right to say that you should be a Christian because your parents were Christians, or because Christianity is the dominant religion in your country. These are not good enough reasons. Christianity stands or falls on the claim that it is true. Authentic worship is a response to revealed truth. "If the Lord is God, follow Him."

The people found it very difficult to respond to Elijah's challenge. "The people said nothing" (v. 21). Elijah's question assumed categories of truth and error, and the people found it very difficult to think in these terms. They had been brought up on a syncretism that said, "The God you worship is a personal choice, faith is a private matter in the realm of your own heart, and every individual must find a way to worship that fits their own personality."

When Elijah challenged the people to decide what was true, they didn't know what to say. So Elijah's first task was to confront the people with the claims of truth. Before you can truly worship, you need to know who God is. Authentic worship is a response to revealed truth. So if worship is to be restored, truth must be proclaimed. The whole of a public service of worship should be built around the truth. We should sing the truth, read the truth, pray the truth, and preach the truth.

If you want to know a greater depth of worship in your life, get your Bible open and engage with the truth. Soak your mind in it. The Holy Spirit will use the truth to stimulate a response within your heart, and this will help your prayers.

AUTHENTIC WORSHIP FOCUSES ON THE LIVING GOD

Elijah invited the prophets of Baal to prepare a sacrifice and then call on the name of Baal to manifest himself by sending fire. The prophets of Baal gave themselves to the challenge and called on their god. "Oh, Baal, hear us." They danced around the altar, working themselves into a frenzy.

This went on hour after hour. You have to give them top marks for sincerity and effort. Perhaps they would have said that they felt that this form of worship was very meaningful, or that it made them feel good. And they probably did feel good; after all, six hours of dancing would be a pretty good workout!

But after all of this intense activity, "There was no response, no one answered" (v. 29). That is the tragedy of false religion. When they had done everything with total sincerity and at great personal cost, there was no one there.

Their worship was nothing more than an exercise in self-expression. They were talking to themselves, because nobody else was listening. Baal worship evolved because at some point in history, people made up mythical stories about Baal and wrote them down. Then other people made images of Baal and carved them out of wood. But there was nothing in the worship of Baal beyond what human minds had dreamed up and what human hands had made. The whole thing was a cultural creation, and for that reason, it had no authority and no power. Elijah wanted to save the people from that.

There are many people today who have concluded that Christianity evolved in precisely the same way as the worship of Baal did. They assume that the Bible is also a book of ancient myths, and because they assume that it is a creation of human culture, they insist that it has no authority. If they are right in their assumption, then they are right in their conclusion. A religion created by one culture should not be imposed on another; a religion that was merely the choice of one generation should not be foisted on another. If all religions are human creations, then none of them can claim to be true.

But Elijah knew that the living God was no cultural creation. He longed that the knowledge of the living God should be restored in the land. So he began to pray:

> "O LORD, God of Abraham, Isaac and Israel, let it be known
> today that you are God....Answer me, O LORD, answer me, so
> these people will know that you, O LORD, are God." (vv. 36–37)

Elijah was talking about the most fundamental truth in the Bible: "In the beginning God." Before the world began, before cultures developed, before religious writing, before animal, vegetable, or mineral, in the beginning there was God. The world and all that is in it are His handiwork. The living God had revealed Himself to Abraham, Isaac, and Jacob, and the tragedy of our world is that the knowledge of God has been drowned out in the noise created around a thousand substitutes. Elijah longed that his own people should know who God is.

Authentic worship is directed toward the living God. Churches today are often struggling to find ways to stimulate worship. We are in difficulties over worship because we have lost a sense of the weight and glory of the LORD. If we put the living God in the same category as Baal and swallow the world's conviction that all religion is a creation of human minds, we will be in profound difficulties over worship. Like the prophets of Baal, we may find ourselves increasingly desperate in our efforts to provoke a response.

Elijah's approach was very different. He knew that where God's glory was known there would not be a problem over worship. He simply stepped forward and prayed that God would make Himself known. Questions of worship style are entirely secondary.

AUTHENTIC WORSHIP FOCUSES ON AN ACCEPTABLE SACRIFICE

Elijah acted very deliberately as he built the altar of God. He took twelve stones, representing the twelve tribes of Jacob. That was politically incorrect. His audience from the northern tribes would have preferred him to take ten stones. But Elijah took twelve, because he was about to offer a sacrifice to the God of all Israel.

He prepared the sacrifice on the altar, and then in order to make the revelation of the power of God compelling even to skeptics, he poured water over the altar and drenched the sacrifice. And then came a miracle both astonishing and profound in its significance:

> The fire of the LORD fell and burned up the sacrifice. (v. 38)

Try to imagine yourself in the crowd at that moment. You have bought into the prevailing belief of your culture, that all religions are a human creation, and that one religion is essentially the same as another. Now you are sitting on the top of Mount Carmel, and as you watch Elijah praying, suddenly the sky is filled with fire. In an instant, your mind is lucid, and everything falls into place. *Elijah had been speaking the truth. The Lord is God, and now the fire of His judgment is falling on us!*

Here we come to the most wonderful part of the story: "The fire of God fell on the sacrifice." There were thousands of people there, but when God's fire came, it did not fall on them. God's fire was diverted away from them, and onto the altar, where the sacrifice had been prepared.

Something similar happened when the first man and the first woman sinned in the garden and God pronounced judgment. God looked at the serpent and said, "Cursed are you." Then God looked at Adam and said, "Cursed is *the ground* because of you" (Genesis 3:17, italics added). Adam must have expected the curse, but God diverted His judgment to the ground instead. The same thing happened here on Mount Carmel. The fire of God fell, but it did not fall on the people; God struck the sacrifice instead.

SPOTLIGHT ON CHRIST

On another day on a different hill, another sacrifice was offered. When Jesus Christ died at Calvary, the judgment of God fell. But it did not fall on the people; it fell on the sacrifice. It struck Him, and in this way, God created room for men and women from every culture and in every generation to be reconciled to Himself.

The sacrifice of Jesus is the focal point of Christian worship. The worship of heaven is centered around all that Jesus Christ has done for His people. The same should be true of our worship. Authentic worship is truth based, God centered, Christ focused, and Spirit inspired.

When the representatives of the twelve tribes saw the fire, they fell prostrate and cried, "The LORD—he is God! The LORD—he is God!" (v. 39). Watching His awesome power and amazing grace, a group of people made a new and decisive commitment as they confessed their faith in the living God.

This is where true worship brings us. The Scripture makes it clear that it is the work of the Spirit to bring us to the point of confessing the Lord (1 Corinthians 12:3). A man I'll call Bill had been attending a church occasionally for years. His wife was a Christian, and other members of his family were praying for him, but somehow he never made any spiritual progress. One day as Bill was leaving the service, his pastor asked him if he was any nearer becoming a Christian.

"Well, I don't know," he said.

"Don't you think this is a bit pathetic?" said his pastor pointedly. "You say you believe in God and Christ and His death and resurrection. Why don't you confess Christ?"

Later that night Bill's wife phoned the pastor.

"What have you been saying to my husband? He's been phoning up all his colleagues at work and telling them that he is a Christian." The Holy Spirit, through a caring yet candid pastor, had convicted the man of his need to worship the Savior.

Years later, I had the opportunity to speak with Bill. He had grown to have a profound faith and an effective ministry. He laughed as we talked about the story. "I think that I was head-butted into the kingdom," he said. "But it was the greatest thing that has ever happened in my life."

Have you come to a place of decisive commitment to Christ in your own life?

Maybe as you have been learning God's truth, you have seen something of the glory of the living God and His grace to you in Jesus Christ. Why don't you confess faith in Christ today? The Scripture promises, "If you confess with your mouth, 'Jesus is Lord,' and believe in your heart that God raised him from the dead, you will be saved" (Romans 10:9).

UNLOCKED

Authentic worship is always a response to revealed truth. It is directed towards the living God, focused around the Lord Jesus Christ, and inspired by the Holy Spirit.

True worship will be fostered where God's truth is proclaimed, where Jesus Christ is exalted, and where God's people give freedom to the work of the Holy Spirit in their lives. Everything else is secondary.

If you want to grow in your own worship, take time to meditate on who God is. Soak your mind in what God says about Himself in Scripture. Ask God's Spirit to enlarge the capacity of your own heart to appreciate what God has done for you in Christ.

PAUSE FOR PRAYER

O God my Father,

Your word speaks to me today because I see the land where I live, which I love, increasingly filled with false religion. I see a new generation that does not believe in truth and does not know the living God.

Send forth Your Word. Establish Your truth. Let Your glory be known. May I worship You wholly in spirit and truth. Through Jesus Christ my Lord I pray. Amen.

Sin

2 KINGS 17

What is sin and

why is it serious?

21 Sin

2 KINGS 17

900 B.C.

KINGS OF THE NORTH (CONTINUED)

874–853   AHAB

853–852   AHAZIAH

852–841   JORAM

841–814   JEHU

814–798   JEHOAHAZ

800

798–782   JEHOASH

793–753   JEROBOAM II (COREGENT)

753   ZECHARIAH

752   SHALLUM

752–742   MENEHEM

742–740   PEKAHIAH

752–732   PEKAH

732–722   HOSHEA

722   FALL OF THE NORTH

700

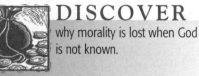

DISCOVER
why morality is lost when God is not known.

LEARN
the story of the ten northern tribes of Israel.

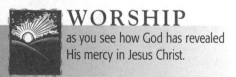

WORSHIP
as you see how God has revealed His mercy in Jesus Christ.

FOR many of our contemporaries, the word *sin* belongs on the dessert menu! When I was in the grocery store recently, I was struck by the names of some of the cookies a shopper could purchase. Two that caught my eye were called "raspberry temptations" and "sinful selections." Those cookies were described as "sinful" because of the amount of chocolate they contained, a fact that would make them attractive to all normal people, except of course for those who had chosen the miserable path of a disciplined diet!

For many people in our culture, *sin* has become a word that describes slightly indulgent things that are entirely legitimate, and which would make most normal people turn a wry smile.

THE BIBLE IN THE BASEMENT

Imagine a thirty-five-year-old husband and father at home on a Sunday morning; let's call him Bob. He has finished reading the Sunday *Tribune* and decides that he will tackle that often postponed task of sorting out his basement. As he sorts through the boxes, Bob comes across an old family Bible that belonged to his grandmother. Something inside tells him he should not throw it away; after all it's rather old, and there are notes in his grandmother's rather frail handwriting on many of the pages. He opens it up to see what it says and he reads that "Christ Jesus came into the world to save sinners" (1 Timothy 1:15).

This strikes Bob as rather quaint. This person Jesus Christ has come into the world to save overindulgent people! Bob likes to enjoy a cream pie and knows that he probably shouldn't, but he does work out in the gym twice a week and is generally in good health. He doesn't particularly need saving. He flicks over a few pages in the Bible to see what else it says, and he reads that God was angry with people who sinned (Hebrews 3:10). This doesn't make any sense to Bob. Why would sin (as he understands it) make God angry? What kind of God would be angry towards people who indulge in a little bit of pleasure?

Even among Christian people, the word *sin* is falling into disuse.

So he closes the Bible reassured that he made the right choice to spend his Sunday morning at home. He loves his wife and his kids and cannot really see why it was that his grandmother thought that the Bible was such a wonderful book.

Clearly the word *sin* has been assigned a new meaning in our culture, one Christians must be careful not to adopt. We must always recognize that sin is disobeying God and His laws. It is rebellion against God, not a harmless pleasure.

Sadly, even among Christian people, the word *sin* is falling into disuse. People used to come to church to confess their sins. Catholics did it personally through the confessional, and Protestant pastors led in a prayer to confess the sins of the whole congregation, and the people would say "Amen" because they all felt that they could identify with what he was saying. But "God, have mercy on me, a sinner" (Luke 18:13) the humble cry in the New Testament, is a prayer that is fast disappearing even from evangelical churches. We celebrate grace, but we do not confess sin.

If we did, it would probably be couched in contemporary language. "As we come to prayer this morning, let us confess our struggles to get in touch with ourselves, and especially our need to be more authentic. Lord be merciful to me, a person who needs to be more intentional about developing my full potential."

As long as we hide behind politically correct verbiage, we will never understand what God says about sin, and if you do not feel that sin is your greatest problem, you will not be able to make sense of Christianity. Jesus Christ came to save His people from their sins.

SIN IN THE NORTHERN KINGDOM

As we noted in the previous chapter, God's people became divided after the death of Solomon. The ten tribes in the north declared their independence from the two tribes in the south. The tragedy of the northern tribes was that they separated themselves from the blessing of God. God had promised He would bless the line of

David's descendants, who continued to rule from Jerusalem in the south. There the royal line of David continued, with the king typically transferring power to his son as he approached death.

In the north, however, with no established royal house, most of the kings came to power by murdering their predecessor. Political intrigue and sin abounded. The northern kingdom lasted about two hundred years. There were nineteen kings altogether, and every one of them "did evil in the eyes of the Lord."

Eventually, God allowed enemies to overrun the northern kingdom. The people were deported and the whole area became a kind of wasteland. Second Kings 17 is an important chapter in the Bible story because it tells us why God brought the northern kingdom down.

THE PRIORITY OF GODLINESS

> *All this took place because the Israelites had sinned against the* LORD *their God....They worshiped other gods....They worshiped idols, though the* LORD *had said, "You shall not do this." (17:7, 12)*

Jeroboam, who was the first king of the ten northern tribes, did not want his people going to Jerusalem to worship God. So he established his own religion at Dan and Bethel, where he set up two golden calves (see page 253). This was the beginning of two hundred years in which these people turned away from the LORD, so that by the time of Ahab, a prophet who spoke about the living God did so under threat of his life.

If you want to get a sense of what life was like in the later years of the northern kingdom, read the book of Amos. He describes a community where the rich lived in opulence and showed a total disregard for the poor. The streets were filled with violence. One of the greatest atrocities in Israel was an obscene practice in which parents gave up unwanted children and allowed them to be burned in the fire. This society had become sick at the core.

But it is very significant that the first charge God brought against His people was not the violence, the murder, the greed, or the cruelty. The first complaint against them was that they had worshiped other gods (17:7).

This should not surprise us, as the first four commandments are all about God Himself. "You shall have no other gods before me. You shall not make for yourself an idol....You shall not misuse the name of the LORD your God...Remember the

Sabbath day by keeping it holy" (Exodus 20:3–4, 7–8). These are God's funda-mental requirements for His people.

Our first calling is to give God His place. The Bible calls this *godliness*, or a God-centered life. The priority of godliness is confirmed by the teaching of Jesus. When asked, " 'Which is the greatest commandment in the Law?' Jesus replied: 'Love the LORD your God with all your heart and with all your soul and with all your mind' " (Matthew 22:36–37).

THE PRIORITY OF RIGHTEOUSNESS

After God calls us to godliness, He speaks about our attitudes and actions towards other people. "Honor your father and your mother…You shall not murder. You shall not commit adultery. You shall not steal. You shall not [lie]. You shall not covet" (Exodus 20:12–17).

This is God's second calling for His people. The Bible calls such restraint *righteousness*. Righteous living is a faithful reflection of the attitudes and actions of God in our relationships with other people. Christ confirmed this as the second priority, when He said that the second commandment is, "Love your neighbor as yourself" (Matthew 22:39).

It's crucial we understand the order of these two priorities. True godliness—a God-centered life—will result in increasing evidence of righteousness. Put another way, godliness will cause us to reflect the attitudes and actions of God in our relationships with other people. Righteousness is built on the foundation of godliness, and so when people reject godliness, they find that righteousness is beyond their grasp. You cannot have righteousness if you do not have godliness. You cannot reflect the attitudes and actions of God until you have a God-centered life!

This is the message of 2 Kings (and 1 Kings 12; 15:25–22:53), which gives us a record of two hundred years of history. The story teaches us that when a nation turns away from the living God, the result will be moral confusion and the unleash-ing of sin and evil. In the northern kingdom, sin began with the people rejecting God, and it ended with them putting their children through the fire. The reason they lost the morality of the Bible is that they rejected the God of the Bible. You cannot have righteousness without godliness.

BOB'S BIGGEST PROBLEM: LIFE WITHOUT GOD

This is a truth that our culture desperately needs to hear: *You cannot have righteousness without godliness.* Our friend Bob, who is clearing out his basement on Sunday morning, wants his family to enjoy the benefits of righteousness. He wants to have an ordered family life and his kids to respect him. He wants his children to be free from the fear of violence. He wants his marriage to succeed, and he would like the people who do business with him, to be honest and keep to their word. He expects public officials not to tell lies, and he wants his own property to be protected and safe.

Bob wants all the benefits of righteousness, but he does not want God, and that is his first and greatest sin. Bob is godless. Bob is a successful, laid-back, regular family man who wants the best for himself and his family, but he will not let God be God! The book of 2 Kings is telling us that when people turn away from God, they lose the benefits of righteousness.

It is a great mistake to think that our hearts are filled with a natural love for God. "The sinful mind is hostile to God" (Romans 8:7). Unless God changes our hearts, it is natural for us to resent God because His power seems to threaten our freedom. Further, we resent God because His holiness offends our pride, and His complete knowledge of us seems like an invasion of privacy. And the fact that He will never change means that there will never be a time when He steps down from power, or becomes more tolerant of things that He presently disapproves, or when His memory fails and our deeds slip beyond His recall!

Unless God changes our hearts, this is what we feel about Him. The sinful mind is hostile to God, and that is the root of our sin. Sin originates with the rejection of God.

PROVOKING THE ANGER OF GOD

> *They did wicked things that* provoked *the LORD to anger…*
> *They practiced divination and sorcery and sold themselves*
> *to do evil in the eyes of the LORD, provoking him to anger.*
> (17:11, 17, EMPHASIS ADDED)

The anger of God is one of the most misunderstood truths of the Bible. Notice the word *provoked*. Anger is not a part of the nature of God. God is always holy, He is always love, and He is always true, but He is not always angry.

Many of the pagan gods were angry in their nature. They were always smoldering and constantly needing to be appeased. So offerings were given to placate them and settle them down. But their anger never went away, it was never spent, it was only contained. But when you come to the Bible, you find something entirely different.

"The LORD is…slow to anger" (Psalm 103:8). It is not a part of God's nature to be angry, but He can be provoked to anger.

This is part of the perfection of God. A God who was not provoked when people made their children pass through a fire could hardly be worshiped. We do not admire those who stand idly by while others are being abused.

God is immensely patient. For two hundred years, He restrained judgment and sent the prophets to call the people back to godliness and righteousness, but the people "would not listen" (2 Kings 17:14). Eventually, God was provoked.

Notice what God does when He is provoked to anger:

> So the LORD was very angry with Israel and removed them from his presence…The LORD removed them from his presence, as he had warned through all his servants the prophets. (17:18, 23)

Where it says "his presence," it means the land where God had put His name. God acted upon His repeated warnings through the prophets. And then we are told how this happened: "The people of Israel were taken from their homeland into exile in Assyria" (v. 23).

That is hell: eternity outside the blessing of God.

This pattern began in the Garden of Eden. Adam decided that he did not want to live under the rule of God. His ungodliness led to unrighteousness as he broke God's commandment, with the result that he was driven out of the presence of God. Now in the two books of Kings we find that the people turned away from worshiping the living God, and that led to all kinds of unrighteousness, with the result that God drove His people out from the land that He had promised to bless.

At the end of the Bible story, we are told that every person who has ever lived will stand before God, and the ungodly and the unrighteous will be driven from the presence of God. That is hell: eternity outside the blessing of God. If a person refuses to bow before God and say, "Your will be done," a time will come when God will say to that person, "Your will be done. Depart from me forever."

The book of Romans, which contains the most systematic explanation of the Christian faith in the Bible begins with the apostle Paul reminding readers that "the wrath of God is revealed from heaven against all the *ungodliness* and *unrighteousness* of men" (Romans 1:18 NKJV, italics added).

That is the fundamental issue. The message to an unbelieving world is not that following Jesus is the best way to a more satisfying life. Paul was saying, "You need to understand that you are facing an immense problem. The wrath of God is revealed from heaven against all the godlessness and unrighteousness of men!" This is why what he had to say about Jesus Christ is so urgent. This is why he was so passionate about it, and why we must use all possible means to communicate this same message today.

AN OPPORTUNITY FOR THE MERCY OF GOD

The people had rejected the Lord and refused His invitation to return to Him. God was provoked to anger, and He removed them from His presence. The land God had promised to bless lay desolate and uninhabited.

But it wasn't long before the king of Assyria repopulated the area by bringing people from all over his empire and settling these people in the area previously occupied by the ten northern tribes. Immigrants came from Babylon, Cuthah, Avva, Hamath, and Sepharvaim and settled in the land (17:24).

Apparently while the Promised Land was left desolate, the number of wild animals increased; so when these new immigrants arrived, they faced some unexpected problems. A number of them were attacked by lions that seemed to be roaming freely. The new immigrants didn't have the faintest idea of what to do about this problem. They would have been brought up to believe that a different god is responsible for each area of countryside, so they naturally assumed that the lions were some kind of plague from whichever god was in charge of this area.

Word of the problem got back to the king of Assyria, who thought that the best way to deal with the situation would be to find a priest from among the people who used to live there. He assumed that a local priest would know what to do to placate whatever god was causing this problem, and so he gave orders for a priest to be found and sent back to Israel. But this priest did more than the king intended. According to the Scripture,

> One of the priests who had been exiled from Samaria came to
> live in Bethel and taught them how to worship the LORD. (v. 28)

Here was God's mercy in action. He brought people from the north, south, east, and west into the place He had promised to bless, and when they were there, God sent one of His own people to them so that they could discover the truth of the living God. Those who were outside the scope of God's kingdom were brought near. God's promise was not just to bless Israel, but that through Israel all the nations of the earth would be blessed (see Genesis 22:18).

Over a period of time this multiethnic population became confused because each national group made its own gods as well (17:29). So these people had some truth mixed with a lot of error, but there was a witness to the truth among them for the first time.

The story of these immigrant people soon would intertwine with that of the Hebrew people. One hundred and fifty years later, the people of the southern kingdom were also taken into exile. Seventy years later, a group of these Hebrew people came back under the leadership of Ezra and Nehemiah to rebuild the temple of God. Ezra tells us that these northern settlers—foreigners who worshiped God (and sometimes other gods as well)—offered to help in the rebuilding of the Jerusalem temple. The Jews quickly refused their offer of help (see Ezra 4:1–3). They made it plain that the temple was to be built by the people of God, and that the northern settlers could have nothing to do with it.

After that, the Samaritans, as these people came to be known, opposed the work that was going on and became bitter enemies of the Jews. Later they decided that they would build their own temple, on Mount Gerizim, where the blessings of God had been spoken when God's people came into the land. From then on, the Jews would have nothing to do with Samaritans.

SPOTLIGHT ON CHRIST

Four hundred years later Jesus Christ came into the world. John tells us that "he had to go through Samaria" (John 4:4). He met a woman there who, not surprisingly considering her Samaritan background, had some knowledge of the truth, with a great deal of confusion mixed in. She also had a disastrous personal life, having had five husbands and now living with a man out of wedlock. She was hung up on some questions about the appropriate place to worship. She wondered whether people had to worship in the Jewish temple in Jerusalem or whether the Samaritan temple on Mount Gerizim would do (John 4:20).

This woman was both godless and unrighteous. But notice that as Christ counseled her, He did not begin by telling her that God was angry about her sins. Christ tells her that God is seeking "worshipers [who] will worship the Father in spirit and truth" (4:23). He began by guiding her toward a right relationship with God.

Godliness is the foundation of righteousness, and there is little point in talking about issues of righteousness to people who do not know God. Christ began by speaking to the Samaritan woman about knowing God because things could only change for her when she discovered the transforming power of a God-centered life!

Christ died to deal with our ungodliness and our unrighteousness. On the cross, the Father treated the Son as if He had lived a godless life, and as if He were guilty of every kind of unrighteousness that had been known in the history of the human race. The Father turned away from the Son, and Christ was shut out from the presence of God. That is why He cried out, "My God, my God, why have You forsaken me?" (Matthew 27:46)

Christ became the godless one and the unrighteous one. He did this in order to bring us back into a right relationship with God and restore us to a righteous life. "Christ died for sins once and for all, the righteous for the unrighteous, to bring you to God" (1 Peter 3:18).

Jesus Christ is able to bring godless and unrighteous people to God. If you will come to Him, He will make you godly. He will lead you into a God-centered life that will be the foundation of growing in righteousness.

Paul begins the book of Romans by telling us that "the wrath of God is being revealed from heaven against all godlessness and wickedness of men." But then he explains what Christ has achieved on the cross and says, "There is now no condemnation for those who are in Christ Jesus" (Romans 1:18; 8:1).

I've sometimes been asked why God created the world if He knew that Adam would sin. One of the answers to that is that if there had never been sin, the mercy of God would never have been known or revealed.

Angels have experienced God's holiness, His truth, and His love, but because they have never sinned, they have never experienced God's mercy. It must have been quite staggering for them to watch as Jesus Christ came into the world and they saw what it meant for the one they had always worshiped to bear the sins of others. A whole new dimension of the character of God was revealed to them—and to us. God has always been merciful, but it was our sin that caused that mercy to be revealed.

UNLOCKED

Sin is breaking the law of God. Jesus summed up the law when He said that we are to love God with our whole heart and our neighbors as ourselves. God's two great priorities for His people are godliness and righteousness.

The northern tribes took the wrong path when they allowed idols to take the place of God. The decline of the nation began with them losing the knowledge of God; it ended with them putting their children in the fire. Morality cannot be sustained when a people lose the knowledge of God.

Eventually, God's anger was provoked, and He brought judgment to the ten northern tribes. They were invaded by the armies of Assyria, and the people were scattered. Eventually they were replaced by an immigrant population who became known as the Samaritans, and God's grace came to these people also.

Christ came into the world to save His people from sin and its consequences. When we come to Him, He will lead us in paths of righteousness.

PAUSE FOR PRAYER

Father in heaven,

I recognize that I am a sinner by nature and by practice. I thank You that You sent Christ into the world to save sinners.

Help me to live a godly life and to love You with my whole heart. Then help me to love others, and to reflect Your character to them in my attitudes and actions. May Your name be known and honored in our nation, through Jesus Christ our Lord. Amen.

22

Righteousness

2 KINGS 22–23

What is

righteousness,

and how can

it be established

in our land?

22Righteousness

2 KINGS 22–23

DISCOVER
why one of the greatest attempts to call the nation back to the Bible failed.

LEARN
why no government can enforce righteousness.

WORSHIP
as you see how Christ brings our hearts into line with God's law.

HOW would you feel if, in the news one morning, you discovered that forty-two of the fifty American states had left the union? Each of the forty-two had a completely independent government and armed forces, and refused to pay taxes. Then, what if several years later, those forty-two independent states collapsed and were overrun by enemies?

As a citizen in one of the eight remaining united states, you would no longer be part of a world superpower. Instead, you would be a citizen of a rather small and vulnerable country. Enemies who were once thousands of miles away could now move military installations very close to your border. What once seemed strong and secure would now seem weak and vulnerable.

That must have been how it was for the people of God in the two tribes that made up the southern kingdom of Judah. In the time of David, Israel had been a dominant power, with the twelve tribes united and the kings—Saul, David, and Solomon—ruling from the south. During Solomon's reign, admiring heads of state came to Jerusalem to see the achievements of the world's leading country.

But after ten of the twelve tribes declared their independence, things changed radically for the south. The nation was diminished militarily and economically. And within two hundred years, the whole of the northern area would be overrun by enemies, and the ten tribes were scattered.

If you were in the south at that point, you were among the remaining few of a once-magnificent kingdom; you were part of a vulnerable group of the descendants of Judah and Benjamin. All that remained was two tribes.

God's promise to bless the descendants of Abraham and then to bring blessing to all the nations of the world through them at that point must have looked very doubtful. But God's promise to bless His people had never been revoked, and although the people of the southern kingdom, usually referred to in the Bible as Judah, went through some harrowing times, God was faithful to His promise.

THE UPS AND DOWNS OF LEADERSHIP

For many years, the people of Judah had the benefit of better leadership than their brothers and sisters in the north. Both 1 and 2 Kings say that every one of the nineteen northern kings "did evil in the eyes of the LORD" or "did not turn away from any of the sins of [the previous king],"[1] but in the south, there were a number of kings who "did what was right in the eyes of the LORD." (2 Kings 15:3).

Things took a turn for the worse when Manasseh came to the throne. He was to the south what Ahab had been in the north. He reigned for fifty-five years (21:1) and brought more trouble to God's people than anyone else. "Manasseh led them astray, so that they did more evil than the nations the LORD had destroyed before the Israelites" (21:9).

God had driven the Canaanites and Perizzites out of the land because of their sins, but now God's own people were doing things that were worse! Manasseh promoted the worship of Molech, which included an evil rite in which children were sacrificed in a fire (21:6). After half a century of this, God's anger was provoked. If God judged the Amorites for their sins, then how could He restrain judgment on His own people when they did the same things? (See 21:11.) They were called to be a light in a dark place, but the reality was that they were living in the same darkness as the people around them!

At the end of Manasseh's reign, his son Amon came to the throne, but he lasted only two years before he was murdered, and so a boy by the name of Josiah became king when he was only eight years old.

THE INFLUENCE OF A GODLY LEADER

> [Josiah] did what was right in the eyes of the LORD and walked in all the ways of his father David, not turning aside to the right or to the left. (22:2)

This was one remarkable kid! He began to seek the Lord in the eighth year of his reign (2 Chronicles 34:3), which would be at age sixteen. As a teenager he developed a heart for God, and that became the foundation of the character of a great man. It is never too early to seek God.

So here we have a godly young leader who wanted to get Judah back on the right lines. What was he to do? He had no Bible training to draw on. His father (Amon) and grandfather (Manasseh) certainly had not given him any kind of model to follow. Josiah grew up in what we would call a spiritually confused and biblically illiterate culture, and yet deep within his heart, there was a longing to know God.

REDISCOVERING THE BIBLE

Josiah knew that the living God was to be worshiped in the temple, so he decided that he would begin his attempt at turning things around by refurbishing the temple of God. That would take money, so he set about raising the money through taxes, which were collected at the temple.

Then in the eighteenth year of his reign (at age twenty-six), the king and his people began the renovation (22:3). Josiah sent his secretary Shaphan to tell Hilkiah the high priest to hand the money over to the supervisors, who would pay the builders. Hilkiah entered the temple to collect the money, which presumably was being stored in some kind of vault, and while in the vault the high priest discovered a dusty old book that would change the direction of the nation.

> Hilkiah the high priest said to Shaphan the secretary, "I have
> found the Book of the Law in the temple of the LORD." (22:8)

It is extraordinary that the leading religious figure of the day did not know where to find a copy of the Word of God! This "Book of the Law" was almost certainly a copy of the book of Deuteronomy, and one wonders how it could possibly have become lost in, of all places, the temple!

Remember that Judah had gone through half a century in which the pattern of national life had been to resist the LORD and push against the boundaries of every area of His law. The Word of God did not sit comfortably with the prevailing trend of the culture. God's Law roundly condemned most of the things that Manasseh had done, and everybody knew what had happened to the brave prophets who had spoken the Word of God in the north: Jezebel had put them to death.

So it is not very difficult to imagine why the priests in the time of Manasseh ignored the Scripture. If the priests had preached from the Word of God, they would have found themselves on a collision course with some of the central values of the culture. If the high priest had preached from the Scriptures, he would have had to say that there is one living God and that the worship of all other gods is an offense to God's glory. That would have led to trouble in Judah during Manasseh's time, just as such a statement would lead to trouble today.

> The priests ran the entire program of the temple without ever needing to open the Scriptures.

So the high priest in Manasseh's day probably placed the Bible in the vault of the temple and offered in its place short talks that gave encouragement to everyone. Now, fifty years later a new generation of the people of God arose that did not know the law of God, and so lacked any idea of what righteousness is.

The amazing thing is that the priests continued their work in the temple without ever using the Scriptures. What were they doing all day? Presumably they became experts in administration, pastoral counseling, and organizing social events, but apparently the priests ran the entire program of the temple without ever needing to open the Scriptures.

That practice has returned today. The apostle Paul warned us that "the time will come when [people] will not put up with sound doctrine…[but] will gather around them a number of teachers to say what their itching ears want to hear" (2 Timothy 4:3). They will not want preaching that talks about righteousness. Indeed, many people today seek pastors who tell a few stories, crack a few jokes, and offer the people something along the lines of "chicken soup for the soul." You don't need the Bible to do that. But if the church chooses this path, then within a generation they may well have young people like Josiah growing up, who long to know God but do not know where to find Him. They go to church, but they do not find Him there.

Until age twenty-six, that's where Josiah was—longing to know God but not knowing where to find Him. Then Shaphan turned up with the long-lost Book of the Law and read it to the king.

REDISCOVERING RIGHT AND WRONG

The book of Deuteronomy contains the Ten Commandments and all the regulations about how God's people were to live when they entered the land. It contains the blessings and the cursings that would follow obedience or disobedience, and it ends with a record of how the people of God renewed their covenant with God and committed themselves to live according to His law.

All this was read to the king, and "when the king heard the words of the Book of the Law, he tore his robes" (22:11). Josiah took the Bible seriously. When the commandments were read to him, he said, "We are not doing this."

How could they have strayed so far from what God required? Without the Word, the people had no criteria for telling right from wrong. So they were reduced to operating on consensus, and that seemed to change with every generation! By the time of Manasseh there had been a consensus that it is sometimes right to put your children in the fire.

The Bible has a very simple definition of righteousness and of evil. What God says is right, is right, and what God says is evil, is evil. Righteousness is revealed in the Word of God. And if righteousness is to be restored to our nation, then the Bible must be restored to the churches, and those who love God must get serious about putting the Bible into practice.

Josiah gives us a wonderful model of this. He heard the Word of God, took it seriously, and then he said, "This is how I am going to live." He did more than read the Bible. He wanted to put it into practice, and he wanted to begin with his own life at the age of twenty-six. As he listened to the Scriptures, he was gripped by a radical new vision of obedience to the Word of God. What would it be like if life was lived fully according to the Law of God?

This was the vision that fired up D. L. Moody after he arrived in England. An English evangelist said to him, "The world is yet to see what God will do with a man who is wholeheartedly given to Him." Moody said, "By the grace of God, I will be that man."

Josiah also wanted to be that man, so he gathered the elders and the people together for a rally at the temple. Imagine the sea of faces as a great crowd gathered around the temple area. Josiah read the whole of the book of Deuteronomy to the people, and then he stood by the pillar of the temple and made a personal and public commitment to obey the Lord (23:2–3). Then he had all the rest of the people make the same commitment (2 Chronicles 34:32).

LEADING A REFORMATION

Then Josiah went through the country on a kind of "reformation tour." Wherever he found altars, Asherah poles, or other evidences of idolatry in the land, he completely destroyed them. It was the greatest onslaught against pagan practices in the history of Israel. Josiah went right through the area of Judah and even extended his activity into the now desolate areas of the north.

The significance of Josiah's reform can be measured from the fact that he destroyed the altars that Solomon had authorized for the sake of his foreign wives (23:13). These altars had stood for three hundred years. No other king had been prepared to do anything about them. Then, when Josiah went to the north, he destroyed the altar in Bethel, where Jeroboam had set up a golden calf. That altar had also stood for three hundred years. Other kings had promoted the worship of God but none of Josiah's predecessors in the north or the south had the courage and political will to destroy the pagan altars in the land. Josiah was doing what no other king before him had been prepared to do.

Later, when Josiah sent a delegation to a prophetess named Huldah, she sent him this message:

> "Tell the king of Judah, who sent you to inquire of the LORD, 'This is what the LORD, the God of Israel, says concerning the words you heard: Because your heart was responsive and you humbled yourself before the LORD…I have heard you, declares the LORD. Therefore I will gather you to your fathers, and you will be buried in peace. Your eyes will not see all the disaster I am going to bring on this place.'" (22:18–20)

God honored Josiah's leadership and held back judgment on the nation during his lifetime. King Josiah died in peace, and the book of Kings gives Josiah a sterling epitaph that reflects praise for his personal integrity.

> Neither before nor after Josiah was there a king like him who turned to the LORD as he did—with all his heart and with all his soul and with all his strength, in accordance with all the Law of Moses. (23:25)

You couldn't ask for a much better personal epitaph than that. But there were limitations to his achievement. "Nevertheless, the LORD did not turn away from the heat of his fierce anger, which burned against Judah because of all that Manasseh had done to provoke him to anger" (v. 26).

The explanation lay in the hearts of the people. A holy God observed their past and present evils. Consequences would still come.

RIGHTEOUSNESS BEGINS IN EACH PERSON'S HEART

God had said, "If my people...will humble themselves and pray and seek my face and turn from their wicked ways...[I] will heal their land" (2 Chronicles 7:14). But there was precious little evidence of a change of heart among the people during Josiah's reign.

Most of the change came as the direct result of Josiah's own activity. He had to go around the country and personally oversee the destruction of these altars. It was not a popular uprising of the people; it was all done by state intervention! It was Josiah who did away with the pagan priests (2 Kings 23:5) and took the Asherah pole from the temple of the Lord (v. 6) and "tore down the quarters of the male shrine prostitutes,...desecrated Topheth, which was in the Valley of Ben Himmon,...[and] pulled down the altars the kings of Judah had erected on the roof" (vv. 7, 10, 12).

There was a strong element of coercion involved in all of this. When Josiah held his great rally to renew commitment to the covenant, we are told that "he had everyone in Jerusalem and Benjamin pledge themselves to it" (2 Chronicles 34:32). So it is not surprising to find that "as long as he lived, they did not fail to follow the LORD, the God of their fathers" (2 Chronicles 34:33). But as soon as Josiah died, the inevitable happened. Things went back to the way they were before.

The book of Jeremiah gives us a fascinating insight into the limitations of Josiah's reform. God said to the prophet, "'Judah did not return to me with all her heart, but only in pretense,' declares the LORD" (Jeremiah 3:10).

> *"I will put my law in their minds and write it on their hearts."*
> (JEREMIAH 31:33)

With the right leader you can change the laws of the land. But unless the hearts of the people are changed at the same time, it will only lead to disappointment in the long term.

When Josiah used his political power in an attempt to change the face of the nation, the people conformed to the tide of cultural pressure. But that was as far as the change went. Under a new king, the tide moved in a different direction.

It is not difficult to conform to the expected patterns of Christian behavior. But if all you do is conform to the expectations of others, then you will find that when you are with a different crowd, you adapt to a new tide of cultural pressure. Patterns of behavior can sometimes be little more than a reflection of our environment.

As long as there was no change in the people's hearts, a reformation of morals led by the king would not last long after the king died. Righteousness must flow from the heart! The greatest question for the church is not how to change the laws of the land, but how to change the hearts of the people.

Some years after Josiah's bold attempt to change the face of the nation, God spoke again to the prophet Jeremiah. It must have been hard for Jeremiah to see the people slide back into their old idolatrous ways after the death of the good king, but that was when God gave one of the most wonderful promises in the whole of the Old Testament: "'The time is coming,' declares the LORD, 'when I will make a new covenant with the house of Israel and with the house of Judah....*I will put my law in their minds and write it on their hearts*. I will be their God, and they will be my people" (Jeremiah 31:31, 33; italics added).

Some years later, God gave the same promise through the prophet Ezekiel: "I will give you a new heart and put a new spirit in you; I will remove from you your heart of stone and give you a heart of flesh. And I will put my Spirit in you and move you to follow my decrees and be careful to keep my laws" (Ezekiel 36:26–27).

That must have sounded like a dream to the prophets. Josiah had been able to put the law on the statute book, but he could not put the law into the people's minds. He could enforce the law of God in the courts, but he could not put it into people's hearts. But now God was promising to do what no state, no church, and no parent could ever do: to get His law into the minds and the hearts of the people. God was promising to bring a fundamental change in the thinking of His people, so that they thought along the same lines as the law of God.

He would bring a change in their hearts so that they would want what God commanded. They would have a new hunger and thirst for righteousness. Jeremiah must have wondered how on earth God would do it.

SPOTLIGHT ON CHRIST

Six hundred years later another King was born into the line of Josiah. One night, He went into an upper room, and He took a cup filled with wine. He said, "This cup is the new covenant in my blood, which is poured out for you" (Luke 22:20). He was talking about the new covenant God had promised to Jeremiah, in which God would bring an inner change to the way His people think and feel.

Then, He went out from the upper room, down into a garden where He was arrested, and the next day He was crucified. On the third day, He rose from the dead.

This King, the risen LORD Jesus Christ, invites all to come to Him. He invites us to come as we are, with our confused minds and our stubborn hearts.

When we come to Him, He puts the desire for righteousness in us. That is the promise of the new covenant. God gives us more than His law, He gives us Himself! When God's Spirit enters your soul, He creates new desires and capacities within you. That is why a Christian loves God and longs for righteousness. That is why a Christian prays, and why, when a Christian sins, it is not long before he or she feels the need to come to Christ and be forgiven.

This hunger and thirst for righteousness is one of the greatest blessings of the Christian life. Those who hunger for what God forbids will, in the end, experience emptiness and frustration, but those who have an inner desire for what God wants will be satisfied. Jesus said, "Blessed are those who hunger and thirst for righteousness, for they will be filled" (Matthew 5:6).

Don't rest content with an outward conformity to Christian values when Christ can give you a new heart.

UNLOCKED

God has reserved the right to tell us what is good and what is evil, what is right and what is wrong; and man's first sin in the Garden of Eden was to assume that right for himself. We still want to take God's place and decide what is right for ourselves. When someone says, "It may not be right for you, but it's right for me," he is saying that the individual can determine right and wrong. But God tells us what righteousness is in His law. Righteousness is what God says is right.

Righteousness cannot be imposed by governments because it must flow from the heart. Of course, good laws are better than bad ones, and they have great value in educating people in what is good and restraining what is evil. Good laws backed up with appropriate penalties for breaking them will usually bring some modification of behavior. But the law cannot bring a change of heart, and that is why attempts to impose religion always fail.

God's purpose is not to impose an outward conformity to the law but to cultivate an inward desire for righteousness. This is the work of the Holy Spirit. It involves changing our hearts to give us a hunger and thirst for righteousness, and new capacity to pursue a life that is pleasing to God.

PAUSE FOR PRAYER

Almighty Father,

Forgive me for the arrogance with which I often try to decide what is right and wrong for myself, instead of listening to what You say in Your Word. Bring my mind and my heart into line with Your words, and help me to count what You say is right as right and what You say is wrong as wrong. Help me to agree not only in my head but also in my heart, and help me to follow through by doing what You command and turning from what You forbid.

Create a new hunger and thirst for righteousness in our land. Begin among Your people, but let that hunger sweep into the lives of those who are not yet Your people. Begin a new work in many hearts, by the power of Your Spirit. In the name of Jesus Christ our Lord I pray. Amen.

NOTE

1. Twenty-three times in 1 and 2 Kings we are told that the kings of Israel (that is, the northern kingdom) "did evil in the eyes of the Lord." Of ten of the nineteen kings it was said that the current monarch "did not turn away from any of the sins of [the previous king]."

Joy

NEHEMIAH 8

How can God's

people experience

His joy?

23 Joy
NEHEMIAH 8

DISCOVER
the joy of obedience.

LEARN
how a community was discipled
around the Word of God.

WORSHIP
as you anticipate the joy that God
is preparing for His people.

IN 1999, near the close of the second millennium, scores of earthquakes rocked the world, but the most devastating was in Izmit, Turkey. The Turkey quake, measuring 7.4 on the Richter scale, killed an estimated 15,000 people. Centered 115 miles east of Istanbul, the quake's toll brought enormous grief to families of the victims.

During the early days of the rescue, however, technology gave many families some hope. Rescue teams from twelve countries sent a variety of equipment to locate survivors, including video cameras, sensitive microphones, and locator dogs—all able to detect bodies under rubble that otherwise would go unseen and unheard.

The trapped survivors, weak or even unconscious, could not cry out, but the dogs or equipment would point rescuers to the site, and hours later, survivors were pulled out alive, placed on stretchers, and delivered to hospitals where they'd make a full recovery.

For the parents and spouses of trapped victims, hope remained as long as there were reports of rescues. However, the likelihood of survival decreased with the passing of time. Eventually, after days of no rescues and with fears of airborne disease, a decision was made to call off the search and clear the rubble.

The last glimmer of hope had faded.

In the waning years of the southern kingdom of Judah, Josiah's great attempt to call people back to the Bible was the last glimmer of hope, and after it faded, God allowed enemies to reduce His own city to a pile of rubble.

God used the power of Babylon to bring discipline to His people. The Babylonian army laid siege to Jerusalem. There was a terrible loss of life, and those who survived either fled for their lives or were taken prisoner and marched off to resettlement camps in Babylon.

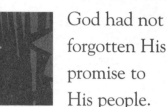

God had not forgotten His promise to His people.

The city where God had put His name became a smoldering ruin, and silence reigned where a community of believers had once lifted their voices in worship. The temple that had once been filled with the cloud of God's presence was completely destroyed.

But God had not forgotten His promise to His people, and after seventy years, the exiled people of Israel watched as the Babylonian empire fell, to the rising empire of the Medes and Persians. Soon the new king, Cyrus, gave the decree that any Jewish exiles who wished to return to Jerusalem and rebuild a temple to the living God were free to do so.

Only about fifty thousand people responded to the challenge (Ezra 2:64–67). But they had caught the vision of rebuilding the temple and forming a new community in the city of God.

It was a small group for such a large task, but they were fired up by the opportunity to return home and serve the LORD. The first challenge was to build homes. Perhaps they would have thought about how, when their ancestors had first come into the land, God had given them homes they did not build and vineyards they did not plant. But there was nothing like that on this occasion. The land had been untended and laid waste. These people had to do it the hard way. They had to saw every timber and hammer every nail.

When their homes were complete, Zerubbabel, who was leading this first group of returning exiles, called the people together to build an altar (Ezra 3:1–2). When it was finished, the people once more began to offer sacrifices as God had commanded Moses. Next they began the task of rebuilding the temple, and when the work was completed, there was great joy.

Then God raised up a man called Ezra. "Ezra came up from Babylon. He was a teacher well versed in the Law of Moses, which the LORD, the God of Israel, had given....The hand of the LORD his God was on him" (Ezra 7:6).

After Ezra arrived in Jerusalem and discovered the spiritual condition of the people, he sat down appalled and remained there in a stunned silence until the end of the day (see Ezra 9:2–4). He could hardly believe that the people of God in the city of God knew so little about the Word of God.

A few years later, God raised up another man named Nehemiah, who was a brilliant planner and organizer. He also came to Jerusalem and saw that, although the temple had been completed, nothing had been done about the walls. The great city of God had no defenses, was underpopulated, and had precious little infrastructure. God put it into Nehemiah's heart to do something about all of this.

The story of the rebuilding of Jerusalem is a wonderful example of how God brings people with different gifts together to get His work done. Despite adversity, they succeeded, finding strength in "the joy of the LORD" (Nehemiah 8:10). God used a builder, a Bible teacher, and a strategic planner, and in His strength God's people achieved great things.

Ezra was faced with the challenge of teaching the Bible to a community of people who thought they knew the Lord, but actually knew very little about the Bible. Most of the people who returned to Jerusalem had spent their whole lives in a pagan culture. They had been surrounded by the language and literature of the Babylonians, and although some, like Daniel, had no doubt maintained the distinctives of their faith, many had become assimilated into their surrounding culture. They knew that they were the people of God, but they knew very little about the God whose people they were.

More than five hundred years had passed since the cloud of God's glory had filled Solomon's temple. By the time of Nehemiah, these events were ancient history! So how could these people be molded into a worshiping community who loved the LORD and were committed to obeying His law? The answer was the Word of God!

BRING OUT THE BIBLE!

On a truly remarkable occasion, fifty thousand people gathered in a public square to worship God. Then they made a request:

> They told Ezra the scribe to bring out the Book of the Law
> of Moses, which the LORD had commanded for Israel.
> (NEHEMIAH 8:1)

Now how do fifty thousand people make a request? They chant! So we have to assume that this crowd, gathered in high spirits and with a great hunger for the Word of God, grew impatient for events to get underway. They began to shout,

"We want the Bible; bring out the Bible!" or something similar.

It must have been a great joy for Ezra to bring out the Scriptures and to teach this vast crowd the Word of God. These people had been starved for Bible teaching for most of their lives, and now they were committing themselves to a new life of faith and obedience to God, and they were hungry for the Word of God.

THE VALUE OF FAMILY WORSHIP

Ezra the priest brought the Law before the assembly, which was made up of men and women and all who were able to understand. (v. 2)

"All who were able to understand" means children were there too. It is a powerful thing to bring children into an environment where they see adults worshiping and taking the Word of God seriously. I thank God for the impact of that in my own life. As a child, I would sit on the pew in a small Baptist church in Scotland with my grandmother, grandfather, mother, father, and younger brother. I usually tried to get near my grandmother because she carried candies in her bag, and I became an expert at taking the wrappers off without the slightest hint of a sound!

My parents and grandparents had their Bibles open on their laps, so I learned to do the same. When the pastor said, "You see it says in verse two," a finger would come out from the left or from the right and land on my Bible right by verse two, just in case I had become distracted by adding up all the numbers of the hymns and seeing how many would divide by five!

Over the years, their example communicated a powerful sense of the importance of the Word. The Bible was speaking to my mother and father in their forties and to my grandparents in their sixties and seventies, and they were deadly serious about learning it! I remember now things that were said from the pulpit when I was twelve years old, and perhaps more significant, I remember the sense of the presence of God.

Seeing my parents worship left a lasting impression. Hearing my father sing or my mother softly saying "Amen" at the end of a prayer conveyed a sense that they were not just sitting in church; they were worshiping! Over a period of about ten years, this set a path I wanted to follow.

I thank God for the influence of Sunday school in my life and am grateful for programs that are geared specifically to our children and young people. But there is something special about bringing children and young people into an environment where they see an adult congregation taking the Word of God seriously. So I encourage parents to bring their children into a worship service as soon as they are "able to understand." If parents do not model a desire to worship God and to receive His Word when their kids are young, it will be difficult for them to feel that this is important when they are older.

GREAT EXPECTATIONS

The crowd watched expectantly, and when Ezra opened the Scriptures, the people all spontaneously stood (v. 5). Then, as Nehemiah reports,

> *Ezra praised the LORD, the great God; and all the people lifted their*
> *hands and responded, "Amen! Amen!" Then they bowed down*
> *and worshiped the LORD with their faces to the ground. (v. 6)*

It was a thousand years since God had spoken these words to Moses, but when the Book was opened and explained, the people clearly believed that God was speaking to them. They recognized that when they heard this Book read and explained, they were not listening to the words of a man, but they were hearing the Word of God, so they gave it their full attention.

Notice that they did not ask Ezra to take a trip to Mount Sinai and see if there were any new words from the LORD. They asked Ezra to open the Book of the Law which was a thousand years old, because they believed that what God said then in that Book was still His Word for them in their day.

Ezra, and the Levites who assisted him, give a great model for preachers to follow:

> *They read from the Book of the Law of God, making it clear*
> *and giving the meaning so that the people could understand*
> *what was being read. (v. 8)*

MAKING THE MEANING CLEAR

Notice that the preaching started from the text of the Bible. Ezra did not create a message to suit his audience; he explained the message that had already been given by God. He did not decide on a message and then come to the Bible to find some verses to support it; he came to the Scripture and allowed the Scripture to determine the message. God has not promised to bless the words of any preacher. But He has promised to bless His own Word. So the task of the preacher is to fill his words with God's words so that the people will be blessed.

Ezra was supported by the Levites in his task. It seems that they were interspersed in the crowd. Ezra would read a part of the law and explain the meaning, and then he would stop. The Levites would then gather people around them in smaller family groups and ask if they had understood and if there were any questions. When everyone in the group was clear, Ezra would continue (see vv. 7–8).

There was a direct connection between Ezra's preaching and a small group setting in which people had the opportunity to ask questions and make applications of the teaching. People had some break-out time to work through the application of the preaching. Of course these small groups would have been based around extended family units, so what we have here is a model of public preaching being confirmed and applied in the home.

One of my heroes of the faith is a man called Richard Baxter. He served as a pastor in the town of Kidderminster, England, in the seventeenth century. When he came, Kidderminster had few believing people, but God used his ministry to transform the whole town. He taught the Bible from the pulpit, and then he had a system of visiting families and talking with them in their homes about what they had learned.

Baxter would ask some questions of each family member, including the children, and if they were confused, he would give some clearer explanation. Families could ask questions, and he would encourage parents to be faithful in teaching their children and praying with them.

> God still speaks through His Word…the bread that sustains the spiritual life of God's people.

Baxter did this for sixteen years, and in this way, he discipled a whole community. The Word was preached in the church, then confirmed and applied in the home, and families were encouraged through the visits of their pastor or an elder. In this way, a biblically illiterate generation was discipled.

God still speaks through His Word. It is the sword of the Spirit, and it is the bread that sustains the spiritual life of God's people. If we lose confidence in the power of the Word, we will soon be trying just about everything else to hold on to our young people, attract our neighbors, or make our services more interesting. But if we want to disciple a community of people, then reading, explaining, and applying the Bible must be central to all that we do.

THE JOY OF GRACE

Then Nehemiah the governor, Ezra the priest and scribe, and the Levites who were instructing the people said to them all, "This day is sacred to the LORD your God. Do not mourn or weep." For all the people had been weeping as they listened to the words of the Law. (v. 9)

As Ezra read the law of God, the people realized how far they were from what God was calling them to be. One of the first effects of receiving the Word of God is that it humbles us. You start to see things in your life that you didn't see before. You become sensitive to attitudes and actions that grieve the heart of God. The Word of God is sharper than a two-edged sword. It pierces and cuts and wounds!

It is often the purpose of God to bring you there, but it is never the purpose of God to leave you there. You may have experienced a legalistic kind of preaching that made you feel small, and that was all it did. You came out saying, "What a miserable person I am; I must do better," but then after years of that you got worn down. Eventually you lost (or will lose) the energy or the strength to keep trying.

Ezra and Nehemiah's ministry was very different. When they taught the Word of God, it reduced many people to tears, but the leaders did not leave the people there. Nehemiah said, "Go and enjoy choice food and sweet drinks, and send some to those who have nothing prepared. This day is sacred to our LORD. Do not grieve, for the joy of the LORD is your strength" (v. 10).

Conviction of sin is never an end in itself. It is always a means to an end, and the end is that we come to a deeper appreciation of God and His Son Jesus Christ. In just a few days' time it would be the Day of Atonement, the day that reminded the people that God would forgive the sins of His people. They could look at the animal to be sacrificed and know that atonement was coming! We can look at the Cross and know that atonement has come!

When Nehemiah spoke about the joy of the LORD, he was not telling them to pull themselves together and cheer up, but reminding them that the grace and mercy of God was enough to wipe away tears from all of their eyes.

It is not your joy that is your strength; it is God's joy that is your strength. This is the joy that Jesus spoke about when He said that there is joy in heaven over one sinner who repents (Luke 15:7). Repentance on earth leads to joy in heaven. Our tears over sin are reflected in God's joy in forgiving, and that joy is our strength.

When you feel your failure and your weakness, look up into the face of God, and you will find that He is gracious. His hand is extended toward you in Christ. His joy will be your strength.

If the Christian life was an endless attempt to fulfill the law of God, our strength would eventually be exhausted. But the message of the Bible is that the mercy and grace of God are extended toward us, and in that, you will find the strength to go forward.

When people left the great service of worship in Jerusalem, they were not going home preoccupied with themselves and their failures. They went home with a fresh glimpse of the grace and mercy of God that had brought them new hope and new joy which had given them new strength to face the challenge of another week.

THE JOY OF OBEDIENCE

The day after the great rally, the men returned for a follow-up session. During a further reading of the Law, they made a discovery:

> They found written in the Law, which the LORD had commanded through Moses, that the Israelites were to live in booths during the feast of the seventh month. (NEHEMIAH 8:14)

This rather unusual festival involved each family making a temporary housing from branches and then living in it for seven days. The festival reminded the people of how God had kept their forefathers in the desert. It was also a reminder that everything in this world is temporary, and that, like Abraham, they were to look for a heavenly city.

I love the spontaneity of their response. These men see the teaching of the Word of God and so they go and do it. "So the people...built themselves booths on their own roofs, in their courtyards, in the courts of the house of God, and in [the market square]" (v. 16). Their obedience was visible in the home, among their neighbors, in their place of worship, and in the workplace. It was a marvelous example of the power of a group of men who are committed to do whatever the Word of God says.

Their obedience to the Word of God was infectious:

> The whole company that had returned from exile built booths and lived in them. From the days of Joshua son of Nun until that day, the Israelites had not celebrated it like this. And their joy was very great. (v. 17)

Eight centuries had passed since the days of Joshua! These people had never been so happy as when they were fully obedient.

God had spoken to His people through His Word. It had humbled them in their sins, but it had lifted them up to see the grace and mercy of God, and then had directed them into a new life of obedience.

In all our desperate searching for ways to find joy, God is telling us that we will never find joy like the joy of knowing God, being humbled in our sins, experiencing His grace, and walking in a life of obedience.

The book of Nehemiah brings us to the end of the Old Testament story. After the people of God returned from exile and rebuilt the city of Jerusalem, there was a break of four hundred years before the central event in the Bible story, when Jesus Christ came into the world.

The rest of the Old Testament comes in two parts. First, there are books of wisdom: Job, Psalms, Proverbs, Ecclesiastes, and Song of Songs. These books contain the timeless wisdom or skills that we need for life. Then there are the prophets: Isaiah and Jeremiah, through to Haggai. The prophets were raised up by God to speak His Word to the nation, but all of them ministered within the period of the story we have already covered. In volume two of *Unlocking the Bible Story*, we will match the words of the prophets with the events that were taking place at the time.

Thus far in the Bible story, we have seen how God chose to reach out to men and women after their sin in the garden.

God pledged that blessing would come to all the nations of the world through an offspring of Abraham. So we have followed the story of Abraham's family becoming a great nation under the blessing of God.

We have seen how God gave His law and the sacrifices to His people. They became a great and powerful nation, but then they were allured by the worship of idols. God warned them that the same love that had blessed them would also discipline them if they turned to idols. The warnings of the prophets fell on deaf ears and eventually, when God's anger was provoked, the ten northern tribes were scattered, and later, many of the people from the two southern tribes were taken into exile, where they remained for seventy years.

But God never gave up on His people. Eventually a small community returned to Jerusalem, and once again there was a gathering of God's people in the place where God had said He would put His name.

Over the next centuries, this small community of God's people suffered all kinds of evil through invading armies and advancing empires. That pattern has never changed. Our world is still plagued with the knowledge of evil.

And when the people of God rebuilt the temple, one thing was missing: the visible manifestation of the presence of God. God had promised to meet His people at the ark, which was in the Most Holy Place at the center of the temple. But the ark had been lost. So when the new temple was built, the Most Holy Place was empty. God's place was an empty room.

On the day when the foundations of the second temple were laid, some of the older people found it hard to join in the celebrations. They could remember Solomon's magnificent temple, and when they saw the size of the foundations for the new building, they knew that it would only be a shadow of the one that had been destroyed, and they couldn't hold back their tears. (See Ezra 3:12 and Haggai 2:3.) They knew that they were living in a "day of small things" (Zechariah 4:10).

So the Old Testament story leaves us with a sense of thankfulness to God for His promises and His faithfulness, but still looking to see how God will deliver people from evil and restore men and women to His presence.

SPOTLIGHT ON CHRIST

When Jesus Christ came into the world, He said, "Blessed are the pure in heart, for they will see God" (Matthew 5:8). If you were pure in heart, you would be free from the knowledge of evil. And Christ spoke of how these people would have the joy of seeing God. Christ also said that His kingdom was not of this world. So we should not expect this world to be free from the knowledge of evil, nor should we expect to see God in this world. But Christ has come to deliver us from the knowledge of evil and to bring us into God's presence.

The whole Bible story is leading up to the great day when Christ will return and bring His people from every tribe and nation into the immediate presence of God. Evil will be destroyed, and human history as we know it will come to an end. Our bodies will be changed, and we will begin a new kind of life of greater joys than Adam ever knew in the garden.

UNLOCKED

God's people experience joy when they discover His grace and respond in obedience. When God's Word is taught, sin will be challenged and God's gracious forgiveness presented. God delights to forgive. Restoring sinners is a joy to the heart of God, and God's joy is the source of our joy.

The Word of God also shows us the path of righteousness, and the same God who offers His grace also calls us to a life of obedience. In Nehemiah's day God's people discovered that there is great joy in wholehearted obedience to all that God had commanded. A large part of our joy in heaven will be that we will serve God and bring Him pleasure. There is great joy in obeying God.

PAUSE FOR PRAYER

Gracious Father,

I believe that in Your presence there is fullness of joy and at Your right hand, there are pleasures forevermore. Forgive me for thinking that I can find joy without You. Help me to know the joy of Your grace and to discover the joy of obedience.

As the psalmist prayed, "Restore to me the joy of your salvation, and grant me a willing spirit, to sustain me." Through Jesus my Lord and Savior I pray. Amen.

You Can Do It!

Can you imagine the insight and joy gained from reading the entire Bible? In as little as 15 minutes a day, *The One Year Bible* will guide you through God's Word with daily readings from the Old Testament, New Testament, Psalms, and Proverbs.

Begin reading *The One Year Bible* from cover to cover and experience the spiritual growth and communion with God that come from daily Bible reading. Available in the clear, accurate New Living Translation. Also available in the NIV and King James Version.

Available wherever Bibles are sold.

for those who thirst.

TYNDALE

☐ **January 1**
Genesis 1:1–2:25
Matthew 1:1–2:12
Psalm 1:1-6
Proverbs 1:1-6

☐ **January 2**
Genesis 3:1–4:26
Matthew 2:13–3:6
Psalm 2:1-12
Proverbs 1:7-9

☐ **January 3**
Genesis 5:1–7:24
Matthew 3:7–4:11
Psalm 3:1-8
Proverbs 1:10-19

☐ **January 4**
Genesis 8:1–10:32
Matthew 4:12-25
Psalm 4:1-8
Proverbs 1:20-23

☐ **January 5**
Genesis 11:1–13:4
Matthew 5:1-26
Psalm 5:1-12
Proverbs 1:24-28

☐ **January 6**
Genesis 13:5–15:21
Matthew 5:27-48
Psalm 6:1-10
Proverbs 1:29-33

☐ **January 7**
Genesis 16:1–18:15
Matthew 6:1-24
Psalm 7:1-17
Proverbs 2:1-5

☐ **January 8**
Genesis 18:16–19:38
Matthew 6:25–7:14
Psalm 8:1-9
Proverbs 2:6-15

☐ **January 9**
Genesis 20:1–22:24
Matthew 7:15-29
Psalm 9:1-12
Proverbs 2:16-22

☐ **January 10**
Genesis 23:1–24:51
Matthew 8:1-17
Psalm 9:13-20
Proverbs 3:1-6

☐ **January 11**
Genesis 24:52–26:16
Matthew 8:18-34
Psalm 10:1-15
Proverbs 3:7-8

☐ **January 12**
Genesis 26:17–27:46
Matthew 9:1-17
Psalm 10:16-18
Proverbs 3:9-10

☐ **January 13**
Genesis 28:1–29:35
Matthew 9:18-38
Psalm 11:1-7
Proverbs 3:11-12

☐ **January 14**
Genesis 30:1–31:16
Matthew 10:1-23
Psalm 12:1-8
Proverbs 3:13-15

☐ **January 15**
Genesis 31:17–32:12
Matthew 10:24–11:6
Psalm 13:1-6
Proverbs 3:16-18

☐ **January 16**
Genesis 32:13–34:31
Matthew 11:7-30
Psalm 14:1-7
Proverbs 3:19-20

☐ **January 17**
Genesis 35:1–36:43
Matthew 12:1-21
Psalm 15:1-5
Proverbs 3:21-26

☐ **January 18**
Genesis 37:1–38:30
Matthew 12:22-45
Psalm 16:1-11
Proverbs 3:27-32

☐ **January 19**
Genesis 39:1–41:16
Matthew 12:46–13:23
Psalm 17:1-15
Proverbs 3:33-35

☐ **January 20**
Genesis 41:17–42:17
Matthew 13:24-46
Psalm 18:1-15
Proverbs 4:1-6

☐ **January 21**
Genesis 42:18–43:34
Matthew 13:47–14:12
Psalm 18:16-36
Proverbs 4:7-10

☐ **January 22**
Genesis 44:1–45:28
Matthew 14:13-36
Psalm 18:37-50
Proverbs 4:11-13

☐ **January 23**
Genesis 46:1–47:31
Matthew 15:1-28
Psalm 19:1-14
Proverbs 4:14-19

☐ **January 24**
Genesis 48:1–49:33
Matthew 15:29–16:12
Psalm 20:1-9
Proverbs 4:20-27

☐ **January 25**
Genesis 50:1—Exodus 2:10
Matthew 16:13–17:9
Psalm 21:1-13
Proverbs 5:1-6

☐ **January 26**
Exodus 2:11–3:22
Matthew 17:10-27
Psalm 22:1-18
Proverbs 5:7-14

☐ **January 27**
Exodus 4:1–5:21
Matthew 18:1-22
Psalm 22:19-31
Proverbs 5:15-21

☐ **January 28**
Exodus 5:22–7:25
Matthew 18:23–19:12
Psalm 23:1-6
Proverbs 5:22-23

☐ **January 29**
Exodus 8:1–9:35
Matthew 19:13-30
Psalm 24:1-10
Proverbs 6:1-5

☐ **January 30**
Exodus 10:1–12:13
Matthew 20:1-28
Psalm 25:1-15
Proverbs 6:6-11

☐ **January 31**
Exodus 12:14–13:16
Matthew 20:29–21:22
Psalm 25:16-22
Proverbs 6:12-15

☐ **February 1**
Exodus 13:17–15:18
Matthew 21:23-46
Psalm 26:1-12
Proverbs 6:16-19

☐ **February 2**
Exodus 15:19–17:7
Matthew 22:1-33
Psalm 27:1-6
Proverbs 6:20-26

☐ **February 3**
Exodus 17:8–19:15
Matthew 22:34–23:12
Psalm 27:7-14
Proverbs 6:27-35

☐ **February 4**
Exodus 19:16–21:21
Matthew 23:13-39
Psalm 28:1-9
Proverbs 7:1-5

☐ **February 5**
Exodus 21:22–23:13
Matthew 24:1-28
Psalm 29:1-11
Proverbs 7:6-23

☐ **February 6**
Exodus 23:14–25:40
Matthew 24:29-51
Psalm 30:1-12
Proverbs 7:24-27

☐ **February 7**
Exodus 26:1–27:21
Matthew 25:1-30
Psalm 31:1-8
Proverbs 8:1-11

☐ **February 8**
Exodus 28:1-43
Matthew 25:31–26:13
Psalm 31:9-18
Proverbs 8:12-13

☐ **February 9**
Exodus 29:1–30:10
Matthew 26:14-46
Psalm 31:19-24
Proverbs 8:14-26

☐ **February 10**
Exodus 30:11–31:18
Matthew 26:47-68
Psalm 32:1-11
Proverbs 8:27-32

☐ **February 11**
Exodus 32:1–33:23
Matthew 26:69–27:14
Psalm 33:1-11
Proverbs 8:33-36

☐ **February 12**
Exodus 34:1–35:9
Matthew 27:15-31
Psalm 33:12-22
Proverbs 9:1-6

☐ **February 13**
Exodus 35:10–36:38
Matthew 27:32-66
Psalm 34:1-10
Proverbs 9:7-8

☐ **February 14**
Exodus 37:1–38:31
Matthew 28:1-20
Psalm 34:11-22
Proverbs 9:9-10

☐ **February 15**
Exodus 39:1–40:38
Mark 1:1-28
Psalm 35:1-16
Proverbs 9:11-12

☐ **February 16**
Leviticus 1:1–3:17
Mark 1:29–2:12
Psalm 35:17-28
Proverbs 9:13-18

☐ **February 17**
Leviticus 4:1–5:19
Mark 2:13–3:6
Psalm 36:1-12
Proverbs 10:1-2

☐ **February 18**
Leviticus 6:1–7:27
Mark 3:7-30
Psalm 37:1-11
Proverbs 10:3-4

☐ **February 19**
Leviticus 7:28–9:6
Mark 3:31–4:25
Psalm 37:12-29
Proverbs 10:5

☐ **February 20**
Leviticus 9:7–10:20
Mark 4:26–5:20
Psalm 37:30-40
Proverbs 10:6-7

☐ **February 21**
Leviticus 11:1–12:8
Mark 5:21-43
Psalm 38:1-22
Proverbs 10:8-9

☐ **February 22**
Leviticus 13:1-59
Mark 6:1-29
Psalm 39:1-13
Proverbs 10:10

☐ **February 23**
Leviticus 14:1-57
Mark 6:30-56
Psalm 40:1-10
Proverbs 10:11-12

☐ **February 24**
Leviticus 15:1–16:28
Mark 7:1-23
Psalm 40:11-17
Proverbs 10:13-14

☐ **February 25**
Leviticus 16:29–18:30
Mark 7:24–8:10
Psalm 41:1-13
Proverbs 10:15-16

☐ **February 26**
Leviticus 19:1–20:21
Mark 8:11-38
Psalm 42:1-11
Proverbs 10:17

☐ **February 27**
Leviticus 20:22–22:16
Mark 9:1-29
Psalm 43:1-5
Proverbs 10:18

☐ **February 28**
Leviticus 22:17–23:44
Mark 9:30–10:12
Psalm 44:1-8
Proverbs 10:19

☐ **March 1**
Leviticus 24:1–25:46
Mark 10:13-31
Psalm 44:9-26
Proverbs 10:20-21

☐ **March 2**
Leviticus 25:47–27:13
Mark 10:32-52
Psalm 45:1-17
Proverbs 10:22

☐ **March 3**
Leviticus 27:14—Numbers 1:54
Mark 11:1-25
Psalm 46:1-11
Proverbs 10:23

☐ **March 4**
Numbers 2:1–3:51
Mark 11:27–12:17
Psalm 47:1-9
Proverbs 10:24-25

☐ **March 5**
Numbers 4:1–5:31
Mark 12:18-37
Psalm 48:1-14
Proverbs 10:26

☐ **March 6**
Numbers 6:1–7:89
Mark 12:38–13:13
Psalm 49:1-20
Proverbs 10:27-28

☐ **March 7**
Numbers 8:1–9:23
Mark 13:14-37
Psalm 50:1-23
Proverbs 10:29-30

☐ **March 8**
Numbers 10:1–11:23
Mark 14:1-21
Psalm 51:1-19
Proverbs 10:31-32

☐ **March 9**
Numbers 11:24–13:33
Mark 14:22-52
Psalm 52:1-9
Proverbs 11:1-3

☐ **March 10**
Numbers 14:1–15:16
Mark 14:53-72
Psalm 53:1-6
Proverbs 11:4

☐ **March 11**
Numbers 15:17–16:40
Mark 15:1-47
Psalm 54:1-7
Proverbs 11:5-6

☐ **March 12**
Numbers 16:41–18:32
Mark 16:1-20
Psalm 55:1-23
Proverbs 11:7

☐ **March 13**
Numbers 19:1–20:29
Luke 1:1-25
Psalm 56:1-13
Proverbs 11:8

☐ **March 14**
Numbers 21:1–22:20
Luke 1:26-56
Psalm 57:1-11
Proverbs 11:9-11

☐ **March 15**
Numbers 22:21–23:30
Luke 1:57-80
Psalm 58:1-11
Proverbs 11:12-13

☐ **March 16**
Numbers 24:1–25:18
Luke 2:1-35
Psalm 59:1-17
Proverbs 11:14

☐ **March 17**
Numbers 26:1-51
Luke 2:36-52
Psalm 60:1-12
Proverbs 11:15

☐ **March 18**
Numbers 26:52–28:15
Luke 3:1-22
Psalm 61:1-8
Proverbs 11:16-17

☐ **March 19**
Numbers 28:16–29:40
Luke 3:23-38
Psalm 62:1-12
Proverbs 11:18-19

☐ **March 20**
Numbers 30:1–31:54
Luke 4:1-30
Psalm 63:1-11
Proverbs 11:20-21

☐ **March 21**
Numbers 32:1–33:39
Luke 4:31–5:11
Psalm 64:1-10
Proverbs 11:22

☐ **March 22**
Numbers 33:40–35:34
Luke 5:12-28
Psalm 65:1-13
Proverbs 11:23

☐ **March 23**
Numbers 36:1—Deuteronomy 1:46
Luke 5:29–6:11
Psalm 66:1-20
Proverbs 11:24-26

☐ **March 24**
Deuteronomy 2:1–3:29
Luke 6:12-38
Psalm 67:1-7
Proverbs 11:27

☐ **March 25**
Deuteronomy 4:1-49
Luke 6:39–7:10
Psalm 68:1-18
Proverbs 11:28

☐ March 26
Deuteronomy 5:1–6:25
Luke 7:11-35
Psalm 68:19-35
Proverbs 11:29-31

☐ March 27
Deuteronomy 7:1–8:20
Luke 7:36–8:3
Psalm 69:1-18
Proverbs 12:1

☐ March 28
Deuteronomy 9:1–10:22
Luke 8:4-21
Psalm 69:19-36
Proverbs 12:2-3

☐ March 29
Deuteronomy 11:1–12:32
Luke 8:22-39
Psalm 70:1-5
Proverbs 12:4

☐ March 30
Deuteronomy 13:1–15:23
Luke 8:40–9:6
Psalm 71:1-24
Proverbs 12:5-7

☐ March 31
Deuteronomy 16:1–17:20
Luke 9:7-27
Psalm 72:1-20
Proverbs 12:8-9

☐ April 1
Deuteronomy 18:1–20:20
Luke 9:28-50
Psalm 73:1-28
Proverbs 12:10

☐ April 2
Deuteronomy 21:1–22:30
Luke 9:51–10:12
Psalm 74:1-23
Proverbs 12:11

☐ April 3
Deuteronomy 23:1–25:19
Luke 10:13-37
Psalm 75:1-10
Proverbs 12:12-14

☐ April 4
Deuteronomy 26:1–27:26
Luke 10:38–11:13
Psalm 76:1-12
Proverbs 12:15-17

☐ April 5
Deuteronomy 28:1-68
Luke 11:14-36
Psalm 77:1-20
Proverbs 12:18

☐ April 6
Deuteronomy 29:1–30:20
Luke 11:37–12:7
Psalm 78:1-31
Proverbs 12:19-20

☐ April 7
Deuteronomy 31:1–32:27
Luke 12:8-34
Psalm 78:32-55
Proverbs 12:21-23

☐ April 8
Deuteronomy 32:28-52
Luke 12:35-59
Psalm 78:56-64
Proverbs 12:24

☐ April 9
Deuteronomy 33:1-29
Luke 13:1-21
Psalm 78:65-72
Proverbs 12:25

☐ April 10
Deuteronomy 34:1—Joshua 2:24
Luke 13:22–14:6
Psalm 79:1-13
Proverbs 12:26

☐ April 11
Joshua 3:1–4:24
Luke 14:7-35
Psalm 80:1-19
Proverbs 12:27-28

☐ April 12
Joshua 5:1–7:15
Luke 15:1-32
Psalm 81:1-16
Proverbs 13:1

☐ April 13
Joshua 7:16–9:2
Luke 16:1-18
Psalm 82:1-8
Proverbs 13:2-3

☐ April 14
Joshua 9:3–10:43
Luke 16:19–17:10
Psalm 83:1-18
Proverbs 13:4

☐ April 15
Joshua 11:1–12:24
Luke 17:11-37
Psalm 84:1-12
Proverbs 13:5-6

☐ April 16
Joshua 13:1–14:15
Luke 18:1-17
Psalm 85:1-13
Proverbs 13:7-8

☐ April 17
Joshua 15:1-63
Luke 18:18-43
Psalm 86:1-17
Proverbs 13:9-10

☐ April 18
Joshua 16:1–18:28
Luke 19:1-27
Psalm 87:1-7
Proverbs 13:11

☐ April 19
Joshua 19:1–20:9
Luke 19:28-48
Psalm 88:1-18
Proverbs 13:12-14

☐ April 20
Joshua 21:1–22:20
Luke 20:1-26
Psalm 89:1-13
Proverbs 13:15-16

☐ April 21
Joshua 22:21–23:16
Luke 20:27-47
Psalm 89:14-37
Proverbs 13:17-19

☐ April 22
Joshua 24:1-33
Luke 21:1-28
Psalm 89:38-52
Proverbs 13:20-23

☐ **April 23**
Judges 1:1–2:9
Luke 21:29–22:13
Psalm 90:1–91:16
Proverbs 13:24-25

☐ **April 24**
Judges 2:10–3:31
Luke 22:14-34
Psalm 92:1–93:5
Proverbs 14:1-2

☐ **April 25**
Judges 4:1–5:31
Luke 22:35-53
Psalm 94:1-23
Proverbs 14:3-4

☐ **April 26**
Judges 6:1-40
Luke 22:54–23:12
Psalm 95:1–96:13
Proverbs 14:5-6

☐ **April 27**
Judges 7:1–8:17
Luke 23:13-43
Psalm 97:1–98:9
Proverbs 14:7-8

☐ **April 28**
Judges 8:18–9:21
Luke 23:44–24:12
Psalm 99:1-9
Proverbs 14:9-10

☐ **April 29**
Judges 9:22–10:18
Luke 24:13-53
Psalm 100:1-5
Proverbs 14:11-12

☐ **April 30**
Judges 11:1–12:15
John 1:1-28
Psalm 101:1-8
Proverbs 14:13-14

☐ **May 1**
Judges 13:1–14:20
John 1:29-51
Psalm 102:1-28
Proverbs 14:15-16

☐ **May 2**
Judges 15:1–16:31
John 2:1-25
Psalm 103:1-22
Proverbs 14:17-19

☐ **May 3**
Judges 17:1–18:31
John 3:1-21
Psalm 104:1-23
Proverbs 14:20-21

☐ **May 4**
Judges 19:1–20:48
John 3:22–4:3
Psalm 104:24-35
Proverbs 14:22-24

☐ **May 5**
Judges 21:1—Ruth 1:22
John 4:4-42
Psalm 105:1-15
Proverbs 14:25

☐ **May 6**
Ruth 2:1–4:22
John 4:43-54
Psalm 105:16-36
Proverbs 14:26-27

☐ **May 7**
1 Samuel 1:1–2:21
John 5:1-23
Psalm 105:37-45
Proverbs 14:28-29

☐ **May 8**
1 Samuel 2:22–4:22
John 5:24-47
Psalm 106:1-12
Proverbs 14:30-31

☐ **May 9**
1 Samuel 5:1–7:17
John 6:1-21
Psalm 106:13-31
Proverbs 14:32-33

☐ **May 10**
1 Samuel 8:1–9:27
John 6:22-42
Psalm 106:32-48
Proverbs 14:34-35

☐ **May 11**
1 Samuel 10:1–11:15
John 6:43-71
Psalm 107:1-43
Proverbs 15:1-3

☐ **May 12**
1 Samuel 12:1–13:23
John 7:1-30
Psalm 108:1-13
Proverbs 15:4

☐ **May 13**
1 Samuel 14:1–14:52
John 7:31-53
Psalm 109:1-31
Proverbs 15:5-7

☐ **May 14**
1 Samuel 15:1–16:23
John 8:1-20
Psalm 110:1-7
Proverbs 15:8-10

☐ **May 15**
1 Samuel 17:1–18:4
John 8:21-30
Psalm 111:1-10
Proverbs 15:11

☐ **May 16**
1 Samuel 18:5–19:24
John 8:31-59
Psalm 112:1-10
Proverbs 15:12-14

☐ **May 17**
1 Samuel 20:1–21:15
John 9:1-41
Psalm 113:1–114:8
Proverbs 15:15-17

☐ **May 18**
1 Samuel 22:1–23:29
John 10:1-21
Psalm 115:1-18
Proverbs 15:18-19

☐ **May 19**
1 Samuel 24:1–25:44
John 10:22-42
Psalm 116:1-19
Proverbs 15:20-21

☐ **May 20**
1 Samuel 26:1–28:25
John 11:1-54
Psalm 117:1-2
Proverbs 15:22-23

☐ **May 21**
1 Samuel 29:1–31:13
John 11:55–12:19
Psalm 118:1-18
Proverbs 15:24-26

☐ **May 22**
2 Samuel 1:1–2:11
John 12:20-50
Psalm 118:19-29
Proverbs 15:27-28

☐ **May 23**
2 Samuel 2:12–3:39
John 13:1-30
Psalm 119:1-16
Proverbs 15:29-30

☐ **May 24**
2 Samuel 4:1–6:23
John 13:31–14:14
Psalm 119:17-32
Proverbs 15:31-32

☐ **May 25**
2 Samuel 7:1–8:18
John 14:15-31
Psalm 119:33-48
Proverbs 15:33

☐ **May 26**
2 Samuel 9:1–11:27
John 15:1-27
Psalm 119:49-64
Proverbs 16:1-3

☐ **May 27**
2 Samuel 12:1-31
John 16:1-33
Psalm 119:65-80
Proverbs 16:4-5

☐ **May 28**
2 Samuel 13:1-39
John 17:1-26
Psalm 119:81-96
Proverbs 16:6-7

☐ **May 29**
2 Samuel 14:1–15:22
John 18:1-24
Psalm 119:97-112
Proverbs 16:8-9

☐ **May 30**
2 Samuel 15:23–16:23
John 18:25–19:22
Psalm 119:113-128
Proverbs 16:10-11

☐ **May 31**
2 Samuel 17:1-29
John 19:23-42
Psalm 119:129-152
Proverbs 16:12-13

☐ **June 1**
2 Samuel 18:1–19:10
John 20:1-31
Psalm 119:153-176
Proverbs 16:14-15

☐ **June 2**
2 Samuel 19:11–20:13
John 21:1-25
Psalm 120:1-7 |
Proverbs 16:16-17

☐ **June 3**
2 Samuel 20:14–21:22
Acts 1:1-26
Psalm 121:1-8
Proverbs 16:18

☐ **June 4**
2 Samuel 22:1–23:23
Acts 2:1-47
Psalm 122:1-9
Proverbs 16:19-20

☐ **June 5**
2 Samuel 23:24–24:25
Acts 3:1-26
Psalm 123:1-4
Proverbs 16:21-23

☐ **June 6**
1 Kings 1:1-53
Acts 4:1-37
Psalm 124:1-8
Proverbs 16:24

☐ **June 7**
1 Kings 2:1–3:2
Acts 5:1-42
Psalm 125:1-5
Proverbs 16:25

☐ **June 8**
1 Kings 3:3–4:34
Acts 6:1-15
Psalm 126:1-6
Proverbs 16:26-27

☐ **June 9**
1 Kings 5:1–6:38
Acts 7:1-29
Psalm 127:1-5
Proverbs 16:28-30

☐ **June 10**
1 Kings 7:1-51
Acts 7:30-50
Psalm 128:1-6
Proverbs 16:31-33

☐ **June 11**
1 Kings 8:1-66
Acts 7:51–8:13
Psalm 129:1-8
Proverbs 17:1

☐ **June 12**
1 Kings 9:1–10:29
Acts 8:14-40
Psalm 130:1-8
Proverbs 17:2-3

☐ **June 13**
1 Kings 11:1–12:19
Acts 9:1-25
Psalm 131:1-3
Proverbs 17:4-5

☐ **June 14**
1 Kings 12:20–13:34
Acts 9:26-43
Psalm 132:1-18
Proverbs 17:6

☐ **June 15**
1 Kings 14:1–15:24
Acts 10:1-23
Psalm 133:1-3
Proverbs 17:7-8

☐ **June 16**
1 Kings 15:25–17:24
Acts 10:24-48
Psalm 134:1-3
Proverbs 17:9-11

☐ **June 17**
1 Kings 18:1-46
Acts 11:1-30
Psalm 135:1-21
Proverbs 17:12-13

☐ June 18
1 Kings 19:1-21
Acts 12:1-23
Psalm 136:1-26
Proverbs 17:14-15

☐ June 19
1 Kings 20:1–21:29
Acts 12:24–13:15
Psalm 137:1-9
Proverbs 17:16

☐ June 20
1 Kings 22:1-53
Acts 13:16-41
Psalm 138:1-8
Proverbs 17:17-18

☐ June 21
2 Kings 1:1–2:25
Acts 13:42–14:7
Psalm 139:1-24
Proverbs 17:19-21

☐ June 22
2 Kings 3:1–4:17
Acts 14:8-28
Psalm 140:1-13
Proverbs 17:22

☐ June 23
2 Kings 4:18–5:27
Acts 15:1-35
Psalm 141:1-10
Proverbs 17:23

☐ June 24
2 Kings 6:1–7:20
Acts 15:36–16:15
Psalm 142:1-7
Proverbs 17:24-25

☐ June 25
2 Kings 8:1–9:13
Acts 16:16-40
Psalm 143:1-12
Proverbs 17:26

☐ June 26
2 Kings 9:14–10:31
Acts 17:1-34
Psalm 144:1-15
Proverbs 17:27-28

☐ June 27
2 Kings 10:32–12:21
Acts 18:1-22
Psalm 145:1-21
Proverbs 18:1

☐ June 28
2 Kings 13:1–14:29
Acts 18:23–19:12
Psalm 146:1-10
Proverbs 18:2-3

☐ June 29
2 Kings 15:1–16:20
Acts 19:13-41
Psalm 147:1-20
Proverbs 18:4-5

☐ June 30
2 Kings 17:1–18:12
Acts 20:1-38
Psalm 148:1-14
Proverbs 18:6-7

☐ July 1
2 Kings 18:13–19:37
Acts 21:1-17
Psalm 149:1-9
Proverbs 18:8

☐ July 2
2 Kings 20:1–22:2
Acts 21:18-36
Psalm 150:1-6
Proverbs 18:9-10

☐ July 3
2 Kings 22:3–23:30
Acts 21:37–22:16
Psalm 1:1-6
Proverbs 18:11-12

☐ July 4
2 Kings 23:31–25:30
Acts 22:17–23:10
Psalm 2:1-12
Proverbs 18:13

☐ July 5
1 Chronicles 1:1–2:17
Acts 23:11-35
Psalm 3:1-8
Proverbs 18:14-15

☐ July 6
1 Chronicles 2:18–4:4
Acts 24:1-27
Psalm 4:1-8
Proverbs 18:16-18

☐ July 7
1 Chronicles 4:5–5:17
Acts 25:1-27
Psalm 5:1-12
Proverbs 18:19

☐ July 8
1 Chronicles 5:18–6:81
Acts 26:1-32
Psalm 6:1-10
Proverbs 18:20-21

☐ July 9
1 Chronicles 7:1–8:40
Acts 27:1-20
Psalm 7:1-17
Proverbs 18:22

☐ July 10
1 Chronicles 9:1–10:14
Acts 27:21-44
Psalm 8:1-9
Proverbs 18:23-24

☐ July 11
1 Chronicles 11:1–12:18
Acts 28:1-31
Psalm 9:1-12
Proverbs 19:1-3

☐ July 12
1 Chronicles 12:19–14:17
Romans 1:1-17
Psalm 9:13-20
Proverbs 19:4-5

☐ July 13
1 Chronicles 15:1–16:36
Romans 1:18-32
Psalm 10:1-15
Proverbs 19:6-7

☐ July 14
1 Chronicles 16:37–18:17
Romans 2:1-24
Psalm 10:16-18
Proverbs 19:8-9

☐ July 15
1 Chronicles 19:1–21:30
Romans 2:25–3:8
Psalm 11:1-7
Proverbs 19:10-12

☐ July 16
1 Chronicles 22:1–23:32
Romans 3:9-31
Psalm 12:1-8
Proverbs 19:13-14

☐ July 17
1 Chronicles 24:1–26:11
Romans 4:1-12
Psalm 13:1-6
Proverbs 19:15-16

☐ July 18
1 Chronicles 26:12–27:34
Romans 4:13–5:5
Psalm 14:1-7
Proverbs 19:17

☐ July 19
1 Chronicles 28:1–29:30
Romans 5:6-21
Psalm 15:1-5
Proverbs 19:18-19

☐ July 20
2 Chronicles 1:1–3:17
Romans 6:1-23
Psalm 16:1-11
Proverbs 19:20-21

☐ July 21
2 Chronicles 4:1–6:11
Romans 7:1-13
Psalm 17:1-15
Proverbs 19:22-23

☐ July 22
2 Chronicles 6:12–8:10
Romans 7:14–8:8
Psalm 18:1-15
Proverbs 19:24-25

☐ July 23
2 Chronicles 8:11–10:19
Romans 8:9-25
Psalm 18:16-36
Proverbs 19:26

☐ July 24
2 Chronicles 11:1–13:22
Romans 8:26-39
Psalm 18:37-50
Proverbs 19:27-29

☐ July 25
2 Chronicles 14:1–16:14
Romans 9:1-24
Psalm 19:1-14
Proverbs 20:1

☐ July 26
2 Chronicles 17:1–18:34
Romans 9:25–10:13
Psalm 20:1-9
Proverbs 20:2-3

☐ July 27
2 Chronicles 19:1–20:37
Romans 10:14–11:12
Psalm 21:1-13
Proverbs 20:4-6

☐ July 28
2 Chronicles 21:1–23:21
Romans 11:13-36
Psalm 22:1-18
Proverbs 20:7

☐ July 29
2 Chronicles 24:1–25:28
Romans 12:1-21
Psalm 22:19-31
Proverbs 20:8-10

□ July 30
2 Chronicles 26:1–28:27
Romans 13:1-14
Psalm 23:1-6
Proverbs 20:11

□ July 31
2 Chronicles 29:1-36
Romans 14:1-23
Psalm 24:1-10
Proverbs 20:12

□ August 1
2 Chronicles 30:1–31:21
Romans 15:1-22
Psalm 25:1-15
Proverbs 20:13-15

□ August 2
2 Chronicles 32:1–33:13
Romans 15:23–16:9
Psalm 25:16-22
Proverbs 20:16-18

□ August 3
2 Chronicles 33:14–34:33
Romans 16:10-27
Psalm 26:1-12
Proverbs 20:19

□ August 4
2 Chronicles 35:1–36:23
1 Corinthians 1:1-17
Psalm 27:1-6
Proverbs 20:20-21

□ August 5
Ezra 1:1–2:70
1 Corinthians
Psalm 27:7-14
Proverbs 20:22-23

□ August 6
Ezra 3:1–4:24
1 Corinthians 2:6–3:4
Psalm 28:1-9
Proverbs 20:24-25

□ August 7
Ezra 5:1–6:22
1 Corinthians 3:5-23
Psalm 29:1-11
Proverbs 20:26-27

□ August 8
Ezra 7:1–8:20
1 Corinthians 4:1-21
Psalm 30:1-12
Proverbs 20:28-30

□ August 9
Ezra 8:21–9:15
1 Corinthians 5:1-13
Psalm 31:1-8
Proverbs 21:1-2

□ August 10
Ezra 10:1-44
1 Corinthians 6:1-20
Psalm 31:9-18
Proverbs 21:3

□ August 11
Nehemiah 1:1–3:14
1 Corinthians 7:1-24
Psalm 31:19-24
Proverbs 21:4

□ August 12
Nehemiah 3:15–5:13
1 Corinthians 7:25-40
Psalm 32:1-11
Proverbs 21:5-7

☐ **August 13**
Nehemiah 5:14–7:60
1 Corinthians 8:1-13
Psalm 33:1-11
Proverbs 21:8-10

☐ **August 14**
Nehemiah 7:61–9:21
1 Corinthians 9:1-18
Psalm 33:12-22
Proverbs 21:11-12

☐ **August 15**
Nehemiah 9:22–10:39
1 Corinthians 9:19–10:13
Psalm 34:1-10
Proverbs 21:13

☐ **August 16**
Nehemiah 11:1–12:26
1 Corinthians 10:14-33
Psalm 34:11-22
Proverbs 21:14-16

☐ **August 17**
Nehemiah 12:27–13:31
1 Corinthians 11:1-16
Psalm 35:1-16
Proverbs 21:17-18

☐ **August 18**
Esther 1:1–3:15
1 Corinthians 11:17-34
Psalm 35:17-28
Proverbs 21:19-20

☐ **August 19**
Esther 4:1–7:10
1 Corinthians 12:1-26
Psalm 36:1-12
Proverbs 21:21-22

☐ **August 20**
Esther 8:1–10:3
1 Corinthians 12:27–13:13
Psalm 37:1-11
Proverbs 21:23-24

☐ **August 21**
Job 1:1–3:26
1 Corinthians 14:1-17
Psalm 37:12-29
Proverbs 21:25-26

☐ **August 22**
Job 4:1–7:21
1 Corinthians 14:18-40
Psalm 37:30-40
Proverbs 21:27

☐ **August 23**
Job 8:1–11:20
1 Corinthians 15:1-28
Psalm 38:1-22
Proverbs 21:28-29

☐ **August 24**
Job 12:1–15:35
1 Corinthians 15:29-58
Psalm 39:1-13
Proverbs 21:30-31

☐ **August 25**
Job 16:1–19:29
1 Corinthians 16:1-24
Psalm 40:1-10
Proverbs 22:1

☐ **August 26**
Job 20:1–22:30
2 Corinthians 1:1-11
Psalm 40:11-17
Proverbs 22:2-4

☐ **August 27**
Job 23:1–27:23
2 Corinthians 1:12–2:11
Psalm 41:1-13
Proverbs 22:5-6

☐ **August 28**
Job 28:1–30:31
2 Corinthians 2:12-17
Psalm 42:1-11
Proverbs 22:7

☐ **August 29**
Job 31:1–33:33
2 Corinthians 3:1-18
Psalm 43:1-5
Proverbs 22:8-9

☐ **August 30**
Job 34:1–36:33
2 Corinthians 4:1-12
Psalm 44:1-8
Proverbs 22:10-12

☐ **August 31**
Job 37:1–39:30
2 Corinthians 4:13–5:10
Psalm 44:9-26
Proverbs 22:13

☐ **September 1**
Job 40:1–42:17
2 Corinthians 5:11-21
Psalm 45:1-17
Proverbs 22:14

☐ **September 2**
Ecclesiastes 1:1–3:22
2 Corinthians 6:1-13
Psalm 46:1-11
Proverbs 22:15

☐ **September 3**
Ecclesiastes 4:1–6:12
2 Corinthians 6:14–7:7
Psalm 47:1-9
Proverbs 22:16

☐ **September 4**
Ecclesiastes 7:1–9:18
2 Corinthians 7:8-16
Psalm 48:1-14
Proverbs 22:17-19

☐ **September 5**
Ecclesiastes 10:1–12:14
2 Corinthians 8:1-15
Psalm 49:1-20
Proverbs 22:20-21

☐ **September 6**
Song of songs 1:1–4:16
2 Corinthians 8:16-24
Psalm 50:1-23
Proverbs 22:22-23

☐ **September 7**
Song of songs 5:1–8:14
2 Corinthians 9:1-15
Psalm 51:1-19
Proverbs 22:24-25

☐ **September 8**
Isaiah 1:1–2:22
2 Corinthians 10:1-18
Psalm 52:1-9
Proverbs 22:26-27

☐ **September 9**
Isaiah 3:1–5:30
2 Corinthians 11:1-15
Psalm 53:1-6
Proverbs 22:28-29

☐ September 10
Isaiah 6:1–7:25
2 Corinthians 11:16-33
Psalm 54:1-7
Proverbs 23:1-3

☐ September 11
Isaiah 8:1–9:21
2 Corinthians 12:1-10
Psalm 55:1-23
Proverbs 23:4-5

☐ September 12
Isaiah 10:1–11:16
2 Corinthians 12:11-21
Psalm 56:1-13
Proverbs 23:6-8

☐ September 13
Isaiah 12:1–14:32
2 Corinthians 13:1-13
Psalm 57:1-11
Proverbs 23:9-11

☐ September 14
Isaiah 15:1–18:7
Galatians 1:1-24
Psalm 58:1-11
Proverbs 23:12

☐ September 15
Isaiah 19:1–21:17
Galatians 2:1-16
Psalm 59:1-17
Proverbs 23:13-14

☐ September 16
Isaiah 22:1–24:23
Galatians 2:17–3:9
Psalm 60:1-12
Proverbs 23:15-16

☐ September 17
Isaiah 25:1–28:13
Galatians 3:10-22
Psalm 61:1-8
Proverbs 23:17-18

☐ September 18
Isaiah 28:14–30:11
Galatians 3:23–4:31
Psalm 62:1-12
Proverbs 23:19-21

☐ September 19
Isaiah 30:12–33:9
Galatians 5:1-12
Psalm 63:1-11
Proverbs 23:22

☐ September 20
Isaiah 33:10–36:22
Galatians 5:13-26
Psalm 64:1-10
Proverbs 23:23

☐ September 21
Isaiah 37:1–38:22
Galatians 6:1-18
Psalm 65:1-13
Proverbs 23:24

☐ September 22
Isaiah 39:1–41:16
Ephesians 1:1-23
Psalm 66:1-20
Proverbs 23:25-28

☐ September 23
Isaiah 41:17–43:13
Ephesians 2:1-22
Psalm 67:1-7
Proverbs 23:29-35

☐ **September 24**
Isaiah 43:14–45:10
Ephesians 3:1-21
Psalm 68:1-18
Proverbs 24:1-2

☐ **September 25**
Isaiah 45:11–48:11
Ephesians 4:1-16
Psalm 68:19-35
Proverbs 24:3-4

☐ **September 26**
Isaiah 48:12–50:11
Ephesians 4:17-32
Psalm 69:1-18
Proverbs 24:5-6

☐ **September 27**
Isaiah 51:1–53:12
Ephesians 5:1-33
Psalm 69:19-36
Proverbs 24:7

☐ **September 28**
Isaiah 54:1–57:14
Ephesians 6:1-24
Psalm 70:1-5
Proverbs 24:8

☐ **September 29**
Isaiah 57:15–59:21
Philippians 1:1-26
Psalm 71:1-24
Proverbs 24:9-10

☐ **September 30**
Isaiah 60:1–62:5
Philippians 1:27–2:18
Psalm 72:1-20
Proverbs 24:11-12

☐ **October 1**
Isaiah 62:6–65:25
Philippians 2:19–3:3
Psalm 73:1-28
Proverbs 24:13-14

☐ **October 2**
Isaiah 66:1-24
Philippians 3:4-21
Psalm 74:1-23
Proverbs 24:15-16

☐ **October 3**
Jeremiah 1:1–2:30
Philippians 4:1-23
Psalm 75:1-10
Proverbs 24:17-20

☐ **October 4**
Jeremiah 2:31–4:18
Colossians 1:1-17
Psalm 76:1-12 |
Proverbs 24:21-22

☐ **October 5**
Jeremiah 4:19–6:15
Colossians 1:18–2:7
Psalm 77:1-20
Proverbs 24:23-25

☐ **October 6**
Jeremiah 6:16–8:7
Colossians 2:8-23
Psalm 78:1-31
Proverbs 24:26

☐ **October 7**
Jeremiah 8:8–9:26
Colossians 3:1-17
Psalm 78:32-55
Proverbs 24:27

☐ October 8
Jeremiah 10:1–11:23
Colossians 3:18–4:18
Psalm 78:56-72
Proverbs 24:28-29

☐ October 9
Jeremiah 12:1–14:10
1 Thessalonians 1:1–2:8
Psalm 79:1-13
Proverbs 24:30-34

☐ October 10
Jeremiah 14:11–16:15
1 Thessalonians 2:9–3:13
Psalm 80:1-19
Proverbs 25:1-5

☐ October 11
Jeremiah 16:16–18:23
1 Thessalonians 4:1–5:3
Psalm 81:1-16
Proverbs 25:6-8

☐ October 12
Jeremiah 19:1–21:14
1 Thessalonians 5:4-28
Psalm 82:1-8
Proverbs 25:9-10

☐ October 13
Jeremiah 22:1–23:20
2 Thessalonians 1:1-12
Psalm 83:1-18
Proverbs 25:11-14

☐ October 14
Jeremiah 23:21–25:38
2 Thessalonians 2:1-17
Psalm 84:1-12
Proverbs 25:15

☐ October 15
Jeremiah 26:1–27:22
2 Thessalonians 3:1-18
Psalm 85:1-13
Proverbs 25:16

☐ October 16
Jeremiah 28:1–29:32
1 Timothy 1:1-20
Psalm 86:1-17
Proverbs 25:17

☐ October 17
Jeremiah 30:1–31:26
1 Timothy 2:1-15
Psalm 87:1-7
Proverbs 25:18-19

☐ October 18
Jeremiah 31:27–32:44
1 Timothy 3:1-16
Psalm 88:1-18
Proverbs 25:20-22

☐ October 19
Jeremiah 33:1–34:22
1 Timothy 4:1-16
Psalm 89:1-13
Proverbs 25:23-24

☐ October 20
Jeremiah 35:1–36:32
1 Timothy 5:1-25
Psalm 89:14-37
Proverbs 25:25-27

☐ October 21
Jeremiah 37:1–38:28
1 Timothy 6:1-21
Psalm 89:38-52
Proverbs 25:28

☐ October 22
Jeremiah 39:1–41:18
2 Timothy 1:1-18
Psalm 90:1–91:16
Proverbs 26:1-2

☐ October 23
Jeremiah 42:1–44:23
2 Timothy 2:1-21
Psalm 92:1–93:5
Proverbs 26:3-5

☐ October 24
Jeremiah 44:24–47:7
2 Timothy 2:22–3:17
Psalm 94:1-23
Proverbs 26:6-8

☐ October 25
Jeremiah 48:1–49:22
2 Timothy 4:1-22
Psalm 95:1–96:13
Proverbs 26:9-12

☐ October 26
Jeremiah 49:23–50:46
Titus 1:1-16
Psalm 97:1–98:9
Proverbs 26:13-16

☐ October 27
Jeremiah 51:1-53
Titus 2:1-15
Psalm 99:1-9
Proverbs 26:17

☐ October 28
Jeremiah 51:54–52:34
Titus 3:1-15
Psalm 100:1-5
Proverbs 26:18-19

☐ October 29
Lamentations 1:1–2:19
Philippians 1:1-25
Psalm 101:1-8
Proverbs 26:20

☐ October 30
Lamentations 2:20–3:66
Hebrews 1:1-14
Psalm 102:1-28
Proverbs 26:21-22

☐ October 31
Lamentations 4:1–5:22
Hebrews 2:1-18
Psalm 103:1-22
Proverbs 26:23

☐ November 1
Ezekiel 1:1–3:15
Hebrews 3:1-19
Psalm 104:1-23
Proverbs 26:24-26

☐ November 2
Ezekiel 3:16–6:14
Hebrews 4:1-16
Psalm 104:24-35
Proverbs 26:27

☐ November 3
Ezekiel 7:1–9:11
Hebrews 5:1-14
Psalm 105:1-15
Proverbs 26:28

☐ November 4
Ezekiel 10:1–11:25
Hebrews 6:1-20
Psalm 105:16-36
Proverbs 27:1-2

□ November 5
Ezekiel 12:1–14:11
Hebrews 7:1-17
Psalm 105:37-45
Proverbs 27:3

□ November 6
Ezekiel 14:12–16:41
Hebrews 7:18-28
Psalm 106:1-12
Proverbs 27:4-6

□ November 7
Ezekiel 16:42–17:24
Hebrews 8:1-13
Psalm 106:13-31
Proverbs 27:7-9

□ November 8
Ezekiel 18:1–19:14
Hebrews 9:1-10
Psalm 106:32-48
Proverbs 27:10

□ November 9
Ezekiel 20:1-49
Hebrews 9:11-28
Psalm 107:1-43
Proverbs 27:11

□ November 10
Ezekiel 21:1–22:31
Hebrews 10:1-17
Psalm 108:1-13
Proverbs 27:12

□ November 11
Ezekiel 23:1-49
Hebrews 10:18-39
Psalm 109:1-31
Proverbs 27:13

□ November 12
Ezekiel 24:1–26:21
Hebrews 11:1-16
Psalm 110:1-7
Proverbs 27:14

□ November 13
Ezekiel 27:1–28:26
Hebrews 11:17-31
Psalm 111:1-10
Proverbs 27:15-16

□ November 14
Ezekiel 29:1–30:26
Hebrews 11:32–12:13
Psalm 112:1-10
Proverbs 27:17

□ November 15
Ezekiel 31:1–32:32
Hebrews 12:14-29
Psalm 113:1–114:8
Proverbs 27:18-20

□ November 16
Ezekiel 33:1–34:31
Hebrews 13:1-25
Psalm 115:1-18
Proverbs 27:21-22

□ November 17
Ezekiel 35:1–36:38
James 1:1-18
Psalm 116:1-19
Proverbs 27:23-27

□ November 18
Ezekiel 37:1–38:23
James 1:19–2:17
Psalm 117:1-2 l
Proverbs 28:1

☐ 19
Ezekiel 39:1–40:27
James 2:18–3:18
Psalm 118:1-18
Proverbs 28:2

☐ November 20
Ezekiel 40:28–41:26
James 4:1-17
Psalm 118:19-29
Proverbs 28:3-5

☐ November 21
Ezekiel 42:1–43:27
James 5:1-20
Psalm 119:1-16
Proverbs 28:6-7

☐ November 22
Ezekiel 44:1–45:12
1 Peter 1:1-12
Psalm 119:17-32
Proverbs 28:8-10

☐ November 23
Ezekiel 45:13–46:24
1 Peter 1:13–2:10
Psalm 119:33-48
Proverbs 28:11

☐ November 24
Ezekiel 47:1–48:35
1 Peter 2:11–3:7
Psalm 119:49-64
Proverbs 28:12-13

☐ November 25
Daniel 1:1–2:23
1 Peter 3:8–4:6
Psalm 119:65-80
Proverbs 28:14

☐ November 26
Daniel 2:24–3:30
1 Peter 4:7–5:14
Psalm 119:81-96
Proverbs 28:15-16

☐ November 27
Daniel 4:1-37
2 Peter 1:1-21
Psalm 119:97-112
Proverbs 28:17-18

☐ November 28
Daniel 5:1-31
2 Peter 2:1-22
Psalm 119:113-128
Proverbs 28:19-20

☐ November 29
Daniel 6:1-28
2 Peter 3:1-18
Psalm 119:129-152
Proverbs 28:21-22

☐ November 30
Daniel 7:1-28
1 John 1:1-10
Psalm 119:153-176
Proverbs 28:23-24

☐ December 1
Daniel 8:1-27
1 John 2:1-17
Psalm 120:1-7
Proverbs 28:25-26

☐ December 2
Daniel 9:1–11:1
1 John 2:18–3:6
Psalm 121:1-8
Proverbs 28:27-28

☐ **December 3**
Daniel 11:2-35
1 John 3:7-24
Psalm 122:1-9
Proverbs 29:1

☐ **December 4**
Daniel 11:36–12:13
1 John 4:1-21
Psalm 123:1-4
Proverbs 29:2-4

☐ **December 5**
Hosea 1:1–3:5
1 John 5:1-21
Psalm 124:1-8
Proverbs 29:5-8

☐ **December 6**
Hosea 4:1–5:15
2 John 1:1-13
Psalm 125:1-5
Proverbs 29:9-11

☐ **December 7**
Hosea 6:1–9:17
3 John 1:1-15
Psalm 126:1-6
Proverbs 29:12-14

☐ **December 8**
Hosea 10:1–14:9
Jude 1:1-25
Psalm 127:1-5
Proverbs 29:15-17

☐ **December 9**
Joel 1:1–3:21
Revelation 1:1-20
Psalm 128:1-6
Proverbs 29:18

☐ **December 10**
Amos 1:1–3:15
Revelation 2:1-17
Psalm 129:1-8
Proverbs 29:19-20

☐ **December 11**
Amos 4:1–6:14
Revelation 2:18–3:6
Psalm 130:1-8
Proverbs 29:21-22

☐ **December 12**
Amos 7:1–9:15
Revelation 3:7-22
Psalm 131:1-3
Proverbs 29:23

☐ **December 13**
Obadiah 1:1-21
Revelation 4:1-11
Psalm 132:1-18
Proverbs 29:24-25

☐ **December 14**
Jonah 1:1–4:11
Revelation 5:1-14
Psalm 133:1-3
Proverbs 29:26-27

☐ **December 15**
Micah 1:1–4:13
Revelation 6:1-17
Psalm 134:1-3
Proverbs 30:1-4

☐ **December 16**
Micah 5:1–7:20
Revelation 7:1-17
Psalm 135:1-21
Proverbs 30:5-6

☐ **December 17**
Nahum 1:1–3:19
Revelation 8:1-13
Psalm 136:1-26
Proverbs 30:7-9

☐ **December 18**
Habakkuk 1:1–3:19
Revelation 9:1-21
Psalm 137:1-9
Proverbs 30:10

☐ **December 19**
Zephaniah 1:1–3:20
Revelation 10:1-11
Psalm 138:1-8
Proverbs 30:11-14

☐ **December 20**
Haggai 1:1–2:23
Revelation 11:1-19
Psalm 139:1-24
Proverbs 30:15-16

☐ **December 21**
Zechariah 1:1-21
Revelation 12:1-17
Psalm 140:1-13
Proverbs 30:17

☐ **December 22**
Zechariah 2:1–3:10
Revelation 12:18-3:18
Psalm 141:1-10
Proverbs 30:18-20

☐ **December 23**
Zechariah 4:1–5:11
Revelation 14:1-20
Psalm 142:1-7
Proverbs 30:21-23

☐ **December 24**
Zechariah 6:1–7:14
Revelation 15:1-8
Psalm 143:1-12
Proverbs 30:24-28

☐ **December 25**
Zechariah 8:1-23
Revelation 16:1-21
Psalm 144:1-15
Proverbs 30:29-31

☐ **December 26**
Zechariah 9:1-17
Revelation 17:1-18
Psalm 145:1-21
Proverbs 30:32

☐ **December 27**
Zechariah 10:1–11:17
Revelation 18:1-24
Psalm 146:1-10
Proverbs 30:33

☐ **December 28**
Zechariah 12:1–13:9
Revelation 19:1-21
Psalm 147:1-20
Proverbs 31:1-7

☐ **December 29**
Zechariah 14:1-21
Revelation 20:1-15
Psalm 148:1-14
Proverbs 31:8-9

☐ **December 30**
Malachi 1:1–2:17
Revelation 21:1-27
Psalm 149:1-9
Proverbs 31:10-24

☐ December 31
Malachi 3:1–4:6
Revelation 22:1-21
Psalm 150:1-6
Proverbs 31:25-31

Unlocking the Bible Story Series

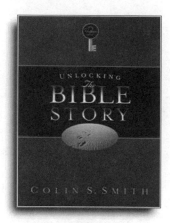

ISBN: 0-8024-6544-7
Volume 2

ISBN: 0-8024-6545-5
Volume 3

There are many people who know stories **from** the Bible, but they have not grasped the story **of** the Bible.

Unlocking the Bible will help you:

• **Discover** - the Bible as one whole marvelous story
• **Learn** - the major themes with the chapter titled with one word taken from the Bible
• **Worship** - as the whole Bible revolves around one central focus, our Lord Jesus Christ.

For all who are wondering how the pieces fit into the jigsaw of God's revelation, Colin Smith has provided an answer, which is refreshingly simple, biblically accurate and will prove phenomenally helpful to the serious Bible student and the new beginner alike.
- Alister Begg, Senior Pastor, Parkside Church

In a postmodern age where many know only of the stories of the Bible, but little of a comprehensive view of Scripture and a biblical worldview, Colin Smith's Unlocking the Bible Story *is a breath of fresh air. Read it to understand how God has worked throughout history and through the ages to provide salvation and redemption for fallen man.*
- Joseph Stowell, President Moody Bible Institute

MOODY
PUBLISHERS
THE NAME YOU CAN TRUST.
1-800-678-6928 www.MoodyPublishers.com

Unlocking the Bible Story Series

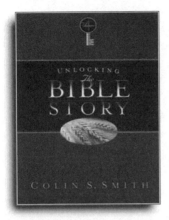

One of the most urgent needs in the church today is for a crisp and comprehensive knowledge of the Bible's storyline. To grasp how the sacred history moves from Genesis to Revelation not only brings fresh insight into how the Bible hangs together, and what each part contributes to the whole, but also is crucial for developing a Christian worldview. Colin Smith has met these needs admirably. I hope these volumes will circulate widely and be read and re-read.
- D.A Carson

ISBN: 0-8024-6546-3
Volume 4

---

10 Keys For Unlocking the Bible

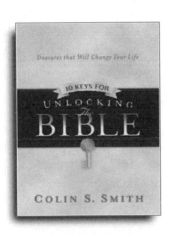

The whole Bible is one story. It begins in a garden, ends in a city and all the way through points us to Jesus Christ.

The 10 Keys included in *Unlocking the Bible Story*, are condensed from a series of four books that cover the story of the Bible in greater detail. If you enjoy the high-altitude flyover and want to get closer to the ground, *Unlocking the Bible Story* will give you a map and a compass. But for those who are new to the Bible or want a quick overview of the Christian faith, this is the place to begin.

ISBN: 0-8024-6547-1

MOODY
PUBLISHERS
THE NAME YOU CAN TRUST.

1-800-678-6928   www.MoodyPublishers.com

Find out More on Colin Smith's
Unlocking the Bible web site

Unlocking the Bible web site was created to help you discover the Bible so that you may know God . . . and there's nothing greater than that.

JOIN online community discussions
HEAR Pastor Colin's weekly radio program
READ through the Bible

Unlocking the Bible is here to help you discover the whole Bible story. We want to help you discover the breathtaking sweep of God's plan as it is unfolded in the Bible story, which begins in a garden and ends in a city, and all the way through is about Jesus Christ.

www.unlockingthebible.org

Unlocking the Bible Story Team

Acquiring Editor:
William L. Thrasher, Jr.

Copy Editor:
Jim Vincent

Back Cover Copy:
Stephanie Pugh

Cover Design:
Smartt Guys Design

Interior Design:
Paetzold Design

Printing and Binding:
Quebecor World Book Services

The typeface for the text of this book is
Goudy